FRANCIA'S REIGN OF TERROR,

BEING THE CONTINUATION OF

LETTERS ON PARAGUAY.

BY

J. P. AND W. P. ROBERTSON.

IN THREE VOLUMES.

VOL. III.

1839

DEDICATION.

TO

HIS EXCELLENCY CAPTAIN PRESCOTT,

R.N.,

GOVERNOR OF NEWFOUNDLAND.

DEAR SIR,

DEDICATIONS, if much expanded, are often so fulsome, and therefore so onerous to the party addressed, that in writing them, we think the Author's motto should be taken from his Latin Rudiments,—" *Vir sapit qui pauca loquitur.*"

Trying, in this instance, to suit the deed to the precept, we shall only farther say, that our Volume is dedicated to Your Excellency as a testimony of sincere respect from both **Authors**; but more particularly as one of cordial friendship from the senior writer, who, after long experienced, and most agreeable intercourse, could testify to qualities of head and heart, upon which, in deference alone to his Motto, he will not permit himself to dilate.

With the greatest sincerity,

We are your faithful Servants,

THE AUTHORS.

London, 1st January, 1839.

PREFACE.

We come now before the Public with our promised Sequel to 'LETTERS ON PARAGUAY.' Such has been the reception accorded to the first two Volumes, that, like favoured actors at the call of the audience, we appear before it to return our unfeigned thanks for the kind indulgence which has fallen to our lot. We find ourselves in the agreeable position of having to thank our critics, one and all. We have not a word of cavil or objection to offer against any one of them. And be it permitted us to record, in honour of the press of England, that in no one instance, directly or indirectly, has influence of any kind, as far as we are concerned, biased a single article in our favour. We acknowledge ourselves highly indebted to the metropolitan as well as to the country press; nor is it any disparagement to the former to say, that among their contemporaries in the counties, there is to be found a talent that would do honour to the first-rate ability with which so many of the London journals are conducted.

And thus we close our Preface. In the present Volume, as well as in its predecessors, we shall only say, that we have aimed at placing simple facts, simply recorded, before our readers; and at drawing from those facts such plain and obvious inferences as we thought they naturally suggested. We have also, throughout our work, endeavoured to keep in view what ought, perhaps, to be considered the only legitimate objects of an author,—the inculcation of *practical good,* and the diffusion of *useful knowledge.*

1st *January,* 1839.

CONTENTS.

LETTER I.

THE AUTHORS TO THEIR READERS.

Page

Introductory and somewhat Retrospective . . . 1

LETTER II.

W. P. R. TO THOMAS FAIR, ESQ.

Francia's Levee—His condescension—Change of Manner and
of System—Takes the Title of Supremo, or Supreme—
Increased austerity—Paralyzation of Commerce—The
Secretary of State, Martinez—Harangue to the Old
Spaniards—The Pelado — The Clergy — Elevation of
Paî Montiel 13

LETTER III.

W. P. R. TO THOMAS FAIR, ESQ.

Dr. Parlett and the Medical Practitioners of Assumption—
Francia's first interview with Parlett—The celebrated
cures he performs—Recalde's daughter—Parlett's death
and destitution 30

LETTER IV.

W. P. R. TO THOMAS FAIR, ESQ.

THE BANISHMENT OF MENDEZ.

Page

The establishment of Mendez—Doña Juanita—Walking-
dress of the Assumpcianas—And of a Montevideana—
Not admitted to the Cathedral—The Tertulia—Intimation of Banishment—Desolation—A Woman's fortitude
—I assist Mendez—His departure—A narrow escape—
Doña Juanita's letter—The Port of Quarepotí—A break-
down in a wood—Further troubles—Reflections—Journey continued — Curuguatí — Mendez's release — And
return to Buenos Ayres   40

LETTER V.

COMMENCEMENT OF THE LETTERS OF J. P. ROBERTSON.

J. P. R. TO THOMAS FAIR, ESQ.

Introductory—Serious aspect of affairs—Preparations for a
return to Paraguay—Interview with the Director Alvear,
and his Secretary Herrera—A fatal letter intrusted to
me, and a fatal shipment made—I sail for Assumption
—Candioti, Governor of Santa Fé—His speech and
conduct—My capture and treatment by Artigueños—A
perilous predicament, and yet more wonderful escape
from it, through an Indian—The Artigueños dressed in
Bond Street clothes, and I in Artigueño attire—I am
forced to play the flute—Arrival at the Bajada—A fortunate encounter—I am lodged in the common gaol—The
inmates of it—My transfer to a solitary cell—The Honourable Captain Jocelyne Percy—His letter to Artigas
—I am set at liberty   63

LETTER VI.

J. P. R. TO THOMAS FAIR, ESQ.

Page

A transition state—The Indian to whom I owed my life—
Artigueño gambling—Restoration of my ship and property, minus what was plundered—Return to Buenos
Ayres—Visit to the head-quarters of Artigas—Short
sketch of him—My interview with him, and a description
of his quarters, occupations, and encampment—Cause
and origin of his vast power—His poverty—Return from
the Purificacion to Corrientes 93-

LETTER VII.

W. P. R. TO THOMAS FAIR, ESQ.

The Letter of the Scotch Serjeant intimating the capture of
J. P. R. My first interview with Francia on the occasion
—His Letter to Hereñú—My second interview with the
Dictator on occasion of my Brother's disaster—My third
interview on the occasion—Francia pronounces Sentence
of Banishment against us both 111

LETTER VIII.

J. P. R. TO THOMAS FAIR, ESQ.

Third visit to Paraguay—News received from Assumption—
Arrival there—Interview with my brother, and with the
Dictator—My banishment—Its effects on the inhabitants
of Assumption—I finally depart from Assumption . 124

LETTER IX.

J. P. R. TO THOMAS FAIR, ESQ.

Return to Corrientes—State of that place, and unforeseen
perils in landing there—Obstacles overcome, and a
second escape from the hands of the Philistines—Their
departure from Corrientes, and my establishment there
—Conclusion of personal observations . . . 136

LETTER X.

W. P. R. TO THOMAS FAIR, ESQ.

Page

Remarks on Francia—Society of Assumption—The Jovellanos family—Their servants—Plain speaking—Sleeping under corridors—Amusements—The Sarandig—The Figueredos—I become a Padrino—My compadre and comadre—A death and a velorio—The funeral of an Angel 140

LETTER XI.

W. P. R. TO THOMAS FAIR, ESQ.

Catholic Lent—Contrasted with Protestant—Reflections—Passion-week—Good Friday—Sermon of Christ's agony on the cross—The funeral service, and conclusion of Good Friday 156

LETTER XII.

W. P. R. TO THOMAS FAIR, ESQ.

Francia sets up as Paviour—Cheap mode of paving—A trip to the Quarries and surrounding Country—Aspect of it —And hospitality of the People—The Paraguay Peasant and his Family—The Estanciero—Don Pedro Francia—A Reduccion—Fiestas of the Indians—The Bull Ring—The Sortija—The Mystery 165

LETTER XIII.

W. P. R. TO THOMAS FAIR, ESQ.

THE PAYAGUA INDIANS.

Their Tolderias—Ornaments—Doctors—Cacique's Wife—A Flitting—A Feast—Their Thefts—and Banishment . 177

LETTER XIV.

W. P. R. TO THOMAS FAIR, ESQ.

Vicissitudes—The winding up of our Affairs—Tenacity about Silver—I prepare to leave—Last Interview with Francia —The Piragua—We are alarmed, boarded, and searched —A temptation resisted—Scene with a Tiger—Arrival at Corrientes 187

LETTER XV.

J. P. R. TO THOMAS FAIR, ESQ.

THE NATURAL PRODUCTIONS OF PARAGUAY.

Page

The Lapacho-tree—Other trees, shrubs, fruit, and vegetables
—Ornithology—Zoology 206

LETTER XVI.

J . P. R. TO THOMAS FAIR, ESQ.

Exports of Paraguay—Destruction of commerce—Revenue
of Paraguay — Expenditure—Francia's imposts—His
parsimony—His opinion of English merchants and manufacturers 216

LETTER XVII.

THE AUTHORS TO THOMAS FAIR, ESQ.

Sources of information—Reflections 230

LETTER XVIII.

W. P. R. TO THOMAS FAIR, ESQ.

MR. OKES'S EXPEDITION TO PARAGUAY.

His character—Suggestion for the voyage of Okes to Paraguay—His departure—His voyage—The Bajada—His
arrival—Francia an Astronomer—Favourable reception
of Okes—Permission to depart—The sequel—Issue of
the adventure—One of Francia's bloody deeds . . 236

LETTER XIX.

W. P. R. TO THOMAS FAIR, ESQ.

DON JOSE DE MARIA.

He visits Francia—A sale of salt—Interference for Foreigners
by Sir Woodbine Parish—Dénouement of the interference
—Effect of Francia's system on the minds of the Détenus—Decree of perpetual silence—Francia's private
secretary—José de Maria's imprisonment—The fate of
Chilaber 253

LETTER XX.

J. P. R. TO THOMAS FAIR, ESQ.

DON PABLO SORIA.

Page

Navigation of the Vermejo—Soria's capture—His treatment
by Francia—His liberation, and return to Buenos Ayres 269

LETTER XXI.

W. P. R. TO THOMAS FAIR, ESQ.

MONS. AIME BONPLAND.

His arrival in Buenos Ayres—He proceeds to Candelaria—
His establishment there—Its total destruction by Francia,
and massacre of his people—Horrible cruelty—Francia's
own account of the transaction—Santa Maria—Attempts
made to procure M. Bonpland's release—Failure of these
attempts — Bonpland's colony at Santa Maria — His
philanthropy — Dismissal from Paraguay—Return to
Buenos Ayres 275

LETTER XXII.

TO THOMAS FAIR, ESQ.

J. P. R. RESUMES, AND CONCLUDES THE SERIES AND THE VOLUME.

The three salient points in Francia's history—His fear of
assassination—His prying and minute organization of
his troops—He sows jealousy of each other among them
—His minuteness — Military insolence encouraged —
Anecdotes of his cruelty and caprice—Courts-Martial—
Increase of dungeons and prisons—The public prison —
Treatment of the prisoners—Females not excepted—State
dungeons 291

LETTER XXIII.

J. P. R. TO THOMAS FAIR, ESQ.

Page

State dungeons—Their inmates—Tevégo made a place of
exile—The torture-chamber—Use made of those instru
ments of tyranny—The Pelado—His fate—Horrible
mode of conducting executions—Fearful progress of
the reign of terror—Case of the shoemaker—The tradesmen's gibbet—Generalization—Application of it to the
shoemaker's case—Dark prospects—Anecdote of a jury
—Inference drawn—Applicable to Francia—Hazael,
Nero, and the Dictator 303

LETTER XXIV.

J. P. R. TO THOMAS FAIR, ESQ.

Francia's growing terrors of assassination—Conspiracy against
him — The conspirators betrayed — Wretched consequences—Fate of the conspirators—Further precautions
taken by Francia—The intrigues of Ramirez, an Artigueño colonel—Executions and torture—Executions continued—Female heroism—Change of the national character—Fate of Don Andres Gomez—General effects
produced by the Reign of Terror 323

LETTER XXV.

J. P. R. TO THOMAS FAIR, ESQ.

Measures adopted against the old Spaniards—The unfortunate mason—False accusations and cruelty—Imprisonment, murder, and mockery—General Velasco—His
history—His humming birds—His butler—The fate of
both—Fate of the Bishop—Fines imposed on the old
Spaniards — Orders to shoot all who looked at the
Government House — Solitude around the Tyrant's
abode 339

LETTER XXVI.

J. P. R. TO THOMAS FAIR, ESQ.

Page

The Dictator's various occupations—General of Dragoons—
His military attire—He gives the word of command—
He turns Land-surveyor—Lays off a town—Demolishes
the old one—Endeavours to build a new one—The job
proves a failure—Francia finds that he cannot make
successful war upon the elements—His sites are staked
off, but not built upon 353

LETTER XXVII.

J. P. R. TO THOMAS FAIR, ESQ.

Reflections preparatory to the closing Review of Francia's
Character—Charges brought by Francia against Mons.
Rengger, " That he is a wretch, assassin, poisoner, seducer, and intriguer ;" "that he wants to marry a Paraguay lady ;" that he is "a mendacious miscreant ;"
"that his work is an essay of lies ;" "that he is an
ungrateful vagabond"—His Letter about Buenos Ayres
—The Dictator's contempt for him . . . 369

LETTER XXVIII.

J. P. R. TO THOMAS FAIR, ESQ.

ANALYSIS OF THE PRECEDING DOCUMENT, AND CONCLUSION OF THE SERIES.

Scurrility of Francia's Exposé—Notoriety of the Facts stated
by Rengger—Lowness of Francia's Imagery and Language—Mons. Rengger's Forbearance—Reason assigned
for this—Credit given to Francia by Mons. Rengger—
Investigation of Francia's Charges—Their Refutation—
Address to Francia, containing a Résumé of the Charges
against Him 381

CONCLUSION 398

LETTER I.

THE AUTHORS TO THEIR READERS.

INTRODUCTORY AND SOMEWHAT RETROSPECTIVE.

London, 1838.

WHEN we published, about three months ago, the first series of these letters, the public and ourselves were utter strangers to each other. Our two volumes constituted our first appearance on the stage of English literature; and many misgivings we confess we had as to the result of our maiden attempt. The difficulty of imparting an interest, and something like a freshness, to events not very recent, enhanced by the apathy which had grown up in regard to South America, gave us no imaginary cause to look forward with an anxious and even dubious eye to the issue of our labours.

They have been received, however, in a way to exceed our most sanguine expectations; and we have not only every reason to be satisfied

but to feel honoured by the reception with which
our first work has met. We trust that the sequel to the strange annals of Dr. Francia, and
the further incidents connected with Paraguay
which we have now to give, may not be deemed
of inferior value to the part upon which the
public has already pronounced so favourable a
judgment.

Before proceeding with our history, we must
take the liberty of detaining our readers at large
for a short time over a few preliminary remarks,
intended principally for the benefit of those who
may not have seen our two first volumes.

The interest which the public has attached to
our sketches of Paraguay, and its Dictator, Francia, only shows the truth of what may pass for
an axiom, that man's curiosity, as a propensity,
and almost an instinct, of his nature, knows no
bounds. It is subject, no doubt, to the many
modifications which time, place, and circumstance
produce : yet while he reserves his stronger sym-
pathies for those scenes and actions which come
within the scope of his own observation, he is
nevertheless ready to take an interest in what is
more distant, and less palpable to his senses;

he concerns himself more or less with the occurrences of the whole world in which he lives, and with all that moves therein.

The fact is, that the utility derivable from the study of man is enhanced rather than diminished by the modifications of climate, education, habits, and institutions. The truly philosophic principle is, "*Homo sum, a me nihil humani alienum puto;*" and while the sentiment is in all cases correct, it applies with double force to those in which some marked peculiarity in the construction of society is discernible, or where the leader or ruler of that society exhibits such broad traits of character as do not, in our previous reading or experience, easily find a parallel.

Such a state of society we think we have so far exhibited in Paraguay, and such a ruler in its living Dictator, Doctor Francia.* Various concurrent circumstances have combined to lend a peculiar interest to the general history of the country of which we treat, and we have already endeavoured to call the attention of our readers to them.

* The Doctor's death, so currently reported three months ago, we now know has not taken place.

Paraguay was a land which, when we took up the subject, was enveloped in a vague and misty celebrity. Most people who had read anything of the New World knew that there was a beautiful and fertile region of that name, a long way inland in some part or other of South America; that it produced a sort of tea, as generally used in those parts as we use the Chinese plant in England; that it had been the seat of the Jesuits; that it had become, in common with all parts of Spanish America, independent of the mother country; and that it had at last come under the rule of a strange and incomprehensible person, called Doctor Francia. Such, in general terms, was the extent of knowledge which the bulk of English readers possessed of Paraguay.

The colonial *régime* of Old Spain, as we have shown in our first volumes, tended to keep all her transatlantic possessions from the public gaze of Europe; and as they receded inland from her principal ports, they became more and more indistinct and fanciful to the vision.* Thus the

* Every one knows how pleasingly Southey has taken advantage of this circumstance in the romantic poem which he has founded on a passage from old Dobritzhoffer, and of which the scene is laid in Paraguay.

very existence of Assumption, the capital of Paraguay, situated 1200 miles up the River Plate, was only known as a city to the learned few, and to Spain herself and her colonies. The country was indeed thrown open for a time after the revolution of 1810; but almost before anything could be seen of it, and transmitted to general knowledge, it was shut up more rigorously than ever by Francia; and while he lives the probability is that it will remain hermetically sealed to all the world.

Yet the beauty, the richness, the luxuriance of Paraguay,—its noble rivers, its magnificent forests, its verdant plains, its picturesque mountains, its fine though warm climate, its fertility in every tropical production of value, and its endless variety of objects of natural history,—all render the country one of the most interesting in the New World, and respecting the peculiar features of which every admirer of the beauties and bounties of nature must be pleased to have some detailed information. Such information we have already, to a certain extent, endeavoured to supply, and we propose to complete it, as well as we can, in the present volume.

Another striking circumstance connected with the history of Paraguay is, that of the rise, progress, and fall of the Jesuits in that country; and this subject we have completed in our first volumes. A short retrospect of the matter here for our present readers shall therefore suffice.

The interest which the history of the Jesuits in Paraguay involves, will be best understood by asking how we should view among ourselves the phenomenon of an organized society, independent of the laws, civil and ecclesiastical, of the realm, yet subordinate to laws of its own, effectual for the restraint of crime, the promotion of corporate aggrandizement, and the working out of a provision, on the principle of a community of goods, for every member of the body politic? Should we not eagerly scan its institutions, investigate its principles, admire its excellencies, or probe its defects? In what variety of speculation should we not indulge as to the legality and utility of such an *imperium in imperio?* How would its proceedings be decried by some, applauded by others, scrutinized by all? And would not such investigation lead to many important and practical results in the constitution of social order?

Now, though the inquiry into such an institution could not proceed as of one existing, or that had existed among ourselves, yet if "history be philosophy teaching by example," it is assuredly true that neither the historical details connected with the government of the Jesuits, nor the inferences deduced can be materially affected by a mere reference to their locality.

The popular account of the Jesuits, embodied in our former letters, was framed either from authentic MSS., which we perused, or from our own personal observation; and we are glad to believe that it has been by many considered to be of an historical importance calculated to instruct the philosopher, as well as to interest the general reader.*

We gave as comprehensive a view as our

---

* We have not been able to refrain from a smile on finding ourselves charged by an otherwise kind and discriminating reviewer as being too deeply imbued with the spirit of John Knox and of Presbyterianism to give a fair account of the Jesuits. Our respected critic will, perhaps, allow us to say that our facts are drawn from, and our reasonings are in accordance with, Roman Catholic writers who have preceded us; and that, as we neither are, nor ever have been, Presbyterians (albeit holding in respect that erudite sect), the doctrines and feelings of that church have in no way influenced our views of the labours of the Jesuits in Paraguay.

limits would permit, first, of the institutions of
the Jesuits, and, next, of the state to which their
communities were reduced after their expulsion.
That expulsion itself, the result of the jealousy
created in the Spanish court of the increase of
power acquired and exercised by the Jesuits,
was attended with great individual oppression;
and it forms an interesting chapter in the history
of their decline and fall.

In little more than forty years after the expulsion of the Jesuits, by order of the King of
Spain, the successor of that monarch was destined in his turn to see his authority on the
wane, and his dominion pass away from him over
countries from which his predecessor had driven
the sons of Loyola.

In the history of the revolution by which the
vast transatlantic possessions of Spain were converted into a number of independent governments or republics, Paraguay comes early into
the field; and though of small comparative importance in the general struggle, the singular
policy it has pursued for twenty-five years has
attracted very general attention in Europe. It
forms a sole exception to the anarchy and confu-

sion which have reigned throughout the other republics, from the time of their colonial emancipation to the present day.

Dr. Francia, the author, and, up to this hour, the inflexible upholder of the non-intercourse policy of Paraguay, is, doubtless, one of the most singular characters of his day. Before this man's real character became known, he received no small credit for the tranquil order which he maintained in his republic, while all the others about him were engaged in apparently interminable broils and civil discords.

But the peace and quiet of Paraguay are as the stillness of the grave. What originated in a deeply-laid plot of oppressive tyranny has been consummated by a universal system of terror. By the most ruthless cruelty,—by the sternest despotism,—Francia established, and now maintains his sway: crimes of a dye so deep,—of a character so appalling as to make human nature shudder and recoil,—have stained his course as he has advanced in his relentless and bloody career. The character of such a man, wherever the theatre of his actions may lie, cannot but excite a strong and general interest; and in proportion as the knowledge of his system and of his acts has been scanty and unauthentic, a desire has arisen to have more credible testimony respecting them.

We have already shown to some extent, and we propose still further to show, that we have the means of placing the history of this tyrant and of his government in an authentic and connected form before the public. We have in our first volumes given some details (now to be followed up by more) of the personal intercourse which we held with Francia while we resided in Paraguay during the early part of his career; and we shall, by-and-by, show the connexion which we kept up with the country after we left it, and the means which were afforded to us, through our own agents and others, of tracking the fiendish course of the cold-blooded and cruel Dictator.

The history of Francia's *mind*, as developed in his actions, is a truly astonishing one. The accusation we have here made against him of progressive oppression and blood-thirsty tyranny will be found to be supported by the most startling facts, attested by a host of witnesses. They

are facts, too, which relate not to some Negro
chieftain of a savage tribe of Africans, but to a
lawyer,—a scholar,—a political chief,—who, in all
probability, exercises, *at this moment*, absolute
sway over a country larger than Great Britain :
a country which, for three centuries, was ruled
by a civilized European power; and a country,
which, though now coerced into the timorous silence of absolute slavery, and laid prostrate at the
feet of a gloomy despot, we ourselves have seen
full of life and activity, teeming with abundance,
and looking, as an effect of the very revolution
which has brought it so low, to perennial prosperity
and wealth. Alas ! where unprincipled ambition
wades through blood to the possession of despotic power,—and maintains that power by a
paralyzing system of terror,—what baneful in-
fluences must we not be prepared to see shedding
their poisonous dews over the length and breadth
of the land !

We have here adverted to some of the claims
which a history of Paraguay has on the attention
of our readers, and which the public at large has
already so promptly recognised. That history
will be successively developed in the course of

this sequel to our first letters ; and, as the whole are not the result of any hasty or superficial survey, but of a personal intercourse, or of correspondence with confidential agents, corroborated by other and high authorities, it is presumed that they may lay claim to some accuracy; and that, while they minister to the general reader instruction and amusement, they may not be destitute of interest to the political, and even to the philosophic inquirer.

THE AUTHORS.

LETTER II.

W. P. R. to Thomas Fair, Esq.

Francia's Levee—His condescension—Change of Manner and
System—Takes the Title of Supremo, or Supreme—Increased austerity—Paralyzation of Commerce—The Secretary
of State, Martinez—Harangue to the Old Spaniards—The
Pelado—The Clergy—Elevation of Paî Montiel.

London, 1838.

THE first series of these letters, which you have
seen, and which we addressed to our friend Mr.
Gilfillan, has so far been stamped by the public
approbation as to warrant our placing your name
in full, without much danger to your reputation,
at the head of our Second Series.   When I state
that you were our partner in business in Buenos
Ayres for a lengthened period of time,—that, as
such, you were leagued with us during the whole
course of our adventures in Paraguay,—and that
a friendship of twenty-five years' standing has
continued to link us together on higher and more
enduring grounds than a mere junction of worldly

interests could effect,—I am sure our readers will
agree that no name can stand more appropriately
at the head of our letters than your own.

Our last volume left off at one of the great political eras of Francia's life,—his nomination for
three years to the dictatorship of Paraguay. You
have seen the manœuvres to which he resorted in
order to insure his popular election to that high
office; and I have informed you that his congress
of a thousand deputies, having gratified the
ambitious consul by a unanimous vote, put a
suicidal end to its own existence after a brief,
though it must be confessed, an important life of
three days' duration.

The two days which followed the election were
graciously set apart by the Dictator as *dias de
Besamanos*, or levee days.

I of course waited on him with the crowd of
courtiers which these two days called into an
ephemeral existence in Assumption. Old and
antiquated Spanish court dresses, which I believe had in some cases been handed down from
father to son, since the days of the first con-
querors of Paraguay, were to be seen in all directions. They were worn by shopkeepers, mer-

chants, and some of the better landed proprietors
of the old school. The prevailing fashion was
very much in the Dr. Bargas style, being a
coat of great amplitude of cuff, pocket and flap,
of "Paño de San Fernando," the best and most
costly superfine of Spain, with monstrously large
flat buttons, and tails reaching to the calf of the
leg. The rest of the dress was in keeping with
this well-preserved heir-loom. Then came the
doctores in court suits of black of an equally
ancient cut; a few (among these, Generals
Yegros, and Cavallero) in fantastic, medley,
and very tight regimentals; and a few more,
young men like myself, who had been to Buenos
Ayres, and adopted the modern European fashion.
But, to me, the most grotesque looking of all the
dictator's visitors at his Besamanos, were the sons
of some of these motley courtiers of a day. Boys
of not more than eight or ten years of age,
strutted by the sides of their fathers, dressed
precisely after the same fashion as their elders,
with gold-headed little canes in their hands,
and conversing with all the gravity and self-
possession of men of sixty. They made their
obeisance to the Dictator with ease and propriety,

and they were received by him not only with cour-
tesy but formality.*   Many belonging to the
classes of a lower grade were admitted to these
levees, held for the first and the last time by the
Dictator.   Among them I remarked my little
Sancho Panza looking friend, Orrego the spy,
decked out in a new, gaudy, and many-coloured
suit, purchased for the all-important occasion.
Whether he had come to spy the Dictator himself or not, I cannot say ; but I caught them
exchanging significant though furtive looks, during Orrego's stay in the saloon.

Francia constrained himself into smiles and
affability to all during his two levees; but the
inward fear and dread of him which filled the
hearts of most of his visitors, they in vain tried,
on their first *entrée,* to hide under an appearance of cordial respect.   I never saw Francia himself look so well as he then did.   He was neatly
dressed in a blue coat, slightly ornamented with
narrow gold lace, white cassemere waistcoat and
breeches, a smart court sword by his side,

* I was forcibly reminded of the style and strut of these
youthful courtiers, by seeing lately the drum-major of the Royal
Military School at Chelsea, as he headed the Liliputian band in
procession to the church.

white silk stockings and thin shoes, with small buckles. He stood in the middle of the room, conversing for a short time with each visitor, and adapting his conversation with much tact to the various capacities of those who surrounded him. Those who had not penetrated into the iron heart of the man might have been excused for indulging a faint and transient hope that, glutted now with the repast of power on which he had gorged, the wolf was about to lie down with the lamb.

The Dictator detained me for a considerable time at his first day's levee. When I entered, I begged to congratulate "his Excellency;"— but here he stopped me short. "Déxe, amigo," said he, "de ' Excelencia,' y conozcame V. y hableme como hasta aqui hemos acostumbrado." "Lay aside ' Your Excellency,' my friend, and know me and address me as you have hitherto done." His title before was Usia (a contraction of Vuestra Señoria) which in Spain is a grade inferior to Excellency. But I knew the man I had to do with too well to avail myself of any such privileged familiarity. I continued " Your

Excellency," and he did not again object to the title.

Francia now began to open up his despotic policy more rapidly, and with less appearance of caution than he had done as Consul of the republic.

His body-guard, as it might properly be termed, of Quarteleros, was now completely organized; and, without his appearing directly to sanction it, an increasing license in their manner of conducting themselves towards the citizens was observable. On the Dictator's daily ride to and from the barracks, the passenger on the way who omitted to uncover as Francia passed, had at first his hat rudely pushed from his head by one of the guards; and ere long this mode of admonishment was changed to the ruffian's riding up with his drawn sabre to the incautious delinquent, and with two or three heavy blows, reminding him of the respect due to the " Supremo ;" for so Francia now ordered that he should be called. In one or two cases before I left Assumption, it happened that the edge instead of the flat side of the sword was used, and then the unhappy victim was cut down, and left to lie bleeding till the Dictator had passed. In all these outrages Francia never appeared to give orders, or in any way to be concerned in the matter. He continued at his unaltered slow pace, with an immovably cold expression in his features, his head bent downwards, and apparently unconscious of what was going forward.

The system of *espionage* was ramified, and more systematically organized; and every day an increasing distrust of each other was introduced and spread among the inhabitants of the capital. This system was afterwards carried into every district and every petty village throughout the republic.

Imprisonments and fines became more frequent, and no man dared to inquire into the cause of his neighbour's loss of liberty. The nature of their imprisonments, and the sufferings of the imprisoned are hereafter to be detailed. The establishment of the *state prisons* was at a period subsequent to that of my residence in Assumption.

I recollect having been told of a Scotch noble-

man who, in order to break his daughters from too
ardent a pursuit of pleasure, would allow them
to accept of an invitation to a ball,—dress for it
in all splendour,—order his equipage to the door;
and who yet, as the buoyant girls were about to
step into the carriage, would suddenly remand
it to the coach-house, order the young ladies
to lay aside their ball dresses, resume their domestic habiliments, and return to the quiet avocations of a family fire-side.

In some such manner did Francia systematically begin, after his dictatorship, to break
the spirit of commercial enterprize in Paraguay.
On some frivolous pretext he would declare the
port of Assumption to be rigorously shut, and
all active trade was immediately paralyzed.
With as little ostensible cause he would, after a
season, open the ports. Then all were on the
alert to load their vessels, and get off their produce to their different markets. But again, just
perhaps as the first vessel was ready to sail,
down would come a fresh order to shut the ports,
—the vessels were to be unloaded,—heavy expenses incurred; and the produce, instead of
rewarding the merchant for his capital employed,

and risk run in supplying the republic with its wants, was remanded to his warehouses, there to deteriorate in value, and perhaps to be altogether lost, The ultimate consequence was that very few were willing to avail themselves of permission to load large vessels, afraid that ere they were ready to sail, they might have to unload, and store their produce once more in a warehouse.

The trade of Paraguay was chiefly in the hands of old Spaniards, whose hatred of Francia was great, but whose fear of him was justly much greater. This he well knew. He, in his turn, not only hated but despised them; and on their ultimate ruin and annihilation, as a body, he had, at an early stage of his career, no doubt determined.

Before the dictatorship, and for some short time after it, a secretaryship of state was kept up, and it was vested in the person of one Martinez, a man of some wealth and much pretension in Assumption.

He was an official personage of routine, and minutely methodical in every thing he did. Like all such persons, his. mind was so little elastic, that he could not distinguish between

the most important and the most trivial affairs
of life. They all received from him the same
degree of minute attention;—he only looked to
detail; and the tiresome prolixity with which he
dissected, and redissected every particular of the
most petty concern with which he had to meddle,
constituted, in his eyes, a talent of the first-rate
order. He was a personification of tautology;
his expletives, and his amplifications knew no
end; and as he was never sure himself that he
understood a thing till he had examined it under
every possible aspect, so he was afraid that
others had the same obesity of mental perception.
Hence his endless repetitions and superfluities of
illustration.

This phraseological phenomenon was of course
a mere tool (and one of the lowest order) in the
hands of Francia. The secretary, however, was
puffed up with the idea of being the next man
in the republic to the Dictator; and while he
was abject servility before his master, he was
pompous, absurd, and inflated to a degree, when
the dread of Francia's keen countenance was not
upon him.

Soon after the dictatorship, Francia desired

Martinez to summon before him the old Spaniards,
to admonish them as to their future conduct, and
to warn them against their supposed inclination
to interfere in state affairs.

Martinez had accordingly the whole of the old
Spaniards, of every grade and profession,—
sailors, artisans, publicans, shopkeepers, and
merchants,—collected together at one point, and
kept there like a flock of sheep. It was on a
hot summer's day, and the operation commenced
while the sun still shot forth its broiling rays,
in all their fury. Martinez himself,—burly in
person, and harsh in feature, yet affecting the air
and manners of a foppish courtier,—sat at his
ease in a large and antiquated elbow chair, under
the veranda, in front of his house. He was
dressed in a mazarine blue silk coat, black satin
breeches and waistcoat, black silk stockings, and
gay slippers. His hair was highly powdered, and
a fine, scented cambric handkerchief was stuck in
his breast. On either side of his chair stood a
young female slave, one to replenish his silver
maté cup, and the other with a richly chased silver
censer, containing charcoal perfumed with pastilla, placed on a salver to correspond with the

censer, and on which lay a few of the best cigars.
He alternately smoked one of these, and sipped
his maté.

The poor old Spaniards, many of them superior to himself, were, indiscriminately, by two
and three at a time, brought up to the bashaw ;
and he successively addressed each little knot
in the following manner : " You are a parcel
of brutes,—do you understand me ? of beasts,
—do you comprehend me ? animals,—eh ? You
are Barbarians and Goths,—are you aware of
what I mean ? Yes, brutes ! you all deserve
to be hanged, or shot like dogs,—do you see ?
for you are a perverse race, and the old and
natural enemies of all South Americans,—eh ? of
the patriots,—do you perceive ? of the natural
born sons of the soil,—do you understand ?

" And what, oh Barbarians ! has been your
conduct in Paraguay ? have you not conspired,—
eh ? rebelled,—do you comprehend ? warred
against his Excellency the Dictator ? Your plots,
your seditions, your conspiracies,—eh ?—do you
see ? your intrigues and your treasons,—do you
now what I mean ?—have been without end ;
and you may thank God,—do you understand

me? you may be grateful to Providence, and no less so to the supreme Dictator,—are you aware? —to his Excellency Don Jose Gaspar de Francia, —do you listen?—that you have not been long ago rooted out,—eh?—extirpated from the land, —do you comprehend?"

In the same strain of eloquence he went on to warn them as to their future conduct; the unfortunate men standing uncovered in the sun, while the pedantic upstart who lectured them sipped his maté, and puffed forth his smoke, fully persuaded that his oratory was making a profound impression on those, whom he termed the trembling caitiffs who listened to him.

I received all the particulars of this unmeaning piece of cruelty to the many respectable inhabitants of Assumption, who were the object of it, from a neighbour of ours, an old Spaniard, whose name I forget, but who went, invariably, under the cognomen of "Pelado," or bald-pate. His tragical end will be related in another place.

Like many other old Spaniards, he indulged in a deeply-rooted hatred of the Creoles, and the indignities to which he was obliged to submit from them sometimes wrought his mind into a state little short of frenzy. He believed that to me, seeing I was a royalist, and supposing that I must hate all republicans, he might give vent to his feelings without restraint or control. I frequently warned him of the risk he ran in talking as he did, and I always cut him short when he began with his bitter invectives. On the occasion in question, however, he was thoroughly roused, and I made allowance for the excitement under which he laboured. He recapitulated all the wrongs which the Spaniards had suffered during the revolution, and then, stamping his foot, and clenching his fist, he exclaimed— " Never, never shall I die in peace, till I have seen the leaders of the revolution in South America pay with their blood for the crimes they have committed ! "

I believe the old man said a great deal more than he ever intended (for he was a good husband, and a kind father to a Creole wife and children), but I suddenly rose up, and, turning to him, said, " How do you know that I may not, *this moment,* go to the Dictator, and report what you have just uttered ? "

These words acted like electricity on the old

Pelado. The stern, the cruel Francia, stood in his imagination before him. He turned deadly pale, and literally sank down on his knees at my feet. " Do not," he exclaimed—" oh, for the. love of God, and in mercy to my family, do not betray me !"

I told him he was perfectly safe in my hands; but I made it a condition that he should never again talk to me in the same strain ; and I earnestly exhorted him to refrain from giving vent to such language in the presence of any other living soul in Paraguay.

There was another class in the republic that Francia hated and contemned as heartily as he did the old Spaniards, and that was the clergy,— secular and regular,—but more especially the latter. He hated the friars for the influence which they exercised over the people, and for the open profligacy of their lives. The simple-minded and superstitious Paraguayans reverenced a paî (or father), as the immediate representative of God ; they blindly and implicitly followed the instructions given to them, and did whatever was required at their hands. Many of the licentious brotherhood took advantage of this superstitious confidence placed in them by the people, to an extent which, in a moral country like England, it would not only shock every feeling of our nature to relate, but would, in the individual instances, appear to be incredible, and, in the aggregate, be counted as slanderous on humanity.

It was so far well for the cause of morality that Francia was not of a character to put up with the baneful influence exercised by these friars on his people; and he prepared accordingly, in his usual slow, sure, and progressive way, not only to destroy the power of the conventuals, but to overthrow the hierarchical government of the church, and to give the power of the Pope to the winds.

The first instrument he made use of for this purpose was our old friend Paî Montiel, the hospitable curate of San Lorenzo. He was called from his rural retreat there, and appointed chaplain to the troops. It was a sorry exchange for the poor paî. From the jovial, warm-hearted, and unsuspicious country curate, he was gradually converted into the crouching slave, the suspicious spy, the crafty and cunning assistant of his new and fearful master. Montiel had

hitherto been under the mild sway of the Bishop
of Paraguay,—a prelate who, from the leniency,
and perhaps apathy of his character, made his
rule to be unfelt by the clergy of his diocese.
He was, as a native of Spain, like all the rest of
his countrymen, much afraid of the Dictator; and
he carried his clerical dignity, therefore, not only
unobtrusively, but with all the trembling timidity
which a latent fear of Francia's ulterior views in-
spired.

The Roman pontiff and his legally-appointed
bishop ceased in the end to have any authority
or sway in Catholic Paraguay; and in their place
Francia became the pope, and Paî Montiel the
vicar-general of the Republic.

Yours, &c.

W. P. R.

LETTER III.

W. P. R. to Thomas Fair, Esq.

Dr. Parlett and the Medical Practitioners of Assumption—Francia's first interview with Parlett—The celebrated cures he performs—Recalde's daughter—Parlett's death and destitution.

London, 1838.

NOTWITHSTANDING the increasing severity of Francia's government, his manner to myself underwent no alteration. I was freely admitted at all times on business, and I was, by his own invitation, his frequent evening's tertuliano, and the chief, if not the only, channel through which he acquired both European and South American news; and of both he was extremely greedy. From October, 1814, to July of the following year, the port of Assumption continued alternately free and under embargo; but Francia now and then stretched a point, in allowing me to get off such produce as I wanted to ship.

Towards the end of July, a person who proved to be one of no small importance to the republic, arrived at Assumption. This was a Dr. Parlett, from Buenos Ayres, an English medical man, very clever in his profession, but unfortunately of very dissipated habits. They had marred his career in the capital of the United Provinces; and learning from my brother that in Paraguay he might make a great deal of money, he came up with letters of introduction to me, and with a view of establishing himself at Assumption.

According to the usual etiquette, I went to present Parlett, the day after his arrival, at the government palace. The Dictator received him standing, as he did most of those who went to see him, nor did he proffer the Señor Medico a chair.

Francia listened gravely to my speech intro-ductory of Parlett, and then, turning suddenly towards him, he said, "Where did you study, Sir?" Parlett answered, as I suppose he had often done before to South Americans, "In London." The Dictator then quietly addressed me thus : "Señor Don Guillermo, I am acquainted with the University of Oxford, and I have read of the University of Cambridge; I know there is one, celebrated for its medical school, in Edinburgh;

that St. Andrews has a university, and that one or two other places in Great Britain also have; but this is the first time I ever heard of the University of London."

Parlett stood aghast; and a sly expression of Francia's eye told me that he enjoyed his little triumph over the medico. I replied, however, that Mr. Parlett alluded to the *College of Surgeons* in London, a famous body, which admitted medical students to practice. "Ay, ay," said the Dictator, "that is all very well; a *college* there may be, but all the world knows there is no *university* in London."

My new medical friend now brushed up; said it was the college, of course, to which he alluded, and in confirmation he pulled his diploma out of his pocket, tendering it to Francia. But the Dictator would not look at it; "Put it up," he said; —"cure the sick of their maladies, and, as far as I am concerned, I desire you to have no better diploma than the approbation and confidence of my people." The one Doctor then waved the other to retire, but the former gave me a nod, intimating to me to stay where I was. When we were alone, he inquired minutely into the whole

history of Parlett, his abilities, his habits, his
temper, his circumstances; and after I had satisfied him candidly on these points, he seemed to
be pleased on the whole to have such a person as
our new comer in the republic. He sent a kind
message by me to Parlett, assuring him that
while he conducted himself with circumspection,
he should have the Dictator's countenance and
support.

The chief anxiety of Francia was for the health,
not of his people, but of his quarteleros and
troops. The irregular lives which most of them
led engendered much sickness among them, and
rendered a good superintendent of the military
hospital extremely desirable. The medical men,
principally old Spaniards, whom Parlett found established in Assumption, were the veriest quacks,
the most arrant *matasanos** that Spain ever produced. I cannot give you a better idea of what
they were than by repeating what one of them
most seriously said to myself. I had remarked
that he made me frequent visits during the
winter, and seemed to have very little or nothing
to do: so one day I told him—" Why," said old

* Literally, killers of healthy persons.

Dominguez, "we give up visiting our patients during the winter,—it is of no use; nature does not then assist · us, and therefore we wait for the spring!"

In a country which had never been under any other regimen than this, it will readily be believed that a clever English doctor soon "astonished the natives." Ere he had been a month in Assumption, the city resounded with accounts of the marvellous cures effected by the "Medico Ingles." It was believed that no disorder could withstand his skill; and spite of every effort on the part of the 'faculty' in Paraguay to keep down his fame, and raise up prejudices against him, Parlett had soon more business than he could attend to. He broke through every received notion in Paraguay of the dignity of his profession, for, although decisive in his business, he was a rattling, off-hand, merry sort of subject, and altogether antipodal to the grave, staid, and stultified facultativos to whom the people had been accustomed;—men who looked wise, felt a pulse, prescribed simples, and left Nature herself to kill or cure according to her humour.

· Parlett could well have dispensed with much of the business that Francia gave him; for where he was called in, I believe he was paid at the rate of only two rials, or a shilling, for each visit to a quartelero. But, on the other hand, he was sometimes magnificently rewarded by the inhabitants for his surgical abilities.

Such a thing as couching the eye had never been heard of in Paraguay, even by the medicos; but Parlett performed this operation on an old estanciero, who had been rendered for years almost blind by a very bad cataract. So successfully did our new medico operate, that he entirely removed the cataract; and he not only received a fee of 2000 hard dollars (400*l.*), but a succession of all the presents which the gratitude of the old man could devise as likely to be prized by his benefactor.

One of the richest old Spaniards in Assumption, Don Antonio Recalde, a shopkeeper and merchant, had a very pretty daughter, twelve or thirteen years of age, on whom her father quite doted. She suddenly complained one morning of violent pain in one of her eyes, and, during the day, Recalde called in, one after another,

every Spanish doctor who resided in Assumption; but all in vain: not one could tell what was
the matter with the orb, the peculiarity of the caso
being, that the eye watered profusely, and without
ceasing, while yet not the slightest inflammation
took place. Recalde, in despair, at length came
to me in the afternoon. He confessed that all
his own countrymen in the medical line had set
him against Parlett; he feared that this gentleman would not now come in if called; and he
begged me to use my influence with my countryman to induce him to visit the distressed patient.

Away Parlett and I went instantly to visit Miss
Recalde,—the Doctor taking a pocket microscope
with him. We found the poor girl suffering great
pain. Parlett began to investigate the affected
organ with his lens, and after a while discovered,
both to his and my great astonishment, a
piqué or *jigger*, adhering to the pupil of the eye.
This insidious and troublesome little insect, so
well known in the West Indies, Brazil, and other
tropical climates, almost invariably confines its
operations on man's body to his *toes*. It works
into the flesh near the nail,—there deposits its
eggs; and where these have not been properly

taken out, mortification, in many cases, has been known to ensue. The streets of Rio Janeiro offer some of the most loathsome spectacles that can be imagined, in the persons of wretched and filthy negroes, suffering from the unheeded inroads of the small and almost invisible piqué.

On cross-questioning the family, Parlett found that when Recalde's daughter first felt the pain, she was opening up a roll of tobacco, into which piqués often find their way. It had jumped into her eye,—stuck its little claws into the pupil, and apparently could not again extricate itself from its novel situation. Parlett ran home, and returned with a little red precipitate; and while I held the eye-lid open, he anointed the pupil with a fine feather. He reasoned that, smarting under the application, the piqué would make an effort to escape; and so it did:—it loosened its hold, and in five minutes Miss Recalde was quite well. Amazement seized the bystanders; and a friar who was present (no old Spaniard's house was ever free from this sort of vermin), said to me, "Este paysano de V. ò es diablo ò es angel,—porque todo, todo lo entiende." "This countryman of yours is either a devil or an angel, for there is nothing on earth which he does not understand."

Recalde,—miserly as a merchant, but generous as a father,—presented Parlett with six doubloons (£20), for his five minutes' operation.

This same Miss Recalde will be found to stand prominently forward in " Francia's diatribe on Rennger," a celebrated paper, of which we have hereafter to speak, and give a copy.

To conclude with Dr. Parlett. His celebrity reached its climax, shortly after the affair of the piqué, by his cure of an old negress who was attacked with a decided case of *pasmo reàl,* or locked-jaw. This fatal disorder is not unfrequent in Paraguay, and it never was even attempted to be cured by the Paraguay doctors. Parlett was of course left to operate as he pleased on the body of the poor negress. If I recollect well, he made some extraordinary experiment upon her: but she recovered under his hands; and thenceforward every other practitioner was fain to "hide his diminished head," as long as Parlett chose to reign lord of the ascendant.

He became a favourite of Francia, who encouraged him in every way, and he made a great deal of money whenever he exerted his professional abilities.   But his habits were too inveterate to yield to new circumstances, new aspirations, or even to established fame and increasing prosperity.   He remained voluntarily for some years in Paraguay, but his anxiety to quit it, after the despotic gloom of Francia had clouded and enveloped the land, was always met by impediments on the part of the Dictator. Parlett became careless, dejected, more than ever a slave to intemperance; and, at last, he so undermined his constitution, in thus seeking a miserable refuge from the real and imaginary ills which surrounded him, that he died, on the very eve of his departure from Paraguay, under circumstances of extreme misery.   He was one of many men of abilities whom I have known in South America; and who, released there from the moral restraint to which they had been accustomed at home, and without sufficient energy of character to resist early temptation, have sunk to their graves unheeded and unlamented, instead of being followed to them by good men sorrowing over departed worth and talent.

Yours, &c.

W. P. R.

LETTER IV.

W. P. R. to Thomas Fair, Esq.

THE BANISHMENT OF MENDEZ.

The establishment of Mendez—Doña Juanita—Walking-dress of
the Assumpcianas—And of a Montevideana—Not admitted
to the Cathedral—The Tertulia—Intimation of Banishment
—Desolation—A Woman's fortitude—I assist Mendez—His
departure—A narrow escape—Doña Juanita's letter—The
Port of Quarepotí—A break-down in a wood—Further
troubles — Reflections — Journey continued —Curuguatí—
Mendez's release—And return to Buenos Ayres.

London, 1838.

Shortly after my arrival in Assumption, I was
followed by a person of the name of Don Manuel
Mendez Caldeyra ; and I purpose in this letter
to give a sketch of his sojourn in Paraguay, as
an illustration, coming under my own notice, of
Francia's mode of banishment, which constituted
so remarkable a feature in his general system of
government.

'Mr. Mendez was of a respectable family of
Montevideo,—had assisted in defending it against
Sir Samuel Auchmuty,—was a shopkeeper, and
sort of general merchant ;—and with all his stock

in trade, with his family and *penates*, he had
come from Buenos Ayres to Paraguay, in the
hope of bettering his fortune. His family consisted of Doña Juanita Mendez de Bianquet, his
wife; of three engaging children,—two boys and
a girl.; and of four or five domestic slaves, as
much part of the family as were the children or
wife themselves. There was Petrona, the ama
de llaves, or housekeeper, and Antonia, the favourite ama de leche, or former nurse; there
was also her daughter, converted into a little
lady's maid, Cosme the cook, and Antonio the
man of all work. Such was the establishment of
Mendez.

He was active in his vocation, honourable in
his dealings ; and he had a good deal of shrewd-
ness, with some humour in his composition. He
was very proud of his wife and children (for what
good citizen either is or can be otherwise ?) ; and
his better half being a " clever woman," Don
Manuel (again as every worthy citizen, under
such circumstances ought to do) *gave in* on all
proper occasions, viz., whenever Doña Juana
preferred her own judgment to his, or whenever
she resolved to have her own way, which was

Doña Juanita was the daughter of Captain Bianquet, who had served under his Catholic Majesty, the King of Spain; and she was, though born in Gallicia, brought, at a tender age, to South America. She was reared and educated in Montevideo,—acquired all the grace of body, and all the liveliness of spirit, for which the Montevideanas are so remarkable, and of course, looking on herself as one of them, she was a "patriota decidida." Don Manuel led her to the hymeneal altar, when she was about sixteen, and he ten years older; they had been married eight years when they came to Paraguay with their little flock; and three finer children than theirs I never saw.

With this happy couple I got very intimate: their manners and mode of life were so much more European than those of any of the worthy Paraguayans who surrounded me; there was so much good nature and good humour in Mendez, —so much sprightliness and conversational talent in his wife; and their *ménage* partook withal so much of the air of an English fireside, that I became a constant *tertuliano* with them.

Doña Juanita was altogether different from anything that the Paraguay ladies had ever

either seen or imagined, and her many innova-
tions on their established customs and habits
were looked upon at first with a somewhat suspicious eye.   Her low dresses, and the extreme
transparency of her lace and gauze veils (Doña
Juana had a very fine skin); the display of her
ankle (it was a very neat one), and the body-
stays (unknown in Assumption) to round off her
taper waist, were, in the eyes of the more scrupulous Paraguayans, all viewed as *contra bonos
mores*.   Doña Juana was made to feel this in a
very mortifying way.   However scantily the native
ladies of rank dressed at home, yet when they
walked abroad, especially when they went to
church, which was almost every day, they were
closely muffled up.   They wore black bombazeen
dresses, reaching nearly to the ground, while the
rebozo, or hood, enveloped their heads and the
upper parts of their bodies.   Their eyes were
bent on the ground, their large rosaries depended from their wrists, and they avoided anything like display in their walking attire.*

With a pride of heart not uncommon to the

* This has strict reference to the higher classes: the lower
were invariably dressed in white, and in a way to develop their
forms precisely as nature had made them.

fair sex, Doña Juanita reserved for the first Sun-
day that she went to mass the triumph of art and
taste to be displayed in her own person, as contrasted with the want of either, in those of the
native females of Paraguay. She put on a superb black satin dress, fringed at bottom with
deep lace, and leaving a happy display of her
well-turned ankle: she wore fine ribbed white
silk stockings, and satin shoes: her hair was
beautifully plaited, and gathered up by a large
and costly tortoise-shell comb; and over her
head, neck, and shoulders was thrown a magnificent black lace veil, disposed in elegant dra-
pery across the breast. White kid gloves, and a
French fan, completed Doña Juana's church dress;
and out she sallied, stepping with the grace of an
Ariadne, and with all the dignity which a conscious feeling of superiority could not fail to en-
gender in her breast. Close behind her walked
her attendant, her handsome little mulatto slave,
prettily dressed, and carrying over her arm the
small but richly-embroidered carpet on which her
mistress was to kneel in church.

As Doña Juanita walked along the streets she
was much admired; but, alas! here her triumph
ended. When she got into the church itself, a

murmur of disapprobation ran through rank and
file of the ladies there assembled.   The dress of
the new comer was a scandal to religion ; whis-
pering in Guarani took place ; the cause of discontent was conveyed to some of the officiating
and officious priests ; a movement among them
was observed ; and the result was, that Doña
Juanita was openly and shamefully ordered out
of the Cathedral!   The hypocritical priests affected to be scandalised ; and it was publicly intimated to Doña Juanita that, if she returned
again to church, it must be in a long bombazeen
dress, and a rebozo.

Doña Juana came home burning with the
indignation of a woman offended in a tender
point : but she was soon brought to join with us
in laughing at the barbarous and ungallant be-
haviour of the rustic priests ; and she was perhaps
soothed by the consideration that she owed her
misfortune to the envy of those of her sex who
could not bear to see themselves eclipsed by her
dazzling superiority.

At the tertulia of Mr. and Mrs. Mendez I
generally met our agreeable friend Don 'Andres
Gomez (who amused us much by the drollery
with which he caricatured his own countrymen

the Paraguayans); Doña Juana Gomez, his
sister, a bas-bleu; and an intelligent young merchant, a native of Spain, called Barbeito, who,
like ourselves, had recently come to Paraguay.
There were other less regular visitors; for, in
spite of the unfortunate affair of the Cathedral,
the Mendezes became favourites in Paraguay;
and this occasional society altogether formed an
agreeable change from the general monotony of my
life in Assumption. As we all came from different
quarters, we had a good stock of observation on
men and manners to throw into the general fund.
We had music, chess, sometimes dancing, and
always a regular set-out of the tea-things, "a la
Inglesa," as Mrs. Mendez had seen them in
Montevideo, after its capture by the English.

Mendez prospered so well in his business that,
in eight months after his arrival at Assumption,
he determined to make a trip with a small cargo
of produce of his own to Buenos Ayres, and to
return immediately with merchandise suitable for
Paraguay. He did this advantageously for himself, his fair partner managing his business in his
absence; and he got back to the republic towards
the end of August, 1815. On his arrival he
waited on the Dictator, as was usual,—was gra-

ciously received by his Excellency, who inquired
minutely into the news stirring in Buenos Ayres,
—and was told "to depart in peace."

It was not more than a week after Mendez's
return that his general tertulianos, including
myself, were assembled in his patio enjoying the
cool and refreshing air of a beautiful moonlight
evening, and in high glee with bad puns and
good impromptus from Gomez and Barbeito,
when suddenly the Government Notary Public
stalked into the circle, and gloomily beckoned
Mendez to retire with him. Fear and trembling
fell on most of the party; nor were we long left
in doubt as to the ominous visit of the man of law.
Mendez returned, pale, trembling, agitated; and
on his wife springing up to enquire what had
happened, his choked utterance would scarcely
permit him to say that sentence of banishment to
Curuguatí had been issued against him by the
malignant despot of Paraguay.

Neither in this, nor in any other case, did
Francia deign to allege a pretext for his proceeding. The sufferer in every instance,—the
almost invariably *innocent* sufferer,—was left
to guess at any proximate cause which he him-

self might fancy of his misfortune. No man, to my knowledge, ever acted more prudently and more circumspectly than did Mendez in Paraguay; so we were left to suppose that the capricious and jealous tyrant had taken umbrage at his victim's simply making a journey to *hated* Buenos Ayres.

From the moment that the news of Mendez's banishment became known, his house, his family, himself, were deserted, as if mortal and contagious disease were within his dwelling. Not a soul but was terrified to go near the banished man, dreading a participation of his doom. His business had been pretty extensive : no one now *dared* to act as his agent, recover his debts, or take charge of his property; no one would pay him; no one would purchase, at any price, anything he had. He could not even, on any terms, get a single person to charter him a vessel which might carry himself and family to the port nearest to his place of banishment. The mark of Cain seemed suddenly to be branded on his forehead. All men fled from him, as from the plague ; in the midst of a populous city, he was at once abandoned to the solitude of the desert.

The weight of his misfortune pressed Mendez to the earth; and had he been left to himself he must have sunk down into utter and hopeless despair. But it is in trying circumstances like these that *woman* frequently displays an unostentatious but active energy of mind, a capability of wrestling with ills of the greatest magnitude, an alacrity and a cheerfulness in meeting and repelling every new and increasing difficulty, which man often hastily pronounces to be beyond his own strength, incredibly beyond that of the frail and tender vessel of the weaker sex.

Doña Juanita Mendez, for one at least, exemplified the truth of my proposition. She saw that the lot of her husband, her own, and her children's, was inevitable; and she gently but firmly urged on Mendez the necessity of a reconciliation to his altered circumstances. She soothed him, assisted him in everything, was active, cheerful, and judicious. The horror of Curuguati, and of banishment to a pestilential desert, *without hope* of returning from it as long as the cruel Francia lived, gradually but rapidly assumed a less frightful aspect under the spirit displayed and fortitude exercised by the wife,—

by the very person of whom it was at first thought that, in sending her into banishment, the cold-blooded Dictator was consigning her to an early and unavoidable grave.

I could not and would not stand by and see the Mendezes abandoned in the hour of their utmost need. Whatever Francia might think of it, I resolved at once substantially and openly to assist them. The day for Mendez leaving Assumption was not fixed by Francia. I had in the port a large brig of our own, called the San José, and in the usual form I presented a petition to government, stating that Don Manuel Mendez had chartered the vessel, and praying that it might be permitted to load for Quarepotí. The license to load was signed by Francia himself that same day. I next went to the government notary public, and had a power of attorney executed by Mendez in my own favour. I intimated to many of his debtors that they were to pay their balances to me; and lastly, I had Mendez's goods and produce, which he could not take with him, transferred to my own stores.

All this occupied about ten days; and during that time I was called by Francia to several in-

terviews, in which he eschewed, and, of course,
so did I, all mention of the name of the banished
man. In the troubles which I then began to
have with the Dictator, and through many angry
moods in which he showed himself to me, he
never once alluded to the banishment of Mendez.

It was a very sorrowful affair when that poor
man, with his amiable wife and engaging children,
accompanied only by myself, and followed by his
faithful domestic slaves, walked slowly down to
the quay, to set sail for his place of banishment.
A death-like silence reigned in the streets as we
passed along; every one inwardly commiserating
the fate of the unhappy family, but none daring
to make any open show of their sympathy. Doña
Juanita's fortitude and constancy failed her not
even on this trying occasion. Whatever her own
feelings might be, she was too intent on cheering
her husband to give the least vent to them; and
I could not but feel very high admiration of
the woman, on witnessing the blended softness,
affection, and noble spirit which characterised her
whole conduct and bearing at this distressing
juncture of her life.

An accident which had nearly proved fatal

to myself, just as I was taking leave of Mendez and his wife, threw them into great consternation. I stood on a long plank, which connected the brig with the quay, and while I there
stood, the vessel, by some mistaken order, was
got under way. I was precipitated into the
river, which is here very deep, and I was swept
into a strong eddy. A peon who stood by,
plunged in after me, and with much exertion,
and very great danger to himself, succeeded in
dragging me out, after I had become quite insensible. I was placed on board the San José,
and, as soon as I recovered, I ordered the patron
once more to get under way, resolving to accompany the exiles a few leagues up the river.
I remained two days with them,—saw that all
was comfortably arranged for their passage,—
and, disembarking about twelve leagues above
Assumption, I returned overland, full of sad reflections on the domestic misery which the hate-
ful and despotic sway of Francia was spreading,
far and near, over the hitherto peaceful and
happy land which had now so irrevocably come
under the grasp of his own iron hand.

The return of the San José brought me ac-

counts from Mendez of his safe arrival in Quarepotí; but my own banishment from the republic
left me without any further news of the exiles
for five months afterwards. I then, being in
Corrientes, received letters from Mendez and
Doña Juanita, and I think I cannot do better
than relate their progress to Curuguatí in the
words of the latter, as detailed to me in her own
communication, which I shall, therefore, now
transcribe. I give a faithful and almost literal
translation of her letter.

           " *Curuguatí*, *3rd February*, 1816.

  " Would you believe, my dear friend, that it
was only after a journey of four months and
twenty days that we arrived at this our ultimate
place of banishment? Such is the fact; and,
although I scarcely know in what colours I am
to depict to you the miseries we have endured
since we left Assumption, I must endeavour to
sketch to you some of the leading and lament-
able events of our journey.

  " We were long detained after we left the San
José by the want of a conductor,* and we had to

  * A carrier with the requisite number of waggons drawn by
bullocks for a journey overland.!

put up with every imaginable wretchedness, in
the mean time, at the miserable port of Quarepoti. The smiling valleys, the shady groves,
the brawling brooks, the green sward, and the
pure air to which we had been accustomed were
exchanged for the unhealthy morass, and the
stagnant pool. Idleness and squalid poverty
sat at the door of each of the dozen mud hovels
which are dignified, as a whole, with the title of
'Villa.' The air and the earth swarmed with
every insect hostile to man, while money, to provide even the necessaries of life, was here of no
avail.

"During our detention at Quarepoti our poor
negro, Cosme, was drowned, while bathing in the
Paraguay. You know what a faithful creature
he was, and what was the strength of his affection for all the family; so you may imagine how
sincerely we grieved over his loss.

" On the 24th of November the conductor, at
length, arrived with his waggons, and that same
day we loaded and despatched them all save one,
which we reserved as our family-carriage, and
which we detained till the following morning.
We expected by the evening to overtake the

main body. We journeyed over an open but
swampy country till six in the evening, when we
entered a dark forest.   Here the road became
so impassable that, ere we had proceeded fifty
yards, down came the crazy cart, and landed us
all in a bed,—not of roses,—but of thorns. We
were a good deal frightened, though not at all
hurt; but our principal anxiety arose from our
being at some distance from any house where we
could take shelter for the night. We walked a
league on foot through a deep and gloomy wood,
Mendez, Antonio, and a peon carrying the children (already tired with a long day's harassing
journey) nearly all the way. I thought we
should never get a sight of the hovel of which
we were in search, and when we came to it at
last, I hailed it as joyfully as if we had come to
a palace. Our beds were ricketty hide stretchers,
without mattress of any kind; we slept in the
clothes which we wore; we were tormented by
venomous insects;—but we had escaped the
tigers, and were safe once more in the dwelling
of man.

    "Next morning, at dawn, Mendez went back
to have our cart repaired, and as he returned

once more to us in the forenoon, his horse at
some distance from the cottage suddenly took
fright; it reared, plunged, and became altogether frantic; it flew off at last like lightning,
—stumbled,—fell; and Mendez being thrown
with great impetuosity to the ground, his right
leg was broken in two places.

 " I still tremble as often as I call to mind the
events of that frightful day. Oh! the agony of
bringing the sufferer from where he lay to the
wretched hut where we were now to take up our
abode. I was almost insensible to every thing
which passed around me. I could only weep,
and implore the aid of Heaven in this my hour of
greatest need and distress. On man I could
not call for help, for I was in a desert where no
human aid was at hand.

 " With a heart brim-full of sorrow, then, but
placing my reliance on the mercy of God, I had
Mendez brought to the cottage; and there, having
not a soul near me who had the slightest idea of
the mode of treating such a case, I myself, as I
best could, set the bones, and bandaged the frac-
tured limb. I knew not what to do for the best.
I immediately, however, despatched a courier to

Assumption with a letter for Dr. Parlett, beg-
ging him to send me specific instructions how to
proceed: I received them at the end of six days,
and by following them closely, my patient began
gradually, though very slowly, to mend.

"We were pent up for nearly two months in
one little close apartment, in which there was
scarcely standing-room for us all. Mendez suffered greatly from the pain of his fractures, and
long confinement to a miserable bed in so miserable a place. I did all I could to alleviate his
sufferings, and I must say he very manfully bore
up against them.

" By the 20th of January we ordered our carts
once more, for, though still not entirely well,
Mendez was able to ride on horseback, and we
were most anxious to get to our journey's end.
He cannot even yet put his foot to the ground,
and he only moves along on crutches. Ah! my
friend, what a difference in our fate in the course
of a few fleeting months! In that short space
we have exchanged health, happiness, and prosperity, for poverty, banishment, and every privation of life; my husband, too, I fear, will never
perfectly recover the use of his limb. Yet have

I great cause to be thankful to a Divine Providence which has spared his life, and vouchsafed
to me a spirit of conformity to bear up against
my heavy trials.

" On the 22nd we left Tacurubì (the place of
Mendez's misfortune); arrived in three days at
San Estanislao, one of the Indian reductions,
where we were kindly received and treated by
the Administrador; and on the 28th we resumed
our journey.

" Never, even in South America, did you see
such roads as we had to travel. Our unwieldy
vehicle, crazing and creaking, now jolting over
huge trunks of trees, now buried in a swamp,
or anon stuck fast in a bog, accomplished two
leagues in three days! Mendez, perceiving that
at such a rate we stood a chance of never seeing
Curuguatí at all, sent back to the town for four
mules to carry us forward, and the following day,
accordingly, we separated from the carts. At
the end of three days we got to this place; but
indeed, indeed, I thought I should have died on
the road. The heat,—you have felt a January
sun in Paraguay,—was truly terrific. Mendez
and I had each one of our children before us on

our mules, and how these little ones bore up
against the burning rays of the sun, and the
fatigue of the mules' pace, I really know not.

"We have been here two days. Why should
I describe a place which, alas! is so well known
to you by report? Yet we have already experienced the utmost kindness, at the hands of
all the poor but hospitable and simple people of
Curuguatí. There are many here you know similarly situated to ourselves; among others, we
have found Loisaga, who is acting the part of
a father to us.

"I have here only given you a sketch of events
since we left Assumption; but when we meet we
have many interesting particulars to recount to
you. Louisa and her little brothers beg their
kind remembrances to you. Mendez writes to
you, and he will tell you how often we recall to
mind and talk over the pleasant times of our
Assumption tertulia. We still laugh at the puns
and the rhymes which we all attempted, and at
the fine words with which my dear and worthy
friend, Doña Juanita Gomez, so often puzzled
us. She writes to me very regularly.

"We are anxious to hear something of you,

as well as of your brother Don Juan, and of Don
Juan Postelfé* (pray don't laugh, you know how
impossible it is to write his name). Do let us
hear from you.

> " Ever your faithful friend,
> " JUANA BIANQUET DE MENDEZ."

Mendez and his wife were at first buoyed up
with a hope that, when Francia came to consider
there was absolutely nothing against them, he
would allow them to depart from the republic;
but their appeals to him only confirmed him in
his determination to keep them where they were.
Months rolled on, years passed away, and still
Mendez and his family were exiles at Curuguatí.
But Doña Juanita was a lively sensible woman;
Don Manuel was an active merchant, and always
ready to make the most of his position. They
did such business as so poor a place would permit, and they conjoined the management of a
farm with their other occupations; they educated
their children, and they drew about them a little
society; they reconciled themselves to the feeling that Curuguatí was to be their home till the

* Postlethwajte.

'grave became Francia's ; they ceased to trouble him, which was, as I told them from the beginning it would be, all in their favour.

In 1826, when most of the foreignets in Paraguay were permitted to leave the republic, Mendez, to his unspeakable joy, found himself and family included in the happy number. You yourself may recollect the rest. Our brig, the San José, the vessel which had taken the Mendez family to Quarepotí, was then in Assumption, where she had for some years lain. Our agent, Don José de Maria, you know, brought the whole family down with him; and, after their banishment for eleven years, I had the pleasure of seeing them safely landed at Buenos Ayres. If time and a bad climate had impaired, in some degree, the charms of Doña Juanita, she had now an interesting daughter grown up, in the wilds of Curuguatí, to woman's estate. This was the pretty little Louisa, with whom I had had many a romp in Assumption, before her long term of exile began. She soon afterwards captivated a young estanciero, of good property, who woo'd her and won her for his bride. Mendez went again into business;

his sons turned out fine young men; and they are still all prospering in Buenos Ayres.

Both Mendez and his wife assured me that twelve months elapsed ere they could rightly comprehend in their own minds that they were beyond the reach and the control of the fearful Francia.

Before I proceed with the further details which I have to give regarding Paraguay, my brother, following as closely as we can the chronological order of events, will now give you his singular adventures from the time of his leaving Buenos Ayres to that of his arrival at Assumption.

Yours, &c.

W. P. R.

63

LETTER V.

COMMENCEMENT OF THE LETTERS OF J. P. ROBERTSON.

J. P. R. to Thomas Fair, Esq.

Introductory—Serious aspect of affairs—Preparations for a return to Paraguay—Interview with the Director Alvear, and his Secretary Herrera—A fatal letter intrusted to me, and a fatal shipment made—I sail for Assumption—Candioti, Governor of Santa Fé—His speech and conduct—My capture and treatment by Artigueños—A perilous predicament, and yet more wonderful escape from it, through an Indian—The Artigueños dressed in Bond Street clothes, and I in Artigueño attire — I am forced to play the flute—Arrival at the Bajada—A fortunate encounter—I am lodged in the common gaol—The inmates of it—My transfer to a solitary cell—The Honourable Captain Jocelyne Percy—His letter to Artigas—I am set at liberty.

London, 1838.

There is seldom any friendship so endearing as that which, having been contracted in early life, proceeds down the stream of time in a smooth and uninterrupted course, till the warm and early associations of youth blend and combine with the graver reflections of more mellowed years. Each *class* of associations belonging to the one period of life imparts pleasure to that of the other;

and there arises from the union the agreeable result of enjoyment, heightened by comparison and contrast, and of confidence in the enduring character of *future* intercourse, fortified by the experienced consistency of *past*.

I can truly say that our friendship, now of so many years' standing, has been of this cast; and it is with no ordinary pleasure I bear the feeble testimony which the addressing of these letters to you may afford, of the sincerity with which I make the declaration.

Of a very few of the events recorded you were yourself a personal witness: in one or two of them you were an actor. But I hope the slight anomaly of inditing to you that which you already know, will be overlooked, not only because it is necessary to keep up the continuity of my tale, but because the substratum of my narrative is laid, in not a few instances, by letters which were addressed to yourself, never copied, and which I have now been able to consult only by your placing them at my disposal.

Without further discourse on what concerns more immediately ourselves than the public, I proceed to take up the thread of my story, which

you will recollect broke off at the forty-seventh
letter of the second volume of our first series of
" Letters on Paraguay." I had then just got to
Buenos Ayres, brimful of news from Assumption,
and if not quite so big as the consul himself with
his European projects, yet desirous of throwing
no obstacle in the way of their realization, by not
proceeding to England. But as I found I could
not do this without prejudice to my individual
concerns, and as the first consul had appointed
me neither the outfit nor the income of an am-
bassador, but only certain specimens of produce,
which, if rejected by the House of Commons, and
carried to market, might have produced me
twenty guineas, I thought I was fairly in a position to mind my own business, even to the dis-
regarding, for the present, of his. To this resolution I the more readily came, because every day
was letting in some new and more extraordinary
light upon the quixotic schemes, the untractable
character, and the inflated aspirations of the
ruler of Paraguay.

During my stay at Buenos Ayres, 1814—1815,
the whole continent of South America was, as
you know, involved in the direst anarchy and

civil war. That city stood in a measure by itself, cut off from intercourse, whether political or mercantile, with every other part of the now heaving and agitated dominions of Old Spain in the southern hemisphere. Chile, having first become a prey to internal feuds, was, after having declared its independence, reconquered by the enemy. Buenos Ayres thus lost the importation of two millions of dollars annually, and the benefit of exporting a like amount of produce and manufactures.

In Upper Peru, the royalist and insurgent armies were disputing every inch of ground beyond Potosi; while the mines in that rich district were left unwrought, or, through want of care, became inundated.

The Banda Oriental, or east side of the River Plate, united under General Artigas, with the pompous title of " Most Excellent Lord Protector," bade defiance to all law and order; while Paraguay, wrapt up by Francia in his isolated, selfish, and malignant policy, stood a silent and inactive spectator of the revolutionary desolation which overspread the land.

During this state of things I was to return to

Paraguay by the river. The journey by land was out of the question. The roads were infested by robbers; and the country was overrun by broken detachments of undisciplined troops scouring the plains, or attacking the straggling villages in search of booty and plunder. One signature alone, as a protection for the person, was respected,—that of Artigas; but I was not in a position to procure it, being a resident in Buenos Ayres, with which he was at open war. He had no vessels, however, in the river. Buenos Ayres had; and this line of communication with Paraguay, especially under a sailing license which I had from the Honourable Captain Jocelyn Percy, then commanding the British forces in the River Plate, was considered quite safe. General Alvear was at the time Director of Buenos Ayres, and my friend Mr. Herrera Secretary of State. Both knew me to be well acquainted with Paraguay, and, more than any other person, in the confidence of the Dictator, if that could be called confidence which was limited to the communication of such matters as it was necessary I should be informed of, in order to be of any use to him. The Director Alvear being anxious to initiate a

correspondence with Francia, of which the object
was to draw recruits from Paraguay, in order
to strengthen the legions of the River Plate, I
was invited to an audience at the Fort (or Government House), for the purpose of being consulted by Alvear as to the probability of Francia's
sending men to Buenos Ayres, in return for which
arms and ammunition should be sent to him from
thence.   I thought the thing very improbable;
but stated how impossible it was that I, a neutral
and a private individual engaged in commercial
pursuits, should agree, in such troublous times,
to be charged with such a proposal. At the same
time I suggested that there could be no objection
to the Government's making such proposal if it
thought proper by letter, which, if put sealed into
the letter-bag of the vessel that was to convey
me to Paraguay, should there be delivered to its
address.   On this suggestion Alvear acted; and
a sealed letter, which I never saw, was, with other
correspondence, sent from the post-office by order
of the Buenos Ayres Government, for conveyance
to Francia.   I have been the more minute in my
observations about this letter, because, as the
event will show, my fate was sealed up in it; and,

in consequence of its contents, my personal intercourse with the Dictator was brought to an
abrupt and disastrous termination.

I bethought me, as the time approached for my
return to the republic, of the grievous disappointment that would be experienced by the Supremo
(or Supreme), as Francia was now styled, on his
finding that I had been unable to proceed on his
mission to England. I therefore determined to
mitigate, as far as possible, the consequences of
this catastrophe, by getting, in Buenos Ayres,
everything I possibly could toward the comple-
tion of Francia's various commissions. Cocked-
hats, sashes, lace, musical instruments, military
clothing, swords, pistols, &c., were all procured
and shipped ; and, on application to the Buenos
Ayres Government, no obstacle was offered to
the shipment of a few muskets, and of some mu-
nitions of war. All this was perfectly legal; for
Paraguay, though in a state of isolated non-intercourse, was yet at war with neither Artigas nor
Buenos Ayres. These countries, it is true, were
all on bad terms with one another : the demons
of discord and jealousy hovered over them in
busy and ominous action, now chafing by fancied

insult their petty prejudices, and anon, by stirring them up respectively to implied acts of partial aggression, drawing them every day nearer to a common point of collision. But they were not actually at *war;* and Paraguay especially claimed the privilege of being considered a neutral party, both by the Government of Buenos Ayres, and by General Artigas. The embarkation, therefore, by me, under the sanction of Alvear, of things wanted by Francia, could on no possible grounds be construed into an illegal act. So convinced of this was Captain Percy, that he did not hesitate, with a full knowledge of all the circumstances of the case, to issue, as I have said, a sailing license for the protection of my vessel and property.

Thus equipped and protected I was piloted in the direction of Paraguay, and found myself in my little bark once more cutting through the waters, and stemming the strong but placid current of the glassy Paraná. By dint of a month's perseverance we reached Santa Fé, then governed by my old friend Candioti. Friend though he was, he was too much pressed by the Indians on one hand, and harassed by civil discord on the other, to think of allowing me to pass his door with so opportune, though limited, a supply of arms as that which I had intended for Francia. He, therefore, told me very civilly, but very determinedly, that he must issue a friendly order for their disembarkation at Santa Fé. It was in vain that I pleaded the circumstances under which they were shipped. "Señor Don Juan," said he, "self-preservation is the first law of nature, and, in fulfilment of this law, we must here detain your muskets. The ornamental finery we will allow to proceed to its destination, as well as the sabres, because we have plenty of them; but there, take the value of the muskets and ammunition in dollars, and tell his Excellency the Dictator, it is a good sign of the tranquillity of his republic that he has leisure to think so much about music, mathematics, and gold-lace. Here, you know, we are not in a position, at present, to think of anything but the enemy, and our only means of meeting him successfully is by the collection of all the muskets and ball which we can possibly procure."

So saying, the princely gaucho paid the full value of the stores, and gave me an. elaborate document to show that neither my poverty nor my will had been consenting to the sale, but that a power superior to either, that of coercion, had enforced it.

Lightened of what I knew would be, in the eyes of the Dictator, the most important part of my cargo, I once more bent my course for Paraguay. I felt assured now that all chance of interruption or hostility was at an end, for Santa Fé was then confederate with General Artigas,— and I sailed under the license of his Lieutenant-Governor, Candioti. How much mistaken I was in my anticipation the sequel will show. The truth is, that all of those petty, and subordinate chiefs and governors were independent the one of the other; and that their supreme lord and master, Artigas, was obliged to wink at the irregularities they committed, as he was often made to feel the want of unity in action, and the disobedience of orders which grew out of them.

I have before told you of the rich and varied beauty of the scenery of the river Paraná, and what admirable pheasant-shooting there is to be met with along its finely-wooded banks. I went forth in my boat one evening in quest of game,

the vessel being then tied to a tree, and waiting
a fair wind a little below the port of Goya. The
evening was one of majestic, but serene splendour, and, as I returned with six brace of pheasants in the stern of the boat, the parting rays of
the sun were tinging, with vivid glow, the rich
and varied plumage of the birds. A little in the
distance lay our silent bark, and up, from beside
it, on the shore, rose the curling smoke from the
fire kindled by the sailors. The river was as
smooth as glass, and as bright too; and the stillness of the magnificent scene was rather heightened than interrupted by the splashing oars of
my little boat's crew. Now and then, too, was
heard in the distance the cackling of a pheasant,
in search of a mate it was destined never to
find; and the uncouth chatter, at intervals, of
monkeys, and of parrots coming to roost, told of
woods thickly tenanted by grotesque images of
the human form, and by feathered mimics of the
human voice.

It was not till we came close to the vessel that
my contemplative associations were broken in
upon, and that with a shock so sudden and so
rude, as to bereave me almost, for a moment, of

my senses. Just as I stood up in the boat, and was preparing to mount the sides of the little ship, a company of tattered and ruffian-looking soldiers, who had heretofore lain concealed behind the bulwarks, rose simultaneously, and, pointing their whole musketry into the skiff, threatened to sink it, and shoot me if we moved one inch in advance. Simultaneously with this terrific reception which was given to me, there came round the stern of the vessel a boat which had been kept on the other side of her, so as not to be seen, with half a dozen more of the brigands, armed with carbines and sabres, and brandishing the latter with fierce gesticulation in the faces of myself and of my little unarmed crew. Resistance to so numerous and well-armed a gang would have been impossible, even if we had been prepared for an attack from them; but, taken, as we were, by surprise, the very shadow of opposition would have been madness. I hastened, therefore, to make every demonstration of complete surrender. Our boat was then taken possession of; while I, deafened and disgusted with oaths, and almost stunned with repeated blows from the flat blades of the ruffians' sabres, was forced by them into the vessel. Here I was immediately pinioned, and fastened by a rope to a ring-bolt on the deck. What a scene of desolation presented itself to my eyes! The crew of Paraguayans had been all put on shore,—the deck was in possession of between thirty and forty of the very worst class of the marauding soldiers of Artigas,—the hatches of the vessel were open, and the cases and bales of merchandise, every one of them more or less violated, lay strewed about;—my own poop-cabin, which I had left the picture of neatness and comfort, was rendered desolate by every evidence of spoliation and debauch;—my scattered wardrobe was partitioned out among the robbers;—wine was spilt and glass broken in every direction;—one man was lying on my bed in a state of intoxication;—by his side sat three more in wrangling contention over a pack of cards;—and, as if gambling were not of itself a sufficient excitement, they were quaffing large libations of raw spirits. Every one of the demon-like gang was, more or less, in a state of intoxication; and while, with frequent reference to me, significant gestures were passing from

one to the other, commingled with open threats
of instantly taking my life unless I discovered
to them all the valuable property, and especially
the money, they supposed to be in the vessel, I
was left in profound ignorance of the cause and
origin of so barbarous a violation of law. As
you may conceive, neither enviable nor comfortable were my forebodings of what was likely to
be the issue of an outrage so ominously commenced. Night came on,—sentinels were placed
over the crew on shore,—I was more tightly
bound,—and, after witnessing for hours a scene
of license and debauch too frightful to be conceived, and too gross to be pourtrayed, I was
thrust down into the hold of the vessel, and had
the hatches closed over my head. Awful as such
a predicament was,—hearing over my head, as I
did, the clanking of steel scabbards, and the
loud jar of contentious words as to what should
be done with me and my property,—my situation
was yet tolerable as compared with what it had
been upon deck. There, discussions were openly
going on before me as to how I should die,—
threats, with brandishing of sabres, followed.
Every glass of spirits which I saw taken by

every man rendered him, visibly to me, more
frantic, and many a time did I inwardly implore,
at the hands of some one more desperate than
the rest, a speedy death as preferable to such
protracted agony. How often, with Shakspeare,
have I since exclaimed—

> " There's a Divinity that shapes our ends,
> Rough-hew them how we will."

Sleepless was the part of the night I had
hitherto passed, but yet, so imperative are the
demands of Nature, so much higher and over-
bearing the laws by which she is regulated than
any mere temporary obstruction that can be offered to them, that, though I was ill at ease in
body and in mind,—pierced by the cords that
bound me,—in the midst of the ruin and devas-
tation of my own property,—my life depending
upon the breath of any one of forty drunken
freebooters;—notwithstanding all this, the noise
of their revelries gradually died away upon my
ears,—neither fear nor sorrow had any longer
terrors for sleep,—and I sank into a repose more
profound than any of which, before or since, I
can bear recollection.

Everybody knows the intensity of pleasure

connected with the awakening out of a horrible
dream, and, upon returning consciousness, finding that he is in the same comfortable bed
on which he last lay down,—and in the midst
of the security, love, and endearment of his
domestic circle,—instead of being in the awful
predicament realised to him by the horrors of
some nightmare, from which it has baffled all his
efforts to escape.

Comparatively few have had *reversed* to them
this state of things. It is only the felon condemned to death,—the exile from his country,—
the prisoner for debt,—the captive in war,—the
bereaved husband or widow,—and a few others,
—exceptions, happily, to the common lot of
humanity,—that are doomed to find *their* nightmare in their waking moments. They may
dream of many of the joys which, in the course
of life, have constituted their Elysium ; but returning consciousness dispels the happy illusion
of the dream, and leaves memory,—with painful
accuracy,—to usher up all the sad realities of
their woe.

This latter case was strictly mine. I had
been away in the woods, among the pheasants,

in my slumbers, and it was only my waking moments that told me I was in a den of thieves. The first intimation that I had of this was from the blow of the flat side of a sabre, followed by a stentorian voice calling upon me to get up, and with many not-to-be-repeated expletives, stigmatising me as a "lazy rascal." "My friend," said I, "my bed is not so very enviable as that you should think it invites me to laziness, but at your command I will get up instantly, if you will only a little relax these bonds." Whether from a feeling of momentary compassion, or from a conviction that I could not move from between the two boxes that hemmed me in on either side, the Artigueño* so far unloosed the cords which bound me, as just to leave me room to struggle from out of my berth, and powers of locomotion sufficient to enable me to follow him to the deck. This man, by birth an Indian, was that day the means of saving my life.

When I came upon deck every sort of menace was resorted to in order to extort from me a secret which I had not to reveal. "Where is your money?—and where are the rest of your

* That is, soldier of Artigas.

arms?" were the oft-reiterated demands. They
had got all I had of both; but my protestations
to this effect seemed of no avail. Twice was I
taken out of the vessel to the shore, and twice
were the men drawn up to shoot me. Never
had I lived to record the horrors of that night
and day, but for the Indian to whom I have alluded.

Those marauders, ungovernable by any system
of civilised discipline, were held together, somewhat in the way in which pirates are, by privileges tacitly understood as appertaining to each,
and corresponding to the relative merits of his
services. In accordance with this view, a custom
prevailed among the Artigueños, which was, that
any soldier who had distinguished himself more,
that is, had committed more daring excesses
than another, was entitled to ask a favour
(" pedir un favor," as they styled it) of his
chief; and it was at the chief's peril that he
refused to grant it. On the present occasion
(and, to me, it was one of some emergency)
the Indian stepped out from the ranks, and
" asked his favour." That favour was not a
light one in my eyes, for it was, that my life

should be spared. " Que no se le fusile," said
the Indian, "let him not be shot." I was loosed
from the tree to which I had been tied; and
becoming from that moment the recognised pro-
tégé of the Indian, I was treated with much less
severity by the whole gang. The cords with
which I had been bound were removed; I was
permitted to dine with my not-over-welcome
guests; threats of taking my life were no longer
the order of the day; and I was graciously allowed to drink a little of my own wine. But I
was not permitted to use any part of my own
wardrobe. That was distributed, without reserve
of either a shirt or pair of stockings, among
my fierce assailants; and the metamorphosis
wrought in them by the assumption of my costume was not less striking than that wrought
in me on being forcibly and scantily clad in
theirs. In exchange for my whole wardrobe, I
had thrown over my shoulders a tattered great-
coat, and tied round my waist a worn-out poncho.
No shirt, no stockings, were allowed me. My
attire was completed with an old blue foraging-
cap, and a cast-off pair of "botas de potro."*

* Boots stripped off the leg of a horse.

Many of the Artigueños, on the other hand, having put off similar garments, were now to be seen strutting about in Bond Street cut coats, leather breeches (they were the fashion in those days), Andre's hats, tight fits of boots, both top and Hessian, with broad-frilled shirts, and large ties of white cravat. Here were my gold chain and seals dangling at the fob of the serjeant, he having preferred them to the watch, which went to the corporal. One man had on a pair of buckskins and Hessian boots, another a pair of Hoby's best tops, over white cord pantaloons; and as this last personage was considered the smartest of the group, my opera hat (now, by the bye, no longer mine) was seized upon by him to crown his attire. So motley a group was never perhaps before exhibited; for as I had not a wardrobe ample enough to clothe forty men, each had only a *part* of it, and this contrasted so strongly with the part of his own which he was still obliged to retain, as to make him look like the centaur, human above, brutal below, or *vice versâ*.

I was now told by the serjeant that General Hereñú, the governor of the Bajada, having heard that I had a great many arms on board for Paraguay, had ordered the party which he commanded to come up in pursuit of the vessel by land, and that, having got tidings of her at Goya, they there embarked, and took possession of us in the way I have already told you. The serjeant added, that his orders were either to shoot me, or to take me back to the Bajada; and having embarked the crew, he ordered the vaqüeano to steer for that port.

Desperate as my predicament seemed, I was made comparatively easy by this intelligence; for, though I knew that at the Bajada I should still be 350 miles from British influence or assistance; and though I was aware that Hereñú was one of the most barbarous of Artigas' subordinates, yet I felt he would be a little more alive to the responsibility of taking my life and property than the troopers in whose clutches I now was. I was glad, therefore, to find myself sailing once more down the stream of which I had but two days before been stemming the current.

I must not here omit to relate to you an incident of the serio-comic kind, which took place three days after my capture. I had in my possession a double flageolet, of which the construction sorely puzzled my barbarian keepers. They blew into it, and produced two distinct yet discordant sounds. After their severity towards me was a little softened, the serjeant asked me what instrument that was, I told him; when he presently requested me to play a tune upon it. Not being much of an adept in music, and certainly never in worse tune for it than at that moment, I begged to be excused, but in vain; the serjeant began by a request and ended by a *command* that I should play the flute. " Toca la flauta," said he, in rather a soothing tone at first; " toca la flauta," he added, in a minute after, in one so fierce and peremptory as made my blood run cold. At the same time he laid his hand on the hilt of his sword in such a menacing way as overruled all farther objections on my part. There, seated on the poop of the vessel, in my scanty Artigueño habiliments, was I fain to play duets to the satyrs, savages, and imps around me, among whom dancing to my music became a frequent amusement. But there are few evils without their corresponding alleviation in this life; and in the present case mine was to perceive that the intercourse brought about by

an unskilful performance on a little reed, had a
softening influence on my captors. I can say that
thenceforward the only real inconvenience to
which I was put by them was that of being
obliged, at their pleasure (how little it could be
at my own you need not be told), to "play the
flute." We reached the Bajada, where a *feu de
joie* was fired on arrival of the vessel. I was
then marched off under an escort of ten or twelve
men towards the town, still in my Artigueño
attire; and as I was ruminating, in melancholy
plight enough, on what was likely to be my fate,
and by what possible means I could get a knowledge of my predicament conveyed to my English
friends, and above all to the commander of the
English forces at Buenos Ayres, whom should I
see coming down the hill but an old and faithful
servant, called Manuel! How happy that principle in our nature which gave rise to the homely
adage, that a drowning man will catch at a straw!
The more deeply we are plunged in the abyss of
despair, the stronger and brighter does the faint-
est ray of hope let in upon us appear. Small in
the scale of my present difficulties as the relief
might seem which Manuel could afford me, I yet

hailed his appearance as an aliment of that hope
which had been fast dying within me. I felt
unspeakable relief as I was hurried past him by
my guards, in being able to say to him these few
words, "Fly to Buenos Ayres, and tell them
there what you have seen and heard." Onwards
I marched, never doubting that I should be
taken in the first place before the governor. I
was mistaken, even in this unenviable supposi-
tion. I was marched to the small and wretched
gaol appropriated to the reception of murderers,
robbers, and other felonious caitiffs of the worst
die. There they sat, each upon the skull of a
bullock, in chains, in nakedness, in squalid filth,
and yet in bestial debauch and revelry. There
was a fire lit in the middle of the floor, amid a
heap of ashes which had been accumulating,
apparently, for months. Around this fire there
were spitted, for the purpose of being roasted,
three or four large pieces of black-looking beef,
into the parts of which already done the felons,
with voracious strife, were cutting with large
gleaming knives. "Aguardiente," or bad rum,
was handed round in a bullock's horn; and as
the fire cast its flickering glare on the swarthy

and horrible countenances of the bacchanals, their chains clanking at every motion of their hands or legs, the picture was truly startling. Here again the reflection was forced upon me that happiness and misery are alike comparative terms, expressive of comparative states; for, miserable as I had been on board of the vessel after her capture, I felt now that that misery was enviable happiness when compared with the horrors, infamy, and degradation connected with my present companions and abode. It is true that the mind, moving within a hallowed circle of its own, is not, if in itself virtuous and serene, to be contaminated by the approximation to it of any mere external form of life or action; but it is also true that by the mysterious link of association which connects and sometimes almost identifies that mind with external things, it is susceptible of shocks so rude as no philosophy can withstand,—home-thrusts so desperate as no stoicism can parry.

Scarcely had I been introduced to my unenviable abode, when a yell of horrid welcome was set up by the prisoners. It was in vain that I tried to find a corner for myself. First one and then another pulled me towards the fire; they insisted upon my drinking out of the bullock's horn; and then demanded, with one accord, that I should pay for some more of the same kind of nauseous beverage as that they had just finished. I had not a farthing, (I cannot say in my pocket, for pocket I had none,) but a farthing I had not in the world. "No matter," said they, "the custom is invariable that every new-comer shall treat the older inmates; and although you should get what we want by the sale of your skin, have it we must, and shall." Without further ceremony, they stripped me of my Artigueño great-coat, and, tattered and wretched as it was, procured in exchange for it a large flask of spirits. I was now left, like many of themselves, naked from the waist upward, and for *this night* I found it impossible to sleep. I sat me down in disconsolate silence by the embers of the fire, and as I viewed the numerous skulls around me, I thought them, even though they had only in their time belonged to bullocks, no bad emblem of the end to which all created things must come, and especially of my own, which I scarcely wished should be de-

ferred.   I felt as if I had been plunged into the
uttermost gulf of human woe; and I almost
desired, as the only means of enabling me to
support it, that my powers of reflection, and what
are commonly deemed advantages of education,
were exchanged for the callous barbarism of the
wretches by whom I was surrounded.

The day of a long, long night at length dawned.
I called in the corporal of the guard, and in-
treated him with all my powers of eloquence
(seldom so effectual as when put forth in cases of
personal outrage) to inform the governor of the
miserable predicament in which I was for want
of clothes.   I begged him to say that I had a
friend in the place who would furnish me with
whatever I required if he (the governor) would
only give his permission.   I added, that whatever I received in prison might pass under his
inspection.   Hours rolled away, and I received
no answer; but towards the afternoon a sergeant
entered with a coat, shirt, and stockings, which
he said had been furnished by my friend, with
Hereñú's permission.   When I had dressed myself (for I was all *but* in a state of nudity), the
same sergeant told me to follow him.   I did so,

with not very comfortable forebodings, for I had been told a dozen times during the day that the Englishman (that was myself) would certainly be shot. The sergeant, however, conducted me to a separate cell, in which were a chair, hide, and jar of water. He told me his orders were to place me where no one should have access to me; but that my meals should be regularly sent in twice a day. So saying, he took his leave; and again thrown for comfort upon the resource of contrast, I was glad this time to find it in my favour. The solitude and clothing of to-day, as contrasted with the nakedness and society to which I had been doomed yesterday, made me once more think myself a comparatively happy man. Dreary enough was my cell, but still I was *alone*. I looked through the iron gratings upon the flocks of vultures and gulls which hovered over the dead carcases of cattle all around; and truly I wished that, like them, I had wings with which to fly from my bondage, were I even, as a consequence, to live upon carrion.

Not to protract this personal subject, I shall simply add, that, after eight days' confinement, and after a series of inquisitorial examinations, to every one of which, when I was called from my cell, I went as if I were going to the gallows, I was liberated.

There was nothing in my case which ingenuity itself could distort into criminality. Little, however, would this have availed me, but for the prompt, resolute, and most opportune interference in my behalf of the Honourable Captain Percy, then commanding the British ships of war in the River Plate. From the moment that my faithful servant Manuel saw me in the predicament in which I was met by him, he gave himself no rest till he was riding post with the news to Buenos Ayres. He performed the distance in an incredibly short time; and no sooner had he delivered his plain, unvarnished tale, than every Englishman in the place (and Captain Percy at their head) was roused to indignation, and moved to compassion by the account. A brig-of-war was instantly despatched to General Artigas' headquarters at Paysandú, with one of those peremptory communications from the British officer in command which so often characterize our naval captains, when they know they have a good cause in hand, the safety of British subjects to insure, and the inviolability of British rights to sustain.

The letter was to this effect :—

"Most Excellent Protector: A British subject, Mr. J. P. Robertson, sailing under my license, and under that of the constituted authorities of the country, ratified by your own subordinate Governor, Candioti, has been seized, most inhumanly treated, and finally imprisoned by persons acting under your authority. I require and demand, as a first step, and unless good cause be shown to the contrary, his instant liberation, as well as the delivery to him of his property; and unless this my application be complied with, I shall forthwith proceed to make reprisals of the property under your flag.

"I have the honor to be, &c. &c.

(Signed)   "JOCELYN PERCY."

This letter, delivered at the head-quarters of Paysandú, by a weather-beaten lieutenant,* with a bold air and an uncompromising cocked-hat, would of itself have brought General Artigas to

* The present distinguished Captain Kirkwood.

his senses; but its effect was irresistible, having been delivered not twelve hours after Artigas had received from his own Governor at the Bajada the process instituted against me, from not a part of which could the remotest criminality be either proven or inferred. Instant orders were despatched for my release, and for the restoration to me of my vessel and property; but before these could reach the Bajada, another messenger, sent by Captain Percy over-land, by way of Santa Fé, had penetrated to my lonely cell, and, in company with the Governor, Hereñú, now rather trembling in his shoes, proclaimed to me that I was once more,—a free man. By this latter messenger Captain Percy had sent to Hereñú a copy of his letter to Artigas; and so alarmed was the village despot by a contemplation of the possible consequences of his atrocious, and, as it turned out to be, unauthorised act, that he lost not a moment in his endeavour to repair the gross misconduct of which he had been guilty. Next day General Artigas' own order for my liberation arrived; and having already too long detained you over the dismal details of my story, I shall not here prolong the subject, by requesting you to accompany me in those feelings of lively and really indescribable delight which *must* have taken possession,—which *did* take possession of my innermost soul, upon a transition from the suffering of all that is horrible to the enjoyment (by contrast doubly enhanced) of most that is dear to man.   I was restored to life, after having numbered myself with the dead; I was restored to liberty, after having resigned myself to imprisonment; and I was restored to friends and relations, whose only farther tidings of me, I had made up my mind, would be borne to their ears by my funeral knell.

What I have yet to unfold of this story (and it is not less eventful than what I have hitherto related) I must defer till I next write.   You will then see the extraordinary effects produced in the mind of Francia by these events; the not less violent and uncompromising breach they produced on his part between us; and, as the consequence of it, the sudden and irrevocable banishment of my brother and myself from Paraguay.

Yours, &c.

J. P. R.

LETTER VI.

J. P. R. to Thomas Fair, Esq.

A transition state—The Indian to whom I owed my life—Artigueño gambling—Restoration of my ship and property, minus
what was plundered—Return to Buenos Ayres—Visit to the
head-quarters of Artigas—Short sketch of him—My interview
with him, and a description of his quarters, occupations, and
encampment—Cause and origin of his vast power—His poverty
—Return from the Purificacion to Corrientes.

London, 1838.

FANCY the transition from the company of murderers and robbers to that of sincere friends and
old acquaintances; from prison walls and iron
gratings to comfortable apartments, with ingress
and egress *ad libitum ;* from hard and cheerless
fare to meals made savoury by the company of
agreeable companions ; from cold and nakedness
to warmth and comfortable clothing ; and, finally,
from the terrors of death to the pleasures of
life ;—fancy to yourself such a transition, and
what would probably be your own feelings under
it, and you may then have some tolerable notion
of what were mine. Only yours must, after all,

be an imaginary case: mine was a real one. Make
ample allowance for that difference before you
allow yourself to infer that you have realised
either the intensity of my suffering, or the plen-
itude of my joy.

One of the earliest uses I made of my liberty
was to find out the swarthy Indian, to whose interference with his less humane comrades I had
owed my life. I was curious to know by what
process a ray of compassion had reached the cold
and ruthless heart of a man connected with such
fierce military brigands; and I was anxious,
whatever might have been his motive for pleading
my cause, to reward him for the highest service
which one man can render to another. I found
him squatted on the mud floor of his barracks,
and engaged at play with his companions over a
pack of cards, of which, to my eye, each presented
only two sides of black, unrelieved by a single dot
or figure capable of distinguishing one from
another. The eager anxiety, the trembling agitation, however, with which the players drew one
card from behind another, showed me how much
more acute were their optics than mine. The
moment they got sight of the mere rim of the

card, an expression of fiendish joy, or of scowling
displeasure, was visible on their countenances,
showing that they instantly knew what the card
was. I suppose the figures of these cards had
died away before their eyes so gradually, or
rather, by degrees, had been so overlaid with
filth and grease, the superadded stains being
probably associated in the minds of the players
with the original painting, that the pack was as
good to them as a new one. When you see an
ace take a king, or a king a queen, in ordinary
play, the process is intelligible; but to see, as I
did, the ferocious Artigueños, who disdained all
other laws, bending implicitly to that by which
one card, all black, was allowed to take another
card all black, was to me a very puzzling sight.

It was with some difficulty I could get the
Indian for a moment to leave his squat position
in the ring of gamblers; and when I asked him
what had induced him to interfere in my behalf,
his reply was, " Se me antojó no mas:" that is,
" the whim of the moment." He here evinced
great impatience to return to his companions, not
seeming to expect any reward for what he evidently considered no great service done to me.

Having elicited thus much, I put into his hand a sum in gold sufficient to testify my gratitude, and more than sufficient to satisfy him, who neither felt that he had done a service, nor merited a re-ward. The truth is, that those marauders cared so little about taking a man's life, that they could conceive it no great favour to spare it ; and this was to me evident from the absolute indifference manifested on the subject by my Indian friend. He had no sooner received the doubloons from me than he resumed his place among the game-sters ; and laying down the gold by his side, be-gan to increase his stakes. I met him next day, and he told me he had lost it all.

I now proceeded to receive my ship and pro-perty out of the hands of the Philistines; and I did receive it, with the exception of about 1200*l.* This amount was pilfered by the gentlemen in office and their subordinates. My wardrobe, the arms, the Dictator's finery (as Candioti called it), the clothing for the troops, with such other things as struck the particular fancy of the Governor, cap-tain of the port, serjeants, and others, were de-tained without scruple. Convinced that that was neither the place nor the time for remonstrance,

I allowed all to pass, despatched the vessel once more for Paraguay, wrote a full account to the Dictator and my brother of what had occurred, and, with my faithful herald Manuel, and Captain Percy's emissary, after crossing to Santa Fé, I took horse for Buenos Ayres.

I was received there as one restored to my friends from the grave. Not the most sanguine of them had allowed himself to hope that I should pass, with life, through the ordeal to which I had been subjected; and their congratulations were proportionately cordial. To Captain Jocelyn Percy, of H. M. S. Hotspur; to Lieutenant, now Captain Kirkwood, who went over to Artigas; to John M'Neile, Esq., now banker in Belfast; and most especially to yourself, you know how essentially indebted I was for the disinterested zeal, and effective co-operation, by which I was liberated. Captain Percy's conduct was above all praise, showing that, where the British flag waves over floating artillery, not a hair of the head of a British subject can be unjustly touched with impunity.

As regards restoration of the property stolen, it was generally agreed that, as it formed so small a proportion of the whole, the best way in which to proceed for its recovery would be by friendly remonstrance with Artigas. It was arranged, therefore, that I should proceed to his head-quarters, which were then established at a village called the Purificacion, founded by himself on the banks of the Uruguay. I was glad of the opportunity thus presented to me of holding intercourse with a man who had raised himself to so singular a pitch of celebrity, and whose word, at that moment, was a law over the whole length and breadth of the late viceroyalty of the River Plate, with the sole exceptions of Paraguay and the town of Buenos Ayres. This latter place he kept in continual alarm, by scouring, with his detachments, the plains in its immediate vicinity, driving away whole herds of cattle, and approaching often to the suburbs of the town.

Artigas, during the time of the old Spanish government, was what might be called the Robin Hood of South America. At the head of a daring band of freebooters, he scoured the Banda Oriental on horseback, now making inroads into the Portuguese territory of Brazil, and driving away whole herds of cattle; and anon coasting the River Plate, protecting smugglers, and participating in their ill-gotten gains.

He was too formidable, and much too erratic a person to be coped with, *vi et armis,* by the Spanish Government. To lure him from his predatory habits, therefore, the Governor of Montevideo conferred on him the rank of captain of blandengues, or horse-militia; and it was wise policy to do so; for, though in the country Artigas continued to be more a governor than the Governor himself, he yet abstained, thenceforward, from open violation of the law.

Such was Artigas at the period at which I was called upon to visit him; and after what fashion I found the mighty Protector living, and issuing his mandates, you shall presently hear. Furnished with letters from Captain Percy, requesting, in civil terms, the restoration of that part of the property detained by the chieftain's satellites at the Bajada, or compensation for it, I sailed across the River Plate, and up the beautiful Uruguay, till I came to the Protector's headquarters of the so-called town of the Purificacion. And there (I pray you do not turn sceptic on my hands), what do you think I saw? Why, the

most excellent Prötector of half of the New World,
seated on a bullock's skull, at a fire kindled on
the mud floor of his hut, eating beef off a spit,
and drinking gin out of a cow-horn! He was surrounded by a dozen officers in weather-beaten
attire, in similar positions, and similarly occupied
with their chief. All were smoking, all gabbling.
The Protector was dictating to two secretaries,
who occupied, at one deal table, the only two
dilapidated rush-bottom chairs in the hovel. It
was the scene of the Bajada prison all over,
except that the parties were not in chains,
nor exactly without coats to their backs. To
complete the singular incongruity of the scene,
the floor of the one apartment of the mud hut
(to be sure it was a pretty large one), in which
the general, his staff, and secretaries were assembled, was strewn with pompous envelopes
from all the provinces (some of them distant
1500 miles from that centre of operations), addressed to " His Excellency the Protector."
At the door stood the reeking horses of couriers
arriving every half-hour, and the fresh ones of
those departing as often. Soldiers, aides-de-
camp, scouts, came galloping in from all quarters.

All was referred to " His Excellency the Protector ;" and his excellency the Protector, seated
on his bullock's skull, smoking, eating, drinking,
dictating, talking, despatched in succession the
various matter brought under his notice, with
that calm, or deliberate, but unintermitted nonchalance, which brought most practically home to
me the truth of the axiom, " Stop a little, that
we may get on the faster."   I believe if the business of the world had been on his shoulders he
would have proceeded in no different manner.
He seemed a man incapable of bustle, and was,
in this single respect (if I may be permitted the
allusion), like the greatest commander of the age.

. In addition to my letter from Captain Percy,
I had one of introduction from a particular friend
of Artigas ; and I delivered this first, as considering it the best way of initiating that part of my
business, which, as it involved a claim, I naturally
thought would be the least agreeable.   On perusal of my introductory letter, his Excellency rose
from his seat and received me, not only with
cordiality, but with what surprised me more,
comparatively gentlemanlike manners, and really
good breeding.   He spoke facetiously about

his state apartment; and begged of me, as my
hams and legs might not be so accustomed to the
squatting position as his, to seat myself on the
edge of a stretcher, or open hide bedstead, which
stood in a corner of the room, and which he desired to be drawn near the fire. Without farther
prelude or apology, he put into my hand his own
knife, and a spit with a piece of beef beautifully
roasted upon it. He desired me to eat, and then
he made me drink, and presently he presented
me with a cigar. I joined the conversation, became unawares a gaucho; and before I had
been five minutes in the room, General Artigas
was again dictating to his secretaries, and getting
through a world of business, at the very time that
he was condoling with me on my treatment at the
Bajada, condemning the authors of it, and telling
me how instantaneously, on the receipt of Captain Percy's just remonstrance, he had given
orders for my liberation.

There was a great deal of talking and writing,
and eating and drinking; for, as there were no
separate apartments in which to carry on these
several operations, so neither did there seem to
be any distinct time allotted for them. The Pro-

tector's business was prolonged from morning till evening, and so were his meals; for as one courier arrived another was despatched; and as one officer rose up from the fire at which the meat was spitted another took his place.

Toward evening His Excellency told me he was going to ride through his encampment and inspect his men, and he invited me to accompany him. In one moment himself and staff were mounted. The horses on which they rode stood all saddled and bridled, day and night, round the Protector's hut; so did the horses of each respective troop around the place of its bivouac; and at five minutes' notice, his whole force could be put in motion, either advancing on the enemy, or retreating from him, at the rate of twelve miles an hour. A forced march of twenty-five leagues (seventy-five miles) in a night was nothing to Artigas; and hence many of the wondrous, the almost incredible feats which he performed, and victories which he gained.

Behold me, now, riding at his right hand through the camp. As a stranger and a foreigner, he gave me precedence of all his officers, of whom about twenty followed in his train. Let it not be supposed, however, when I say "in his train," that there was any affectation of superiority on his part, or any signs of deferential subordination in his followers. They laughed, cracked their respective jokes, shouted, and commingled with a feeling of perfect familiarity. Each called the other by his Christian name, without the preface of either Captain or Don, except that all, in addressing Artigas, did it under the evidently endearing and at the same time familiar appellation of "Mi General,"—"My General."

He had about 1500 tattered followers in his camp, who acted in the double capacity of horse and foot soldiers. They were chiefly Indians, taken from the decayed establishments of the Jesuits, admirable horsemen, and inured to every species of privation and fatigue. The sloping hills and the fertile plains of the Banda Oriental, and Entrerios, furnished abundant pasture for their horses, as well as numerous herds of cattle for slaughter. They wanted little more. A scanty jacket, and one poncho tied round the waist in the form of a Highlander's kilt, while another hung over their shoulders, completed, with a foraging-cap, and a pair of potro boots, large spurs, a sabre, a blunderbuss, and a knife, the Artigueño's attire. Their camp was made up of rows of hide huts and mud hovels ; and these, together with about a dozen cottages of a some-what better description, constituted what was called the "Villa de la Purificacion."

How Artigas, without having crossed to the western side of the Paraná, obtained jurisdiction over nearly the whole territory between that river and the eastern base of the Andes, demands some explanation. Very soon after the breaking out of the revolution, the inhabitants of Buenos Ayres showed a disposition to lord it over the towns and provinces of the interior. All the governors, and most of the principal *employés* were natives of that place ; the towns were garrisoned by troops from thence; an assumption of superiority, and often of arrogance, on the part of the Por-teños, disgusted many of the principal inhabit-ants of the interior, and made them see in their supercilious countrymen only so many delegated substitutes of the old Spanish authorities. No sooner, accordingly, did the arms of Buenos Ayres experience a check in Peru, in Paraguay, and on the Banda Oriental, than the interior towns threw off their allegiance, provided themselves with governors of their own choosing, and called in, to strengthen their hands, the aid of Artigas, the most powerful and popular of the insubordinate chiefs. They were thus enabled to make common cause against Buenos Ayres. Each little town succeeded in achieving its own petty independence, but it was at the expense of all order and law. The resources of the country became every day less available for the purpose of enabling it to lay the basis of permanent and solid prosperity; and while, at this moment, rancorous feuds and party bitterness are daily widening the breach between one part of the South American family and another, their substance is undergoing that process of exhaustion ever attendant on civil war. Their commerce is nearly paralysed by the insecurity thus arising to persons and property.

Having now spent several hours with General Artigas, I delivered to him Captain Percy's letter; and in terms as measured as were compatible with making my case plain, I initiated my claim for compensation.

"You see," said the general, with great candour and nonchalance, " how we live here; and it is as much as we can do, in these hard times, to

compass beef, aguardiente, and cigars. To pay
you 6000 dollars just now is as much beyond
my power as it would be to pay you 60,000, or
600,000. Look here," said he; and, so saying,
he lifted up the lid of an old military chest, and
pointed to a canvas bag at the bottom of it—
"There," he continued, "is my whole stock of
cash; it amounts to 300 dollars; and where the
next supply is to come from, I am as little aware
as you are."

It is a good thing to know when, with a
good grace, to desist from a claim which you
see to be unavailable; and I was soon convinced that in the present instance mine was so.
Making a virtue of necessity, I ceded therefore to
him, voluntarily, what no compulsion could have
enabled me to recover; and standing thus upon
my generosity, I obtained from the Most Excellent Protector, as a token of his gratitude and
good will, some important mercantile privileges
connected with an establishment I had formed
at Corrientes. They shortly more than re-
trieved my loss. With mutual expressions of
regard, we took our leave of each other. The
general insisted upon my having an escort of two
of his own body-guard, and on giving me a pass-

port to the frontiers of Paraguay. This procured for me everything I wanted, horses, entertainment, lodging, on the whole line of route between the Purificacion and Corrientes. The journey occupied me four days; and anxious now, after all I had suffered in Francia's cause, to have an interview with himself, I determined forthwith to proceed to Paraguay.

That my interview would be a propitious one, I could not, for a moment, doubt : because, although I was aware that the Dictator would take in high dudgeon the detention of his arms and ammunition, yet I had been so free from blame in the matter, and had risked so much in order to give effect to his wishes, that I could not conceive ingenuity or cavil themselves capable of raising a point on which to breed a quarrel. How much I was mistaken the sequel will show, and, while it will throw some light upon the inflexibility of Francia's character, it will, at the same time, corroborate what has already been said, and remains yet to be detailed, of his cold and calculating selfishness.

Yours, &c.

J. P. R.

LETTER VII.

W. P. R. to Thomas Fair, Esq.

The Letter of the Scotch Serjeant intimating the capture of J. P.
R.—My first interview with Francia on the occasion—His
Letter to Hereñú—My second interview with the Dictator
on occasion of my Brother's disaster—My third interview on
the occasion—Francia pronounces Sentence of Banishment
against us both.

Towards the end of June, 1815, shortly after
I had heard from my brother from Santa Fé,
and when I was daily looking for further
accounts of his progress towards Assumption,
some vague reports reached my ears of his
having been made prisoner; and, owing to one of
the many irregularities which attended the trans-
mission of letters from the river Plate provinces
to Paraguay, the first authentic information I
received of my brother's disasters was conveyed
in the following epistle from our friend Mr.
Spalding, the Scotch serjeant mentioned in our
first series. I give it *verbatim et literatim*, and

I add some notes, by way of making it intelligible to those of my readers who are not acquainted with the idiom of the Spanish language. To the Spanish scholar I am sure Mr. Spalding's letter will prove amusing.

" Corrientes 23 *of June of* 1815.

" Sir,

" I am verry sory too comunicat to you the novelty wich i Juste finish to receive for fact[1] from Don Agustin the patron off Ysasys Brigh, or Berentim,[2] who tries 11 days of Boighe[3] from the Bajada, he encounter[4] yure Bruther in the Rio of St. Juan, about 3 Liges (leagues) of the port of Cavallo Quatia, who has been brote or devolved from Goya,[5] the saldiers went abord of his vesel with the Bote of Don Manoel Himas,

[1] "The novelty wich i just finish to receive for fact" (la novedad que acabo de recibir por un hecho), the news I have just received as authentic.

[2] Brigautine.

[3] "Who tries 11 days of Boighe" (que trae 11 dias de viage), which has had a passage of 11 days.

[4] "Encounter" (encontró), he met.

[5] "Who has been brote or devolved from Goya" (à quun se ha tracdo ó deveulto desde Goya), who (my brother, not the port of Cavallo Cuatia) has been sent back from Goya.

and Himas hade anof to doo to safe his Life, as it was safe, and i spare⁶ in god it will bee so this Agustin encounter Mr. J. P. R. at that place on the 16 of June.

" When I leagued⁷ in this place i was Tauld there was a English Cavalier⁸ a cummin upe the river who was brining arms to paraguay and their was streched⁹ orders to take him presoner, but i intend¹⁰ that they have folloed him by land from the Bajada to Goya, and their aguarded¹¹ for him, *it is said he bring* a good many arms, espessaly sables.¹² One the 25th i meen to get on May way to that plaice, and if i can bee of any serves to him, i will doo what Layes in may power and may short recorses¹³ and from their i will Lit you to no what gowes on, &c., &c.

" I hop by this time That you will have sould may Mullata girel, and you will be sow good as

⁶ "i spare" (espero), I hope.
⁷ "leagued" (lleguè), arrived.
⁸ "Cavalier" (Cavallero), Gentleman.
⁹ "streched" (estrechas) strict.
¹⁰ "i intend" (entiendo), I understand.
¹¹ "aguarded" (aguardado), waited.
¹² "sables" (sábles), sabres.
¹³ "short recorses" (cortos recursos), within my narrow reach.

to envy me[14] the price off hir in yerba suabe with the first opertunity. I sent from the River side to intrigue[15] to you by Don Inricy (Henrique) Aribalo 1 Gould chane, 1 do. cruz,[16] 4 do. Rings of thos memoriales. Pleese let mi no if you hav got them or not, as i went back that nite and tuck the Mrs., but he had not yet intriged them,—the chane had 2 yards Long.[17]

"Having nothing more particlar to rite to you at the present, i desire you may pass it well, and command as you pleese him who subscribes

"Your attentive servant, &c.

"DAVID SPALDING."

This curious production perplexed and alarmed me in no small degree. The matter was cleared up to me, but my alarm was in no way decreased by the receipt that same day of a letter from our friend Mr. Postlethwaite, who informed me that my brother was prisoner in the Bajada by order of one of Artigas's commandants, in

[14] "envy me" (enviarme), to send me.
[15] "intrigue" (entregar), to deliver.
[16] "1 do. cruz" (una iden cruz), one gold cross.
[17] "the chane had 2 yards Long" (la cadena tenia dos varas de largo), the chain was two yards in length.

consequence of information having been lodged of arms for the Dictator of Paraguay forming part of the cargo of his vessel, in which he was on his way to the republic.

I waited immediately on Francia, and found that the Commandant of Nëembucú had communicated to him the same news which I had received. In the first burst of his indignation, Francia assured me that he would declare war against Artigas if any harm came either to my brother's person or property. He felt assured that the marauders would not *dare* to proceed to extremities with " Su Amigo," his friend, El Señor Don Juan; for whom he gave me that same day a magniloquent official letter, intended to be shown to the Commandant of the Bajada, stating that the swords had been ordered by the Dictator, and expressing his conviction that, on General Artigas, or his officers, learning the true state of the affair, both his (my brother's) person and property would immediately be liberated.

I will pass over the anxiety and suspense under which I laboured till I heard of my brother's being rescued, through the interference of the British commander on the station, from the clutches of the Artigueños at the Bajada. It has been seen,—

First.—That my brother was liberated from prison ;

Secondly.—That the great part of his cargo of *merchandise* was restored to him ; but,—

Thirdly.—That the arms, his wardrobe, and other things, were either plundered by the soldiers, or detained by Artigas's commandant.

The goods were sent on to Paraguay, and my brother, previously to coming up, returned to Buenos Ayres to see and to express his acknowledgments to his friends there.

All this was distasteful, in the highest degree, to the haughty, capricious, yet puerile Dictator. His own letter, he expected, would have liberated the person and merchandise seized. To the British commander he had looked for an imperious order to give up the arms to the mighty and puissant Dictator of Paraguay ; and my brother, he had expected, instead of going to Buenos Ayres, would have flown to Assumption to pour forth the expression of his grateful admiration of the wise and spirited conduct of his Excellency in this affair.

As Francia, therefore, went on learning from me the *dénouement* of the Bajada adventure, he showed increasing symptoms of impatience, and his manner to myself gradually changed from cordial to polite,—from polite to dry,—and from dry to rude. At this time I was with him almost every evening; and when, at last, at one of those interviews, I informed him that my brother was at Corrientes on his way to the republic, and that all hopes of the arms being given up were at an end, he abruptly rose and requested me to return the following evening.

I returned accordingly, and found the Doctor walking up and down his room, holding in his left hand his gold snuff-box, the lid of which he tattooed impatiently with the fingers of his right hand; and he was evidently chafing himself with his own irritating reflections. On seeing me enter he stood still, and, turning towards me abruptly, commenced in this way.

" So, Don Guillermo, you inform me that the arms are not to be given up, eh ? "

" I am sorry to say that is the fact," I answered.

" And pray," demanded Francia, " why have

not the British commander and the British consul insisted on my property being restored?"

"Because," I replied, "the arms were considered as *matériel* of war, and in these cases the British commander abstains from any interference, as I think your Excellency knows."

"I know of no such fooleries," retorted the Dictator peevishly. "So, then," he continued after a short pause, during which he seated himself near me, "your commanders and your consuls cannot ensure to me a free traffic in arms and ammunition?"

"It is beyond their power," said I, shaking my head.

The Doctor embedded his nose in *Princesa*, a subtle snuff of Brazil, and then rose up in great wrath.

"Look you, Mr. Robertson," said this self-constituted expounder of international law, "your brother, in the first place, and yourself, in the second, have been kindly received in this republic, and left to trade to and from it to any extent you pleased. I have freely permitted British commerce, and I have sought, as you know, to open up to your nation a direct intercourse with this

rich country. And behold the payment which I
receive ! When I order the articles I require, I
am told that your authorities cannot guarantee a
free trade in arms ! When my interests are to
be consulted, I am told that what is intended
for my republic is to be left to the mercy of
marauders and cut-throats, while British officers
scandalously overlook my just claims on the gratitude of Great Britain ! Know, then, that I will
no longer permit you, or your brother, or any
other British merchant, to reside in my territory.
If you cannot guarantee to me a free trade in
arms, be assured that I will not concede to you a
commerce in English *rags*."

He threw an angry emphasis on the last word,
and then paced backwards and forwards in great
dudgeon.

"Artigas," he went on, "is a scoundrel, a
robber, a highwayman ; but I know how to
make *him* repent of his rashness in having med-
dled with my affairs. He shall feel the weight
of my indignation, and he shall learn not again
to provoke my wrath. But, sir, both you and
your brother must leave the republic. Go to
your naval commander,—go to your consul,—
and tell them, from Francia, that they are fools,

—ay, that they are fools," he repeated, "and that Francia says so ! "

I knew, if I began to argue the case with the heated Doctor, that his fury would only increase, and that he would probably, in the midst of it, pounce upon me with some arbitrary order, which I might in vain try afterwards to get reversed. So I was fain to acquiesce in his allegation that the most Excellent Protector, Artigas, was a knave, and that his Britannic Majesty's consul, Mr. Staples, was a fool. I was then wise enough myself to retire with all haste from the interview, before the epithets should take a wider range, and come more home to me, perhaps, than they had hitherto done.

Foreseeing the difficulties in which we were likely to be involved, I had been writing to my brother to come on to Assumption without delay; but before he could reach me, our little vessel the Inglesita, arrived with the cargo which had been detained at the Bajada, of the value of 15,000*l.*

I was under the necessity of again going to Francia, and, for the first time, I was not admitted to his chamber. He came to me to the door, in his capote, and drily inquired what I

wanted ? When I told him that the vessel had
arrived, he cut me short by saying that I might
make ready to send her and her cargo back; for
that, till he had a free trade in arms, he was determined that we should do no more business in
Assumption. Vaya V. con Dios. "Good-bye,"
he added, and, turning on his heel, he entered
his dingy apartment,.and civilly shut the door in
my face.

The whole business came to its climax the
following day. In the letter-bag of the Inglesita
had been placed, as has already been mentioned
at page 68, an official communication from the
government of Buenos Ayres to Francia, offering
him *arms* for *recruits*. Artigas, as you have
been told, had got hold of this letter, and caused
it to be blazoned forth that Francia was selling
Paraguayans like dogs for muskets. Of all this
Francia had just received official intelligence.
He determined to fasten the whole affair on my
brother; and, raging like a wild bull, or pre-
tending to do so, he sent for me. I say that he
affected a rage which he did not feel, for, when I
arrived, I found him surrounded by the few em-

ployés whom he still retained in office, and he evidently spoke for effect.

" See," said he, " what your brother has had the insolence and hardihood to do! He has trafficked with the vile Alvear for arms against the blood of the Paraguayans! He has offered men for muskets!—he has dared to attempt to sell my people! Let him beware!—let him at his peril tread this republic! Write to him never to set foot on it again!—and as for yourself, depart immediately with what you have. The world shall still see that, whatever be the provocation, justice and leniency towards neutrals preside over the counsels of Francia."

Taking advantage of this self-appropriated hint of Francia's magnanimity, and fearful that a term of four-and-twenty hours to quit might be given me, I immediately said,—" I hope your Excellency will see that I have had no part in any of these unfortunate doings; and that you will not make me the personal sufferer. I am ready gratefully to acknowledge the kindness I have uniformly experienced in Paraguay, and I bow to your Excellency's decision that I now should leave the republic. But I trust your Excellency will give me time to wind up our affairs, and permission to take away in produce of the country the property which I have under my care, and for a considerable part of which I am to others responsible."

"How long," demanded Francia, "will it take you to wind up your affairs, and ship off your property?"

"Two months," I answered.

"Very well," replied the Dictator, "in two months from this day, or sooner if you can, you will leave the republic."

This point being settled so far to my satisfaction, and so much more favourably than I anticipated, I now despatched a courier to stop my brother, as I was most seriously alarmed for the consequences, should he arrive in Francia's present mood. What I wrote will be found in my brother's detail. It had not the effect of stopping him. He arrived three days after my last interview with Francia; and I shall leave him to tell what happened thereupon.

Yours, &c.

W. P. R.

LETTER VIII.

J. P. R. TO THOMAS FAIR, ESQ.

Third visit to Paraguay—News received from Assumption—
Arrival there—Interview with my brother, and with the Dictator
—My banishment—Its effects on the inhabitants of Assumption
—I finally depart from Assumption.

London, 1838.

SCARCELY had I set foot, on my way to Assumption, in the territory of Paraguay, when I was met by a rocking courier whom my brother had despatched, in order to prevent my leaving Corrientes. Judge of my surprise and indignation when the following letter, written by my brother only two days before, was put into my hands by the agitated and worn-out bearer of it. Dismay was painted on his face as he delivered his credentials, and for a moment it took possession of me, as I read thus:—

"My dear John,—I have just returned from an interview—on his part a most stormy one—with the Dictator; and I lose not an instant in despatching our courier with the fatal tidings I have to communicate, and in the fervent hope that he may reach Corrientes in time to prevent your taking the now perilous step of coming to Paraguay. We are both proscribed men; and instead of your now coming to join me here, I must very shortly, in pursuance of my sentence of expulsion, join you at Corrientes.

"Two hours ago I was sent for by Francia, who received me in his very sternest mood; and putting a printed paper into my hands, asked me what I knew of that, and how you had had the audacity to lend yourself to such a business?

"Upon perusal of the paper, I found it to contain a letter, purporting to be addressed by the Director Alvear to the Dictator Francia, offering him muskets in exchange for men, and with distinct reference, by name, to you, as authorised to treat with Francia on the subject. This letter, it seems, was found in the Inglesita's letter-bag, by the party which took possession of that vessel, and being sent to Artigas, has been by him printed, with various aggravating comments, and distributed for the purpose of creating disaffection among the Paraguayans, who inhabit the frontier-towns of Misiones. Artigas says that here is the Dictator in league with Buenos Ayres, and by means of the agency of a foreigner, going to sell one part of his countrymen for arms, with which to lay prostrate and enslave the other part.

"Nothing could have been more ill-timed; nothing imagined more calculated to irritate and chafe the Dictator. He is, in short, furious; will hear of no extenuating circumstance in your favour; assumes that you *have* been intriguing in the way stated; and indignantly repelled my appeal to him that you should yourself be allowed to state how the things had really been. He desired me to tell you that it would be at your peril if you set foot in Paraguay; and he ordered me to prepare, within two months, to leave the province. You know how irrevocable are his determinations, and how perilous the attempt to thwart or disobey them. I beseech you, therefore, should this find you in Corrientes, not to move; and if you should have set out on your journey before the courier arrives, to retrace your steps, at whatever point of the road you may fall in with him. Although Francia alleges as his chief reason for expelling us from the province the part which he insists upon it you must have taken in producing Alvear's odious proposal, the Dictator is yet scarcely less out of humour with our commanders and our consul than with yourself. 'England,' says his Excellency, 'shall know that, unless she will protect a trade in arms, she shall have none to Paraguay in manufactures. We do not want her rags here unless we can have muskets too; and so you may write to your naval commander, or to your prime minister, if you please.'

"Once more, come not up here; and be assured that I shall do everything of which the exigence of the case admits to render the inconvenience and loss of so suddenly breaking up our establishment as small as possible.

"Yours, &c.

(Signed) "W. P. ROBERTSON."

Not daunted by my brother's warning, and determined to tell my own unvarnished tale to Francia, I did proceed onwards to Assumption. I felt so strong in the truth and innocence of my case, that I would not allow myself to believe that even so cool a tyrant as the one I had to deal with would dare to push his measures of hostility beyond the step he had already taken, of ordering my brother and myself, at a very great sacrifice, to quit the republic. My brother thought otherwise; that there was no conceivable violence to which the Dictator might not resort; and the uneasiness and anxiety of the former were augmented in a tenfold degree when he saw me make my appearance under the corridor of our dwelling. He importuned me still to return, and not to hazard an interview with Francia. It was in vain: my mind was made up; and I resolved to wait upon him next morning at his palace.

The night was spent in my brother's recording, and in my hearing, all the acts of growing despotism, and of unmitigable severity, of which the republic had been the scene, and Francia the author, during my absence of twelve months. The prisons were groaning with their inmates; commerce was paralyzed; vessels were rotting on the river-banks, and produce going to decay in the warehouses; a system of espionage of the most searching kind prevailed; the higher classes were all depressed, the lower brought into notice;

while the caprice of the Dictator was the sole rule
of government, and the insolence of his soldiers
was systematically encouraged, as the best means
of striking terror into the hearts of the crouching
and insulted citizens. Distrust and terror per-
vaded every habitation; the nearest relations and
dearest friends looked as if afraid of each other;
despondency or despair were more or less legibly
written on every countenance you met; and
from the moment you became an object of suspicion or dislike to the Dictator, from that moment every door was barred against you, every
face averted, every act of kindness or civility
withheld, lest it should be construed into mis-
prision of treason, or disregard of the frown of
the tyrant. The only laughter heard in the
city was that of Francia's soldiers over their
revels in the barracks, or in exultation over the
affronts offered to unoffending citizens, as money
was extorted from them openly in the streets by
the quarteleros.

In such a state of things did my brother and
myself sally forth to meet the tyrant, now our
inveterate enemy, in his own palace. Contrary
to the freedom with which I had always been ad-

mitted, and to the little ceremony with which I had before been introduced to the Dictator, I was now stopped at the portal, or outer door, till the serjeant of the guard announced me to his master. My brother and I were then marched into the audience-chamber, escorted by three soldiers; and there, like a lion in his den, stood Francia, his eyes kindling with fire and fury, and every feature knit into an expression of the utmost severity and anger.

"What," said he to me, without farther prelude than a scowl, "*what* has emboldened you to come into my presence, after receiving express orders from me not to dare to set your foot upon my territory?"

"I was already, Sir," I replied, "in your territory before I received that harsh mandate; and if I had received it sooner, I should have found nothing, upon a review of my conduct, that would have rendered me either ashamed or afraid of facing you. On the contrary, I thought all I had suffered and lost on your account would insure for me a very different reception from that I now experience."

During this short reply, the Dictator stood

biting his lips, and refrained by an evident effort from interrupting me. At length he burst forth in this wise: "The letter, Sir, the letter: what have you to say to that?" "That I knew nothing of its contents, and still less authorised either them, or the use by Alvear of my name." "Mentira!" said he: that is a lie. "It is *not* a lie, my Lord Dictator; and if you will consider how you would act yourself by a passenger going from hence to Buenos Ayres, at a time when you had any communication to make to that Government, whether you would leave him any alternative but to carry your letter, you will readily see that the Director of Buenos Ayres did no more by me than you would have done by another, nor I any less by the Director than any passenger leaving Assumption *must* have done by the Dictator.

"That the letter of which I was the bearer should have fallen into the hands of Artigas, and been by him used in the way in which it has, is your misfortune, if you please; but it was no more my *fault* than it was yours; and to punish me for it, as you threaten to do, is as cruel as it is unjust."

To this point was I heard; and the Dictator, then interrupting me, spoke with a vehemence which I had never seen paralleled the words which follow:—"Look ye, Sir: see that, at the expiration of forty-eight hours, you are no longer to be found in Paraguay, or beware—beware of the consequence!"

My brother was evidently so apprehensive of some fatal result from this interview, that I the more willingly acceded to his request to bring it to a close; and he lost not a moment in zealously withdrawing me for good from the presence of the tyrant. I never saw him more: but little versed indeed in the history of the natural progress of tyranny must the man be who, after seeing what I did see, could not too ominously predict that Francia's career of terror was scarcely yet initiated.

Paraguay has since become a scene of bloodshed and of misery, of tyranny more absolute, and of slavery more complete, than any presented to the eyes of the world in the worst days of the Cæsars, or known at present to exist among the most despotically-governed countries of the East.

You may think I delineate Francia's character, and depict his actions, with the acerbity of a disappointed man, or the prejudice of an ill-used one. But time has already made notorious many. of my statements, and ratified all my fears. This extraordinary man has worked out, in circumstances *as* extraordinary, a moral and political phenomenon to be studied by thinking men yet unborn, and calculated to make them shudder as they ask themselves to what fearful and unheard-of excesses the combined passions of insatiable ambition, jealous tyranny, and despotic caprice, unchecked by fear or by control, will stimulate the man who has once formed in his savage breast the fiendish project of placing his foot on the necks of his fellow-creatures.

As my brother and I returned from the palace, the fact of my decreed banishment, and of Francia's irrevocable displeasure, being now matter of notoriety, we were permitted to walk along the nearly solitary streets without a single salutation. Our most intimate friends passed us unnoticed; our acquaintance took the other side of the way, or shut themselves up in their houses till we had passed. Had we been infected by the most contagious plague, we could not have been more sedulously shunned. But this was not to be wondered at; for truly, as Candioti said, the first law of nature is self-preservation: and the slight tenure by which every man held his own in Paraguay, was his waking conviction and his sleeping dream. A nod to us might have ended in banishment, and a shake of the hand conducted the presumptuous caitiff who offered it to prison. One faithful servant alone refused to quit me, and one lowly cottage shut not its door against me. My dog retained his fidelity, and my brother his affection; all the rest was one dreary exhibition of friendship gone, intimacy dissolved, kindness grown callous, hospitality chilled, and mirth and good-fellowship awed into silence and suspicion.

I could have no regret in leaving such a place under such circumstances; and once more loosing my little bark from the now inhospitable city of Assumption, I glided gently down the magnificent stream of the Paraguay, with the same pilot and crew who had been witnesses of all my sufferings at the hands of the soldiers of Artigas, after they took possession of the Inglesita. Of the horrors which awaited me anew on my arrival at Corrientes, for which place I was now sailing, you must be informed in my next letter. Like the dove sent out of the ark, it seemed impossible for me to find a resting-place for the sole of my foot; I had been able for some months to pick up no token to show that the waters of bitterness had departed from my soul. In more homely phraseology, I seemed ever to be out of the frying-pan into the fire; nor could I reach that consoling point referred to by the woman with respect to her eels, when she said, they were accustomed to the process of being flayed, and therefore thought nothing of it. I had been pretty well inured to hardship for some months, and yet I thought each succeeding process to which I was exposed the more objectionable on account of its repetition.

Yours, &c.,
J. P. R.

LETTER IX.

J. P. R. to Thomas Fair, Esq.

Return to Corrientes—State of that place, and unforeseen perils
in landing there—Obstacles overcome, and a second escape
from the hands of the Philistines—Their departure from
Corrientes, and my establishment there—Conclusion of personal observations.

London, 1838.

I SHAPED my course to Corrientes for two reasons;
because it was the nearest friendly port to Assumption, and because I had there laid the foundation of an incipient establishment. But when I
arrived there, I found the town in a state of the
most complete anarchy, uproar, and confusion.
Some men of influence in the place had endeavoured to overthrow the authority of Artigas,
and the usual consequence of such a step immediately ensued. During the short ten days
to which my absence had extended, a party
of his light cavalry, by forced marches, came
suddenly upon the place; and, under neither
discipline nor restraint, attacked and pillaged it
without mercy. When I landed, they were scam-
pering through the streets with drawn sabres,

threatening all, and robbing most of those they
met. Fortunately I had in my possession the
passport and protection with which Artigas had
furnished me at the Purificacion. This, being
exhibited by me to the different parties that were
scouring the town, operated as a charm, and,
added to the donation of a few dollars to each of
them, secured me a free passage to the house of
the governor. He was an old friend of mine,
and received me cordially. At the same time he
assured me that the troops were quite beyond
his control, and advised me on no account to
risk the landing of my property in circumstances
of such peril and excitement. On his agreeing,
however, to give me a guard of six men, and to
circulate among the troops the information that I
had a very formal document, guaranteeing to me
the protection by Artigas of my person and property, I overruled his objection; and the issue
proved that I had better estimated than he the
value of the document I had received from Artigas. I landed the whole property, barricaded
my doors, kept my six guards on the alert by
changing watches night and day; gave porter,
wine, and a little gold, to the more influential

men among the soldiers; and while pillage, rapine, and bloodshed were going on around me, I remained safe and unscathed in my fortified tenement. The object of Artigas being at length attained, and his authority re-established, the detachment of troops was ordered to rejoin him, and all was once more tranquillity and security. Most truly welcome was the departure of the marauding troopers, and not less remarkable the hallowed circle which the protection of Artigas seemed to have drawn around me, keeping from intrusion within it even the most lawless of his own lawless bands. I was not, however, for all that, kept the less in a state of fear and trembling, as I saw others robbed and imprisoned, and some assassinated around me. The associations connected with the Bajada scene were yet too recent and vivid to admit of my being well at ease while the same parties, only at the expense of other victims, were enacting deeds pretty similar to those so lately practised toward myself. Most truly rejoiced was I when I saw the last straggling few of so reckless, fierce, and greedy a gang, take their departure, leaving the town in tranquil possession of my friend Governor Mendez, and a company of his sober militia. For the poor inhabitants, they suffered so much from fright and plunder, that I felt assured they would exhibit no symptoms of insubordination for many a month to come.

My brother now joined me from Paraguay, and the country becoming daily more tranquil, we greatly extended our operations, in the hope of retrieving some of our past losses. These operations were chiefly with the large estancieros, and so singular and curious were both the traffic and the men who pursued it, that I may, at some future time, give an account of both.

Having now, however, finished my *personal* observations on Paraguay, I leave my brother to add a few more of his. In conclusion, I shall resume; give an account of the more awful parts of the tyrant's career, from the time we left till the present date; and, after inserting Francia's defence of himself, I shall close the volume with a review of that defence, and an analysis of the character which it has been the chief aim of these letters fully to develop.

Yours, &c.,

J. P. R.

LETTER X.

W. P. R. TO THOMAS FAIR, ESQ.

Remarks on Francia—Society of Assumption—The Jovellanos
family—Their servants—Plain speaking—Sleeping under corridors—Amusements—The Sarandig—The Figueredos—I become a Padrino—My compadre and comadre—A death and a
velorio—The funeral of an Angel.

London, 1838.

FRANCIA was, doubtless, the great lion of Paraguay, in the popular metaphorical sense by
which we make that noble animal to stand for
whatever is strange and wonderful in man or
thing. In the Dictator's case, to be sure, the
tiger would have suited better than the lion to
represent him; but taking him, not as an individual, but as one of that great class which may
be denominated the " world's wonders," Francia
is a " lion " well worthy of being held up and
exhibited to the rest of mankind.

In showing our lion, we have to a considerable
extent allowed the rest of our exhibition of Para-

guay to remain in the background ; but it may be
well to relieve the eye occasionally from viewing
even so magnificent a lion (I cannot, in London,
say " tiger," where the name designates a very
different sort of biped from the Dictator) as Francia, I imagine, is by this time pretty generally
allowed to be. But, though I propose turning
aside from the Dictator for a while, we have not
yet done with him. You have hitherto only seen
our lion *couchant*—you have but heard his growl.
We have yet to show him *rampant*—you have
still to hear his roar. You have seen as yet little
more than the restrained tiger of Van Amburgh,
—we have to show him in his native wilds, and
in all his untamed and savage and original ferocity of character,—we have yet to show him
first tasting of human blood, and thenceforth,
agreeably to his nature, madly ranging his forests, and disdaining all other aliment than the
flesh of man.

Dropping my simile, it is my intention, before
proceeding farther with the history of Francia, to
give you a few details of matters which seem to
me to be of some interest, connected with Paraguay, and the omission of which might appear to

some of our readers to leave our account of the republic incomplete.

It may naturally be expected that we should say something of the state of *society* in Assumption, the capital of an independent state, yet I assure you it is no very easy matter to do so. Gross immorality was so mixed up with primitive simplicity of manners; politeness and urbanity came before you so denuded of all the conventional forms and delicacy of expression which high civilization demands; the strongest feelings of devotion were so embued with a crazy superstition, very nearly akin to a mockery of what we conceive to be true religion, that the mixture formed altogether something very unlike whatever I have either seen or conceived of society in other parts of the world.

One of the most fashionable families of Assumption was that of Señor Jovellanos, the postmaster-general. His wife was looked up to as an oracle by all the other dames of the place ; and his daughters, who were really handsome women, were regarded with envy as the undisputed leaders of the *haut ton* in the capital. They did not muffle up so closely when they went abroad as others were forced to do by their mothers; they were not always to be found in a loose robe-de-chambre when at home; and they were able to converse in a sprightly and pretty fluent strain in Spanish, when visited by those who could not speak Guaraní.

Shortly after my arrival in Assumption, I was invited by Señor Jovellanos to dinner; and, having accepted the invitation, I went on the following day as appointed, at the late and fashionable hour of two o'clock. Several friends were assembled for the occasion; but at table I was placed between two of the Misses Jovellanos,—young, blooming (for most of the females of Assumption were very fair), and without any doubt very pretty women. Guess, then, my confusion, to find at the dinner-table that we were waited on by half-a-dozen boys and girls, little slaves, all perfectly,—how shall I say it? Their liveries had cost nothing—their shoes and stockings had cost nothing—not one of them had *dressed* for dinner,—they were, one and all, in *statú naturæ*. At first I fidgeted in my chair, and threw furtive glances around; but seeing every one on either side of me, including my fair companions, as composed as if the most rigid decorum had been studied, I gradually recovered my serenity, and learned thenceforward to know that whatever has become *the custom of the country*, is never even *fancied* by the people to have anything *outré* in it. I recollected Goldsmith's story of the nation with a fleshy excrescence under the chin.   How we are, in truth, the creatures of habit !   I got so accustomed to these unclothed attendants, during my sojourn in Paraguay and Corrientes, that on my return to Buenos Ayres I thought there was a great deal of affectation in dressing out the same class there from top to toe.

As the body was left loose and unconstrained by dress in Paraguay, so the conversation of all classes was the most unsophisticated in its construction that can be imagined,—quite of the Doric order.   There was no circumlocution, no metaphoric subtilty, no figure of speech by which one thing was made to stand for another.   On the dinner occasion I have mentioned, Mrs. Jovellanos gave me, before her daughters, a dissertation on " Buchan's Domestic Medicine " (it is translated into Spanish), which made my blood run cold, but which she went through with all the volubility of a clever mother, in her fortieth year, who had reared a large family by dint of her constant application to the system of Buchan, and to which her daughters listened as gravely, through every detail, as if it had been to one of Mrs. Chapone's letters on the improvement of the mind.

There was no police in Assumption; and, what may appear somewhat strange, there was no occasion whatever for anything of the kind. In the principal and only street worthy of the name in the city, a long and continuous corridor, as has been mentioned, ran along one side of it. The principal shopkeepers and merchants inhabited this part of the town; and, on very warm nights of summer, this corridor constituted the common bed-room, if I may so speak, of all those shopkeepers from whose houses the corridor projected. The portable beds of these worthy citizens were drawn out and ranged along the covered way; and it was a singular and a primitive sight to see them, as you passed along towards ten o'clock at night, preparing for, or already enjoying, their night's repose. Some were to be seen sitting on the side of their stretchers, yawning, or smoking their cigars; others undressing with the greatest sang froid; here one snoring, there another conversing with his next neighbour; and every one unconscious of the oddness of the scene which presented itself to the eyes of a stranger. The same custom prevailed, more or less, throughout the city. Beds and sleepers obstructed the way in every direction. I used myself constantly to sleep under the corridor of my patio, closed, however, from public view by a large outer gate.

I am here to be understood as speaking of the habits of the people *before* Francia's system began to spread alarm and distrust among all classes. His quarteleros were feared by day and by night; but when things were in their natural order in Paraguay, such a thing as a robbery or theft committed during the night was unheard of; and in fact a security was felt and enjoyed which produced a happy indifference to bolts and bars, and a total absence of nocturnal fears.

The amusements of the better classes in Assumption were on an extremely limited scale. Indeed I can scarcely say they had any. Their tertulias were never graced by music or dancing;

and I believe there were only two or three old
jingling pianos in the whole town. For a mere
occasional dance they contented themselves with
the guitar, accompanied by the voice; and, instead of the minuet and country-dance of Buenos
Ayres, the Assumpcianas indulged in a barbarous movement called the zarandîg, or heel-
dance. The lower ranks in particular were pas-
sionately fond of this dance, and its accompanying
music. When such a thing as a ball occurred,
which it rarely did, the convents supplied the
music. The ball always commenced with *gen-
teel* dancing; but it as invariably ended with
the homely, the inelegant, and, truth to say, the
immodest dance of the zarandîg.

Conversation,—and that in Guarani,—was the
great resort of men and women in Paraguay for
passing away their evenings; and, during the
day, the female part was very much taken up
with their church-goings and processions. Some
of their *velorios*, or *wakings*, were curious.

The next-door neighbour of our unfortunate
landlord, Echague, was Don Antonio Figueredo,
a fat, easy-going old gentleman, who ate a hearty
dinner early in the day, slept a long siesta after

it, and in the evenings of that warm and cloudless climate, enjoyed his maté and his cigar under the porch of his door. All his domestic concerns he left to the uncontrolled management of Mrs. Figueredo.

She was an active, buxom, and still handsome-looking woman, of two or three and thirty, just beginning to get jealous of her oldest daughter, a pretty girl of fifteen. Mrs. Figueredo was almost the only woman in Assumption who had *blue eyes*; and on the strength of this fact she considered she had a better right to the friendship of "los Ingleses rubios" than any other person. We were accordingly very intimate with Mr. and Mrs. Figueredo, having a sort of passive and quiescent intercourse with the one, and a more active and lively one with the other.

A message came to me one forenoon from Mrs. Figueredo, requesting an immediate call; and when I waited on her, I was ushered into her bed-room, where she lay in state. Her daughter sat at the foot of the bed, and a nurse stood respectfully at her side with a babe in her arms. Mrs. Figueredo had blessed her phlegmatic husband with this addition to his earthly possessions three days previously to that of the visit to which I was called.

"Don Guillermo," said the lady, sitting up in bed as I entered, "I have a favour to ask of you, which I hope you will not refuse, and which, indeed, you must promise not to deny me before I proceed any further."

"You have a right, mi Señora Doña Encarnacion," answered I, "to lay your commands on me in any form you please; and as I know how reasonable ladies always are when left to act without control, I can have no hesitation in promising beforehand to do whatever you desire."

"None of your insinuations," replied Mrs. Figueredo, "but let us to the point. Look there at my little babe, who has so recently seen the light; you see she is 'una rubia' (fair complexioned); her eyes are quite blue—she looks altogether an Inglesita. Well, I wish you to be her godfather, and I am going to call her *Guillerma*" (Wilhelmina).

I knew well what an onerous sort of burthen was about to be laid upon me; but of course, with many acknowledgments of the honour which Doña Encarnacion intended for me, I said I should only be too happy to have such a charming god-child as the daughter, and too much honoured to be able to call so agreeable a mother my comadre. Miss Figueredo ran out of the room to her father, who was sitting in his shirt-sleeves at the door, very philosophically puffing a cigar as usual, and told him that I was to be his compadre. " Me alegro mucho " (I am very glad of it), said Don Antonio, and went on smoking, apparently pleased that, without any bodily exertion, or mental labour on his part, a knotty point of this kind was so satisfactorily settled.

About three months after I had become a padrino, or godfather, one of my comadre's female slaves came to me, and begged, on the part of her mistress, that I would go to her house that evening, in order to enjoy a little diversion (para divertirme un poco). Obeying the summons, I went to Mr. Figueredo's towards eight o'clock. The worthy old gentleman was sitting with his accustomed serenity under his veranda, smoking, of course, and listening to the prior of Saint Domingo, a native of Buenos Ayres, who was busy with an account of the taking of that city by " el famoso General, Don Guillermo Carr

Beresford." "Walk in, compadre," said my host, rising to receive me—" walk in, they are expecting you inside;" and in I walked accordingly, leaving my compadre to the enjoyment of the fresco, of his maté and cigar, and of his loquacious friend the prior.

In the large sala, or drawing-room, a curious scene presented itself to my view. Ranged all round it were guests of every description,—fat old ladies and slender misses,—friars and pay-citos (or young gallants), natives of Assumption, —compadres and comadres without end;—and a great variety of female slaves, sitting at the feet of their respective mistresses. Half a dozen servants were busy handing about cigars, matés, sweetmeats, and wine, to ladies and gentlemen indiscriminately (minus cigars to the misses, who only smoked in private), so the room was redolent of smoke, while the buzz of many voices saluted the ear. A paycito had just finished singing a triste, accompanied by his guitar.

At the head of the room was a blaze of huge wax lights, in candlesticks of carved wood, gilded all over, and of gigantic dimensions. Placed on a species of throne, raised on the estrada, was a small coffin, which, as well as the throne, was ornamented with every variety of artificial flowers, tastefully disposed, while the surrounding part of the wall was decorated with rich brocade. Immediately over the head of the coffin was a massive silver figure of our Saviour on the cross ; and in the coffin itself lay, dressed out in the most splendid style, *the corpse of my infant god-daughter !*

Never had I seen death so divested of every attribute repugnant to humanity,—never had I witnessed its solemnity so fairly put down as here. I could have fancied that the King of Terrors, hiding his sepulchral countenance under a mask, and shrouding his skeleton form in the ample folds of a mantle, had stalked into the room, and laid the coffin and its contents on the gay bier, as his contribution to the hilarity of the night ; while, under his mask, and unseen by the merry-makers, all destined themselves at a future day to be his victims, he " grinned horrible a ghastly smile," and left them for a brief season to their gambols.

I had no time, however, for reflections on the incongruous scene which lay before me ; for, a

soon as Mrs. Figueredo's eye caught my figure
in the room, she hastened to me with a brisk
step and smiling countenance—" Ah, compadre !"
said she, " I'm so glad you have come; we have
been expecting you for an hour: come along,
come along," she added, pulling me by the coat,
—" come and see the angel !"

" But, Doña Encarnacion," said I, as we went
along the room, " are you not afflicted by the loss
of your child?"

" Afflicted !" cried the lady with unfeigned surprise, " why should I be afflicted? Is your little
god-daughter not converted into an *angel*? Do
you heretics not know 'that of such is the kingdom of heaven?' Then, why should I be afflicted? I am only sorry you have no longer a
god-child in my family; but never mind, you
shall be god-father to the next, and then all will
be right."

I might be led—" albeit a custom more honoured in the breach than in the observance "—to
endeavour to assuage, by argument, a mother's
excess of grief for the loss of her child; but to
argue my comadre *into* any such grief would
have been rather impertinent. The universally

instilled, and universally received opinion, that the body of a little child after death was, materially speaking, converted into the body of an angel, I felt no inclination to controvert. It was one of the customs of the country; and the customs of the country I had come to respect, and not quixotically to try to overthrow.

As soon as I properly could, however, I retired from the velorio, agreeing previously to assist at the interment the following day.

The funeral was on the same scale of magnificence, and in the same style of oddity as the velorio. First went the band of music of San Francisco, consisting of violins, violoncello, clarionets, and one or two other shrill instruments: then followed the prior of the convent, with a dozen of his brotherhood, and the curate of the parish, and one or two other clerigos: the splendid little coffin, held aloft, came next in the procession: behind it walked my respectable self, the god-father, with a great wax-candle, four feet long, and proportionably thick, in my hand; with my compadre on my right, and my comadre on my left; and with Miss Figueredo and a Master Figueredo behind me, industriously pulling my coat-tails, and endeavouring to upset the gravity of my countenance. The rear was brought up by a whole bevy of friends, and relatives, and *beatas*, and servants, with whom the female population in the streets gradually incorporated themselves as the procession moved along to the cheerful music of the band, and the lusty chanting of the godly friars. The little " angel " was deposited with great pomp in the body of the church: there the funeral ceremony concluded; and the friends, relatives, and assistants returned to the house of Mr. Figueredo, to partake once more of the good things attendant on the velorio and the interment of an " angel."

Yours, &c.

W. P. R

LETTER XI.

Catholic Lent—Contrasted with Protestant—Reflections—Passion week—Good Friday—Sermon of Christ's agony on the cross—The funeral service, and conclusion of Good Friday.

London, 1838.

THE most important season of the year in Assumption was that of Lent. It was ushered in, as in most other Catholic countries, by three days of carnival, those immediately preceding Ash Wednesday; but the amusement of the people was restricted to the ducking of each other with water, in a variety of forms and ways not worth particularising here. If we come hereafter to treat of the inhabitants of *Buenos Ayres,* we may have something more amusing to say of carnival than the quieter habits of the people of Assumption afford.

But the season of Lent, which has degenerated

into one of so nominal a restraint on the indulgence of appetite, the pursuits of pleasure and
amusement, the vanity of dress, and the avocations and engagements of worldly business,
among Christians of our own church, was very
differently observed in Paraguay.   The people
there fasted during the mornings and evenings,
and devoutly abstained from animal food on
the prohibited days: the few amusements of the
place were suspended: the females laid aside
curls and ornaments, and rigidly dressed in
black bayetilla, a woollen stuff: all classes went
to mass every morning, and many secluded themselves for days, inflicting stripes on their bodies,
or almost starving themselves to death: sermons
which, during the rest of the year, never formed
any part of divine service, were preached twice
a week, and they went into the minutest details
of the moral obligations of life (for these sermons,
of which I heard many, were never doctrinal);
and, in short, Lent in Paraguay was emphatically
the religious season of the year.

Should any one be inclined to advance the
proposition that, under this more than usually

ample cloak of religion, hypocrisy might be found to lurk in many of its folds, I answer, that it is not exactly my business either to gainsay or to confirm the hypothesis. In speaking of the religious habits and observances of a people, it is scarcely within the province of the traveller to dive partially into motives, or to hunt out individual cases where he may find profligacy and immorality skulking behind an open display of religious austerity, and whence he may conceive himself at liberty to generalise on the community. I have already sufficiently remarked, wherever the subject came legitimately before me, on the ignorance and immorality which I found generally to pervade all classes of Paraguay. In speaking of their religious observances, let us charitably hope that, although based on grossly superstitious views, they were accompanied by a *general* sincerity of feeling ; and that, instead of aggravating, they may serve as some extenuation of the loose habits into which the most wretched education, if not the total absence of all right moral or religious education whatever, had certainly sunk the great mass of the population of Paraguay.

As Lent, in its religious observances, was distinguished from the rest of the year, so the Semana Santa, or passion week, stood prominently forward in Lent. Preparations for the solemn anniversary of the sufferings of our Saviour might be observed going forward from the commencement of the week, and by Wednesday business of every kind was laid aside. "Exercicios," or self-inflicted corporal castigations, were now at their height; fastings were severe and continuous; and the churches were crowded by those pious persons who, at this season, sought wholly to abstract their thoughts and feelings from every mundane pursuit, and from every enticement of worldly pleasure.

On Thursday, the whole population of the city was in movement, "rezando las estaciones,"— that is, praying at the *stations*, or making a round of several churches, entering each in succession, and in each repeating a certain number of prayers. All the respectable classes were dressed in deep mourning; and, instead of the noisy church-bells tolling and chiming as usual, a sort of wooden clapper was carried round the streets by a boy, and sounded by him as he went along.

No vehicle of any kind, no horse or other animal, was allowed to be found in the streets. A dense multitude of church-goers alone was to be seen, moving all in one direction, in profound silence; and the scene altogether was of an impressive kind.

But Good Friday, which is, in every christian country, save among Presbyterians and some dissenting Protestants, a day of great solemnity, was in Assumption one of very extraordinary excitement; and to a person not imbued with the feelings which grow out of the material obrsevances of the Roman Catholic Church, Good Friday, in the recluse capital of the Jesuits, offered a spectacle of no ordinary interest.

I found great preparations making at an early hour at the cathedral, for the " Sermon de la Agonia,"—of the agony on the cross. A wooden figure of our Saviour crucified was affixed against the wall, opposite to the pulpit; a large bier was placed in the centre of the cathedral; and the great altar at the eastern extremity was hung with black; while around were disposed lighted wax-candles, or flambeaux, and other insignia of a great funeral.

When the sermon commenced, the cathedral was crowded to suffocation, a great proportion of the audience being females, of every class and age. The discourse was a running lecture on the 26th chapter of St. Matthew; and it was interrupted alternately by the low moans and sobbings of the congregation. These became more audible as the preacher warmed with his discourse, which was partly addressed to his auditory, partly to the figure before him; and when at length he exclaimed, "Behold! Behold! He gives up the ghost!" the head of the figure was slowly depressed by a spring towards the breast, and one simultaneous shriek—loud, piercing, almost appalling,—was uttered by the whole congregation. The women now all struggled for a superiority in giving unbounded vent to apparently the most distracting grief. Some raved like maniacs,—others beat their breasts, and tore their hair. Exclamations, cries, sobs, and shrieks mingled, and united in forming one mighty tide of clamour, uproar, noise, and confusion. In the midst of the raging tempest was to be heard, ever and anon, the stentorian lungs of the preacher, reproaching, in terms of indig-

nation and wrath, the *apathy* of his hearers !
" Can you, oh insensate crowd !" he would cry,—
" can you sit in silence ?"—but here his voice
was drowned in an overwhelming cry of loudest
woe, from every part of the church; and for
five minutes all farther effort to make himself
heard was unavailing. This singular scene
continued for nearly half an hour: then, by degrees, the vehement grief of the congregation
abated; and when I left the cathedral, it had
subsided once more into low sobs and silent
tears.

I now took my way, with many others, to the
church of San Francisco, where, in an open
space in front of the church, I found that the
duty of the day had advanced to the funeral-
service, which was about being celebrated. There
a scaffolding was erected, and the crucifixion
exactly represented by wooden figures, not only
of our Lord but of the two thieves. A pulpit
was erected in front of the scaffold; and the
whole Campo de San Francisco was covered by
the devout inhabitants of the city.

The same kind of scene was being enacted
here as at the cathedral, with the difference,

however, of the circumstantial funeral in place of
the death. The orator's discourse, when I arrived,
was only here and there interrupted by a sup-
pressed moan, or a struggling sigh, to be heard
in the crowd. But when he commenced giving
directions for the taking down of the body from
the cross, the impatience of grief began to manifest itself on all sides. "Mount up," he cried,
"ye holy ministers—mount up, and prepare for
the sad duty which ye have to perform !" Here
six or eight persons from the laity (the spy Orrego was one of them), covered from head to foot
with ample black cloaks, ascended the scaffold.
Now the groans of the people became more
audible; and when at length directions were
given to strike out the first nail, the cathedral-
scene of confusion, which I have just described,
began, and all the rest of the preacher's oratory
was dumb show. The body was at length deposited in the coffin, and the groaning and
shrieking of the assembled multitude ceased.
A solemn funeral ceremony took place : every
respectable person received a great wax-taper
to carry in the procession : the coffin, after being

carried all round the campo, was deposited in the church : the people dispersed; and the great day of passion week was brought to a close.

Yours, &c.

W. P. R.

LETTER XII.

W. P. R. to Thomas Fair, Esq.

Francia sets up as Paviour—Cheap mode of paving—A trip to
the Quarries and surrounding Country—Aspect of it—And
hospitality of the People—The Paraguay Peasant and his
Family—The Estanciero—Don Pedro Francia—A Reduccion
—Fiestas of the Indians—The Bull Ring—The Sortija—
The Mystery.

London, 1838.

During my residence in Assumption, the Dictator one day took it into his head to have some
pavement laid down, for which, however, he had
not the requisite material in or near the city.
But about eighteen leagues above Assumption,
and close upon the borders of the river, a large
quarry of granite had been discovered by the
Jesuits, whence they had extracted all the stone
which they had employed in rearing their edifices
and constructing their public works in the capital
of Paraguay. From the same stratum, Francia

determined to supply himself with the stone which he required.

Any other government than his would have set about contracting, on the best terms to be procured, for the material wanted ; but such an idea never entered into the head of Doctor Francia. As the seller of brooms who stole his merchandise ready-made could afford to under-sell all his brother venders, so the Dictator could easily distance any competitor who might attempt to run against him as a paviour.

The very day he resolved on having his pavement, he called the Captain of the port before him, and directed him to order every vessel in the port to proceed immediately to the quarry, and bring him down a cargo of stones ; and every vessel arriving from that day forward was also commanded to be sent, as soon as unloaded, on the same errand. Francia then wrote to the Commandant of the district, ordering him to see that every man in his jurisdiction gave as many days of his labour in the week as might be ne-cessary for digging out, preparing, and shipping the stones : as these arrived, every cart of traffic was obliged to bring one load of them daily to the point where they were wanted; and, lastly, the inmates of the public prisons, loaded with their chains, were made to construct the pavement, under the superintendence of an unpaid surveyor of roads. In this way the whole work was done, as Francia boasted, without one farthing of expense to the public treasury.

Among the vessels which were ordered up the river on Francia's *hard* expedition, and which thus had the honour of being instrumental in mending his ways, was our own large brig, the San José. That the voyage might not be wholly profitless, I resolved to take advantage of it to see the quarries myself, and thence, making a little tour of the surrounding country, to return by land to Assumption. I told Francia of my intention, and he gave me a letter of introduction to his brother, who was governor of one of the Reducciones, or Indian settlements, which came within my projected route.

I detained the San José for a south wind, and, sailing with it, we had a fine run up to the quarries. There I witnessed a scene of bustle and activity which even the Jesuits could never have equalled. As the vessels poured in for loads of stone, the Commandant increased the number of his labourers, and, when I arrived, the whole traffic and manual labour of Paraguay appeared to be concentrated on this rocky point of the Republic. A mild despotism is said to be the most perfect form of government, and a stony despotism, like Francia's, was perhaps the only plan of government by which, with almost the quickness of thought, a South American town could be paved.

The quarry Commandant gave me a guide, and I proceeded on my tour. I found the country beautiful in the extreme, and refreshed in every direction by the most exquisitely picturesque and crystal streams, murmuring over their pebbled beds, under the rich, soft foliage of every possible variety of tree and shrub. Irrigated by these innumerable rivulets, the plains were verdant and the crops luxuriant everywhere. The population was dense, and made up of detached cottages, each with its patch of ground, on which were cultivated tobacco, cotton, mandioca, and other vegetable productions. The women were as remarkable for their industry, as the men for their lazy and indolent habits. The

peculiarity of the Paraguay labourer is, that while
he is noted and known as the most industrious of
his kind when *out* of Paraguay, he is very unwilling
to work when *in* it. The abundance and richness
of his own native soil, together with the paucity
of his wants, permit this idleness at home.
Stretched out in his hide hammock, which is
slung in the porchway of his cottage, his delight
is to lie there in listlessness the live-long day,
and, in the course of it, to smoke a succession of
cigars, and sip some twenty or thirty cups of his
favourite maté.   While he does this, his wife
and children are employed in all the arts of
husbandry, and thus he sees all his and their
wants provided for, without either care or labour
on his own part.

I travelled from estancia to estancia, and I
found on many of them pleasant country residences. Some of these in the vicinity of the quarries
were of stone.   Flocks and herds grazed in the
fat pastures around,—fields of the sugar-cane,
maize, and of tobacco were on all sides to be
seen ; abundance and unlimited hospitality were
the strong and universal characteristics of the
country.   Wherever I stopped, a feast was im-

mediately prepared, and the surrounding
neighbours invited. My hosts exhibited great
delight when I expressed a desire to see their
farms, or praised the general appearance of the
country. As I moved from one estancia to another I had generally three or four of my substantial and newly-made yeomanry friends in my
train; and, such was the jealousy of one and all
of their character for disinterested service, that,
during an excursion of ten days, I literally could
not contrive to spend or give away more than
a very few dollars,—and this exclusively in
presents of two or three rials at a time, to the
children of the poorest cottagers whom I visited.

When I got to the *reduccion* (I forget the
name of it) of which Francia's brother was the
administrator, I was received by him in the most
cordial manner, and I was invited to remain and
witness a series of Indian fiestas or holidays,
about to commence the next morning.

Don Pedro Francia was a totally different sort
of person from his brother; he was a corpulent,
and apparently good-tempered man, but of
slender capacity. He aspired to no higher post
than that of ruling over a few simple Indians;

and he scarcely ever left the reduccion over which he presided. He was subject to fits of insanity of a harmless character; and he was, on the whole, of an inoffensive turn, and the least likely of all others to interfere with his brother's Dictatorial power.

Yet, even of this poor brother, the suspicious dictator became eventually jealous: he was immured by him in one of his prisons. There the insanity of the unhappy administrator, which had heretofore been only slight and occasional, became confirmed and incurable; and there his ruthless and most unnatural brother left him to expire. But this was many years after my departure from Paraguay: and I now return to my own visit to poor Don Pedro.

These *reducciones*—settlements of reduced or converted Indians, generally Guaranis—were in no respect outwardly different from the *missiones* of the Jesuits. They were built in the same quadrangular form, and they were under the civil and religious superintendence of an administrator and a priest. They had, like the towns of the missiones, a dilapidated and depopulated look; and stillness and inertness, from day to day and from year to year, reigned throughout the little community.

On the occasion of my visit, however, to Don Pedro Francia all was life and activity. Great numbers of the surrounding peasantry kept pouring into the village, to participate in the fiestas; the Indians were all dressed out in their best; the alcaldes and other municipal officers in their robes of office: horses were gaily decked in ribbons: a bull-ring was erected; music and dancing went forward; the *sortija*, racing, and cards formed a large part of the amusements; and, above all, on the second evening, a stage was erected, and a *mystery* was performed. Of the bull-fight, the sortija, and the mystery, I shall give you a short account.

For the bull-fight a temporary ring was formed, with rising benches round for the spectators, and one large box, neatly fitted up, for the administrator and his friends. There was none of the dexterity exhibited by the bull-fighters which you have seen in former days in Buenos Ayres,— the poor Indians being of too timid a character to face even the comparatively tame bulls of Paraguay. However, they amused the spectators, and that was as good as if half-a-dozen bulls had been barbarously slain, two or three horses gored to death, and a picador or two made to bite the dust.

One Indian, somewhat bolder than the rest, advanced to the middle of the ring *para embestir al toro,*—to attack the bull with a short sword in his right hand, and his poncho thrown over his left arm, to serve as a decoy. The bull suddenly made his run: the Indian, who was dressed in gay velveteens, fled; and, just as he was clambering over the ring, the bull's horn caught—not the body, but the hinder part of the velveteen vestment of the flying foe. It was torn from one extremity to the other, and the tatters fluttered in the breeze. Huzzas and laughter arose; and in the midst of the mirth the administrator, clapping his hands in great glee, called out—"There go the rotten English velveteens!"

The Indians, with their fine horses, were much more dexterous at the sortija than the bull-ring. Some of our readers may not have heard of this common but favourite Spanish amusement. A frame, like that of a door, wide enough to allow a horse and his rider to pass through it with ease, is erected, and from the centre of the horizontal part of the frame depends a ring, slightly attached, by a hanging cord, to the top of the frame itself. The horseman, taking his stand about 200 yards from this, rushes towards it at full speed, having a small wooden dagger in his right hand; and he who inserts the point of it through the ring (the sortija), and so carries it off, receives it as the prize of his dexterity. At the full speed of the horse, to carry off the sortija is of course no easy operation.

All the amusements of the Indians were familiar to me, with the exception of the *mystery*, which was indeed a novel sight: and yet it was in every respect precisely what the mysteries represented in England, and in many other countries, used to be some three or four hundred years ago. This revival of an amusement, which, for centuries, has slept in oblivion in Europe (at all events in England; for it may still exist in Spain for aught I know to the contrary), appeared to me extremely curious.

The stage was erected in the open square, in front of the administrator's house, and a large oblong piece of green baize served to separate

the stage from *behind the scenes*, where the performers congregated. The side-scenery was
real,—that is, it consisted of many boughs of
trees, disposed in scenic order; and the spectators stood on the ground, in front of the stage,
and looking up to it. The performance was at
night, and by torch-light.

The actors were all Indians—men and women.
They represented, in the first act, the Na-
tivity; in the second, the Journey of Joseph and
Mary to Jerusalem, and Christ's disputing in
the Temple. The church of the village was
emptied of all its finery for the occasion,—saints'
dresses and ornaments, priests' robes, chalices,
censers,—all were transferred from the church to
the stage, to be used for the representation of
the mystery; and the pastor of the Indian flock
acted as prompter. The different passages of
Scripture on which the representations were
founded were dramatised as literally as possible;
and characters, both divine and human, were introduced without scruple. There was not the
slightest idea in the mind of any one present,
saving in my own, that there was even an approach to impiety in the liberty they were taking

with the sacred writings. All the spectators were delighted with the representation ; and the Indians performed their respective parts with much more propriety than I could have anticipated from individuals belonging to so simple and un-lettered a community.

Yours, &c.

W. P. R.

LETTER XIII.

W. P. R. TO THOMAS FAIR, ESQ.

THE PAYAGUÀ INDIANS.

Their Tolderias—Ornaments—Doctors—Cacique's Wife—A Flitting—A Feast—Their Thefts—and Banishment.

London, 1838.

THE Payaguà Indians, of whom notice has already been incidentally taken, formed a very striking part of the population of the capital of Paraguay. They were the only unconverted barbarians who intermingled with the inhabitants of Assumption.

There were several tribes who claimed and possessed that part of the Gran Chaco which lay in front of Paraguay,—the Mbayàs, the Guanàs, the Mocobies, the Guaycarús, the Abipones, and others. Of these the Mbayàs were the most valiant and warlike tribe; and they had so completely conquered the neighbouring nation of Guanàs, that the latter became the serfs of the former. Wherever a Guanà encountered one of the dreaded Mbayàs he crouched at his feet, and acted as his slave.

The Payaguàs, though they visited and frequented the Chaco in their canoes, had their tolderias, or wigwams, on the Paraguay side, and in the vicinity of the city. These tolderias were to be found in different directions, but they were generally within two or three leagues of the town; and, while their inhabitants maintained their own native predilections and customs, keeping (as regards society) within themselves, they professed a submission to the Spanish authorities, and carried on their traffic without restraint, interruption, or fear.

These Payaguàs were, strictly speaking, savages. Their language was guttural, barbarous, and scanty in its extent: both men and women went generally naked from the waist upwards; their moveable dwellings, or tolderias, were no better than pig-styes,—the aperture, intended as a doorway, being so low that the inmates were obliged to bend themselves double to enter and go out of the wigwam; and their habits were entirely those of savage life.

They were fond of the usual ornaments which

attract barbarians : their cloaks and ponchos were curiously overlaid with them,—principally beads and silver tubes and rings. The women wore long silver bodkins, fastened inside the nether lip, and depending on the breast: the men had round pieces of wood inserted in the skin which forms the lower part of the ear; and, by very gradually increasing the size of these pieces of wood, they came at last to be two inches in diameter,—the skin of the ear forming a narrow and slight *rim* round the large circular piece of wood. I endeavoured, on three or four occasions, when I heard of the death of a Payaguà, to purchase his ears, through the medium of his friends; but they would never consent to have them cut off from their deceased relative,—they would lend no *ear* to my proposal.

I incline to think that they destroyed all imperfect children at their birth, with some rare exceptions; for the Payaguàs were generally fine, well-made, and athletic men, and all of them perfect in their limbs and bodies. He who acted as priest and doctor (for the two professions were united in one) was very often deformed; for, generally, they appointed such to the office in

preference to any other. The obvious reason
was, that he required to work with his mind more
than with his body. If, after the election of a
doctor-priest, three of his patients successively
died under his hands, the *lex non scripta* of the
Payaguàs condemned the doctor himself to death.

A favourite remedy with the Payaguà doctor,
—and I believe, on the whole, in that climate, a
judicious one,—was bleeding. This was done by
suction; and I have witnessed the operation.
The patient was laid flat on his back in the toldo,
—as many of his friends as it would contain sat
around,—the doctor lay over the patient's body
sucking some part of it till the blood came; and
a male Payaguà, who squatted at the entrance
during the operation, lustily blew a horn, and
raised a discordant and grating din.

The women immediately after childbirth
bathed in the river (Paraguay); and I am not
aware that the custom was ever attended with a
fatal result, or with any ill consequences whatever to the " *accouchée.*"

Although, on visiting a tolderia, it was impossible, from the general poverty and wretchedness of all, to distinguish classes, the Paya-

guàs had, nevertheless, an aristocracy of their own. On one of our evening rides Doña Juana Gomez engaged to introduce Mr. and Mrs. Mendez, myself, and one or two others, to the cacique's lady at the principal tolderia. With much difficulty we got into the hovel of the princess. Her carpet was that which Nature had furnished, the grass of the open plain, now blackened with smoke, and besmeared with accumulated and accumulating filth. The apartment was drawing-room, dining-room, bed-room, and kitchen. The smell was intolerable, the closeness was suffocating. Beside the cacique's wife, two or three other females, visitors of the great lady, were squatted in this fœtid enclosure; and, on making some little bustle in the hovel to receive us, the lady cacique said to Doña Juana Gomez, in Guaraní, " You and your friends, Madam, will be pleased to excuse any trifling confusion you may observe in my house, for you know, as well as I do, what difficulty we all have now-a-days with our servants!" The meanest servant I ever knew in England would not have exchanged places with this Payaguà princess.

When the encampment of a tolderia became
so dirty and noxious as to offend even the indurated organs of the Payaguàs, they struck their
toldos ; and, loading donkeys, horses, and women with the *materiel* of their wigwams, and
other scanty moveables, they sat down on some
other patch of ground on the border of the river.

The Payaguàs had the exclusive supply of Assumption with fish and a strong grass called chala,
which they cut on the Chaco side of the river, as
fodder for horses.   They acted also as river-
couriers, going down to Neembucú, Corrientes,
and other places, in their canoes, in an incredibly
short space of time.   It was calculated that the
tribe earned yearly about 5000 dollars by these
branches of industry, four-fifths of which they
expended in ardent spirits.

They had, from time immemorial, held a
great annual feast on St. John's day, whence
many superstitious Paraguayans believed that
St. John himself had visited the Chaco.   On
this great occasion, and on several minor ones
throughout the year, a deputation waited on the
Governor to beg permission to hold their feast ;
and it was always given with a useless admoni-

tion to keep their fighting and drinking within due bounds.

They assembled, accordingly, in some shady place outside of the town, and the men, squatting down in a ring, the cacique took the chair, that is, his position was a little elevated above that of his surrounding company. The women stood or squatted behind, and served the guests when necessary. A huge jar, filled with aguardiente, was placed at the cacique's side, and he held a cocoa-nut, formed into a goblet, in his hand. Having filled this with spirits he made an oration in the Payaguá language, which was listened to with great interest, and occasional demonstrations of pleasure and applause, and then, bowing to all round, he quaffed off the contents of the cup. Each man, in his turn, went through the same ceremony, till the deep potations in which they indulged gradually introduced confusion and discord. Fierce gesticulations followed, and, at last, maddened with drink, one and all rose up, and a general battle pugilistic commenced. Even in drink they were adepts in this enviable science, and the blows which were dealt around soon caused blood to flow in copious streams.

The women, who had kept tolerably sober, now rushed in among their husbands, lovers, and relatives, endeavouring to put an end to the fight, and regardless of the blows which they themselves received. After a given time their efforts were successful;—the Payaguàs shook hands with each other, and again became affectionate friends. The women were regaled with more brandy, and then, by twos, and threes, and fours, linked arm-in-arm, they all came staggering, and reeling, and talking through the town,—in perfect harmony, and many outward demonstrations of good-will. Thus they retired to their tolderias,—satiated at once with pugilism and brandy.

The whole of this Payaguà ceremony,—including the walking arm-in-arm, a custom limited in that country to the tribe itself,—was considered by the Paraguayans to be so completely of a John Bull character, that the Payaguàs were often, jocosely, called "los Indios Ingleses," the English Indians.

I was a chief employer of the Payaguà couriers, and they brought the necessary grass for a couple of horses to my door every morning. I got well acquainted with many of them, and became a sort of banker, or rather pawnbroker, for the higher and more extravagant class of the tribe. They brought me curious specimens of clothing, ornaments, and other things, on which I lent them any money they demanded. I was in hopes they would, in this way, sell me some of these articles, for they had an insuperable objection to part with any of their valuables; but, immediately on their learning that I was about to leave the country, they came and redeemed all their pledges, refusing to sell me one of them.

The Payaguàs were much given to stealing. In such cases, when the theft could be clearly traced to a Payaguà, and, if either by his absconding, or from a difficulty of identification, the particular thief could not be apprehended, the municipal court gave an order to take up the first Payaguà to be met with in the street, and carry him to prison. The invariable consequence was that the tribe at large made up the sum demanded, and liberated the innocent prisoner. It was alleged, and no doubt truly, that the poor Payaguàs were, in this way, made to pay for many petty larcenies which they never

If I rightly understand Mr. Rengger (an author of whom we shall presently have to speak), the harmless and useful tribe of Payaguàs felt, in common with every other class of people in Paraguay, the effects of Francia's capricious cruelty. It appears that in the year 1820 the Chaco Indians began to give the Dictator great trouble by repeated incursions into his territory, and that these roused him, at length, to active warfare against them. He defended the accessible points of the river, and then carried fire and sword into the territories of all the Indians indiscriminately. Every Indian found, —man, woman, and child,—was put to death; and the Payaguà tribe, which was in no way whatever concerned with the Chaco Indians, was banished to Tevego,—an unhealthy and wretched settlement which Francia founded, about sixty leagues above Assumption, at once as a place of banishment for his proscribed victims, and as a check on the Indians in that quarter.

Yours, &c.

W. P. R.

LETTER XIV.

W. P. R. TO THOMAS FAIR, ESQ.

Vicissitudes—The winding up of our Affairs—Tenacity about
Silver—I prepare to leave—Last Interview with Francia—
The Piragua—We are alarmed, boarded, and searched—A
temptation resisted—Scene with a Tiger—Arrival at Corrientes.

London, 1838.

MAN, as he advances from stage to stage in the
great journey of life, is too apt—in the grossness
of his nature—to believe that the clock-work and
machinery of his frame are regulated by *physical*
laws alone. Yet, were the perceptions of the mind
as palpable and acute as the sensations of the
body, the eye of philosophy would probably discern
elements working in our *moral* constitution with
a regularity quite equal to that which distin-
guishes our physical system. Then might the
events of our life which are now designated as

" fortunate chances," " sad reverses," " lucky ac-
cidents," " unaccountable mishaps," be seen
plainly to originate in adequate causes, and
proceed uncrringly to legitimate effects. Then
might the metaphysical course of man be marked
out, into different and consecutive epochs, with
the same precision as that with which Shakspeare
has arranged for us our seven ages.

Of the moral laws which govern and regulate
our various careers, none is more striking than
that which subjects us, *malgré* every scheme of
counteraction of our own, to the oft-recurring and
certain vicissitudes of life. In the infancy of a
vicissitude, if I may so speak, we heed not the
germ which is planted,—we go forward in the
fancied security of our own plans. The vicissitude gathers strength, and we begin our endeavours to counteract it ;—but how vain the effort !
A power superior to our own is going on
with its irresistible work ; and whether for good
or for evil, (mentally blind as moles, we never
know for which,) our own plans are overturned,
and the *vicissitude* has worked out the moral
purpose with which it was entrusted by the
Great Regulator of all.

Such was the train of reflections into which I fell as I returned, in sadness and solitude, from the beach, after seeing my brother sail in our little bark, the Inglesita, for Corrientes. A box of sword-blades (for when he left Santa Fé he had no other arms on board) had gradually brought about all the marvellous changes in our views, prospects, and plans which have been detailed in the early letters which we have here addressed to you. All our own apparently well-laid and flourishing schemes had been upset by this box of sword-blades. The seed was small, but the fruits were abundant and bitter. My brother had nearly lost his life,—our mercantile career in Paraguay had been brought to a sudden and disastrous close,—and, from being persons of the first consideration in the republic, we had become "no better than banished men." Yet the conclusion which we came to, that something like ruin was involved in these ultimate effects, was altogether erroneous. They drove us to another soil, which yielded an ample and profitable harvest to our labours.

As it was now known that I was no longer a court favourite, I was very generally shunned

by my friends; yet, aware as I was that this
arose not from any bad feeling, but from the
terror of Francia, I did not of course at all com-
plain of the altered outward demonstrations of
my old acquaintances. Indeed, I insisted with
several on their refraining from farther intercourse
with me.

But what annoyed me exceedingly, was to find
that some of the Dictator's creatures, men in
subordinate office, did everything in their
power to thwart and perplex me. For a variety of reasons I was anxious to *wind up*, as
much as possible, *within* the term which Francia
had given me: and these, his minions, on the
contrary, were desirous of throwing me *beyond*
the time which Francia had allowed.

Chafed at last one day by their insolence, and
perceiving at the same time their drift, I marched
off to the government-house, and sent in my name
as desirous of seeing the Dictator. I was admitted: Francia was standing at the head of the
room, his arms folded, his capote thrown across
his breast, and his sternest look thrown into his
stern countenance.

"I come here," I said, still under the influence

of angry feelings, " to ask if it be by your Excellency's *orders* that I am insulted, ill-treated, and thwarted at every turn which I take in fulfilling your own command to wind up my affairs, and to quit the republic ?"

"Who has *dared*," said Francia hurriedly and angrily,—"who has *dared* to do so ?"

"The administrator of the custom-house," I promptly answered,—"the captain of the port, and the chief of the resguardo."

"Vaya V. con Dios," replied Francia,—"que eso no volverà à suceder."   Go in peace, and be assured that that will not again happen.

In half an hour afterwards the delinquents were before the Dictator ; and I believe he resorted to his favourite plan of *fining* them, for presuming to step out of their general routine without his orders.   Be that as it may, the parties I have named, and all other parties, were cap-in-hand to me from that day forward ; and they seemed as anxious as myself to hasten my departure.

I had been allowed two months by Francia to wind up our affairs, but I used such dispatch that, at the end of three weeks, I was ready to depart.   With permission previously obtained of

the Dictator, I left in Gomez's hands all such property as I could not realise in produce. I was
allowed to send off empty our own vessel, the San
José, on condition of her having no Paraguay
sailors or peons on board of her; and for the produce which I wished to take with me, license was
given to load a *piragua* of the largest dimensions,
with strict orders to all concerned, that the Paraguay sailors employed should return *instantly* to
Paraguay, or be severely punished if they did not,
wherever and whenever they might be found.

Such was the absurd rigour with which Francia prohibited any extraction from the republic of
the precious metals, that when I applied for leave
to take 200 dollars (£40) with me for expenses
and other contingencies on the way, the Dictator
was consulted, and I was politely requested to go
to the custom-house next day.

"Sir," said the administrator, " 200 dollars is
an extravagant and preposterous sum—(I had
about two-and-twenty people to provide for on
my voyage),—and you can never expend it between this and Corrientes."

"Very well, I answered, "let the sum be 100
dollars."

"No, that is still a great deal too much," replied the Administrator.

"Fifty, then," I suggested, with a smile.

"Sir," retorted the guardian of the circulating medium, with much gravity, and even austerity of manner, "I have consulted the most Excellent Supreme, and he is of opinion that *ten dollars* is a sufficient sum for your expenses; and for that sum I am ready to give you a permit."

"Stop," said I, also very gravely; "will you include a pair of light silver, English-made spurs?"

"I shall put them down," said the gracious minister.

"And a silver bombilla to take my mate?"

He paused. "Well," he said, "I shall also include that; but ask for no more." So a formal permission was written out, and, after inspection by Francia, delivered to me, allowing me to extract from the republic ten silver dollars, a pair of small spurs, and a bombilla (the whole worth about 4*l.*), as an "especial favour" granted by his Excellency the Dictator. To such inconceivable and ridiculous minutiæ did the absolute Lord of Paraguay descend in his government!

I took the liberty of carrying my two hundred dollars with me, albeit unaccompanied by the Dictator's permission; conceiving that the moral duty of providing for my crew was superior to any obedience which I owed to the fiscal regulations of Doctor Francia.

During the two or three last days of my stay in Assumption many old friends paid me furtive visits in the evening, to express their regret at the departure of my brother and myself. In truth, a kinder or more warm-hearted people than the Paraguayans nowhere exists.

The day before that of my departure, having my passport in my pocket, and all things in readiness to start, I called once more on Francia. I was desired, as usual, to walk in; and he seemed prepared to hear some new complaint.

Instead of this, however,—" Sir," said I, "having used all diligence in giving effect to your orders that I should quit the republic, I am now ready to depart; and I could not do so without expressing, personally, to you my acknowledgment of the kindness I have received during my stay here. I further wished to say that, if your Excellency has any orders for Buenos Ayres, or any of the other provinces, I shall be happy to charge myself with them, and fulfil them to the best of my power."

The Dictator's rigid features relaxed as I proceeded in my short harangue; and he could scarcely refrain from a smile on finding me make my congé, as a banished man, with so much politeness.

"Vaya V. con Dios,—Vaya V. con Dios," said Francia,—"Go in peace, go in peace." We bowed to each other with much gravity, first in the middle of the room, and then when I got to the door; and in this courtier-like way I brought my intercourse with the "Supremo" to a close.

I now busied myself about my departure; and, as it was not devoid of incident, I shall give you some account of it.

Of the various keeled and unkeeled vessels that sailed on the waters of the Paraguay and Paraná,—brigs, polaccas, sumacas, sloops, chalanas, garandumbas, valsas, boats, canoes, rafts, and piraguas,—the most curious of all were the latter, in one of which I had been ordered to move bag and baggage from the republic.

The piragua is a huge box, perfectly square

and flat at the bottom, and the four sides coming
out in angular directions, so as to form a square
surface on the top, equal to nearly double the
size of the corresponding square of the bottom.
A sort of gangway or rim is then run round the
box, sufficiently broad to allow rowers to stand
conveniently upon it. The box being then loaded
with bales, square with the top of it, a flooring is
laid over them, and on this a hide-house, or
troja, some eight or nine feet in height, is constructed, and this, again, with the exception of
room for passengers and crew, is loaded with
produce. The machine of this description, which
I purchased and loaded, carried about 1500
bales of yerba, equal to about 200 tons, leaving
space for my own personal convenience, and
that of the master, pilot, and nineteen or twenty
peons.

The piragua has neither prow nor stern,
and sails are of no use in so unmanageable and
unwieldy a body as it presents. We were, in
nautical, and in this case literal phrase, obliged
to *box* about the river the best way we could,
assisted by oars. With these, of a very weighty
description, six men on each side of the piragua

stood rowing; four were on the platform behind, also with oars, which served in place of a
rudder; and four in front were ready to act in
the same way, should the piragua be turned to
the right-about. With the advantage of the
current, and of the rowing, we managed to go
down the stream pretty smoothly, at the rate of
about four miles an-hour. I sat on the house-top,
—for such the deck of my "embarcacion" was ;
and the action of rowing it down, and the constant endeavour to keep it steady, on the part of
the willing and merry crew, was a continued
source of amusement to me. In spite of all the
exertions of the crew, the piragua would, three or
four times a-day, be carried into an eddy, which
was too strong to be resisted by the action of
oars ; and then we went clumsily whirling round
and round, like a great tub, till it pleased the
waters to allow us to stop our nautical waltz.
Sometimes the force of the current obliged us to
attack the pendant boughs of the island-trees with
all the ardour which Don Quixote displayed when
he assailed the windmills; with this difference,
however, that the ponderous weight of our vessel
of war carried everything before it ; and branches,

and even trunks of trees, were crushed and broken, and strewed around, wherever our piragua took it into its head to run up against them.

I sailed in this safe but strange sea-boat towards the close of October, 1815; and I con-fess, as we whirled out of sight of the port, I felt glad that I was fairly off, and had nothing further to fear from Francia. From the first of our outbreak I knew that the turning of a straw might have influenced him in setting all general considerations aside, and in making me to feel his despotic sway and his capricious cruelty. These passing surmises vanished when I found myself a few leagues from Assumption; and when, towards evening, we tied up for the night near the Angostura, my mind rested for the first time from all the anxiety consequent on winding up a large concern, where so much decision and promptitude of action had been required; from the increasing bustle engendered by that action; and from the latent suspicion, as I have said, which accompanied the whole, that Francia might suddenly put a stop to my operations, immure me in a prison, or send me off to Curuguatí, just as the whim of the moment might dictate.

It was a still and beautiful night, the air that of a soft and balmy tropical spring, and the atmosphere so clear that the whole firmament seemed to be one immense brilliant cluster of stars, filling with a dazzling glory the infinitude of space. The distant light came in softened beams to the earth, and shed its faint rays over the face of the placid waters on which we lay: nature was hushed into silence and repose; the richly-clothed woods, the undulating hill and dale, were dimly perceptible around; and, as I sat in solitude, viewing the scene before me, I felt inclined to say with Pope,—

"Here heaven-born, pensive Contemplation dwells."

My musings and meditations, which were fast carrying me "beyond the visible diurnal sphere," were suddenly and somewhat alarmingly disturbed by the report of a musket, fired at no great distance from us. I roused the patrón, who, with the whole crew, had retired, after a hard day's work, at an early hour to rest; and we presently heard the splashing of oars and the hum of voices. While we stood wondering what this might import, another musket was fired, and a bullet whizzed over the piragua.

In a minute after, a large boat rounded a point of the river, and our alarm was by no means diminished on seeing that it was filled with armed men. Yet another musket was discharged, and the ball in this instance struck our vessel. It might just as well have struck one of ourselves, for most of the crew were now on their legs, full of consternation at the hostile demonstrations of our approaching visitors. As the boat came near to us, however, we discovered it to be that of the resguardo, or coast-guard, with an officer of the establishment, and eight or ten soldiers under him. When they got alongside they all mounted our piragua, and the officer desired to speak with me in my own cabin.

When we were alone, said he, " information has been given to the Excelentisimo Supremo Dictador that you have clandestinely and unlawfully carried off with you a large sum in specie, and I have been sent to discharge your vessel, to examine every bale and package, and search your piragua. If such specie be found, my orders are to embargo your property, and carry your person back to Assumption."

I had only twelve doubloons, and these I

knew the officer could never get at. During the whole time of loading my piragua it had been bruited, however, that "Don Guillermo" was going to smuggle a hundred thousand dollars out of the republic; and I now saw that Francia had adopted his present plan of discovering, if possible, how far the rumour had any foundation.

"Sir," I said to the officer, "I have no specie on board; but, of course, I am ready to submit both to the discharge and inspection which you have orders to carry into effect."

Dark as it was, the officer forthwith commenced, by the assistance of his men, a rummage of my cabin, turning everything topsy-turvy, and looking into every nook and corner. The patrón, or master, was examined, the pilot was cross-questioned, the men were promised a reward for evidence; and, when all this produced no effect, orders were given to commence a discharge of the vessel at daybreak: then the officer, allowing his men to go forward and have their supper, came and sat himself down beside me in my cabin.

The prospect before me was not an agreeable one. The discharging and reloading of my

K 3

piragua could not be well effected in less time than a fortnight, it might take a month. The property would be deteriorated,—my time was precious,—and, above all, I was to be, during this additional time, under the surveillance of Francia, and subject to his dark and jealous power. Under these circumstances the officer temptingly offered to let me go at once,—for a consideration. He wanted something reasonable for himself and his men, and he would return and report favourably to the Dictator.

I have not the slightest doubt that Francia himself told the officer to make this proposal, and I feel equally convinced that, had I even wavered for a moment, I should have been a lost man. I saw, however, the snare which was laid for me. I told the officer that in the shape of money I had nothing to offer him; and that, although I could not oppose his *taking* any other property I had, I certainly could not, and would not, *give* him anything to stop him in the course of his duty.

The man, with an apparent simplicity of manner which the Paraguayans are celebrated for being able to assume, argued the matter with me; but I remained firm to my purpose, and, happily, the event justified my course. Finding that I prepared with alacrity in the morning to proceed with the discharge, the resguardo officer told me he was satisfied that all was right. He proceeded *up* the river, and with no small joy I proceeded *down*.

Only one further incident worth relating occurred to us during our passage to Corrientes. With my piragua I had a fine canoe which was often at work, and which I used in little excursions among the islands, as we dropped down the river. I examined the mouth of the Pilcomayo (where we very nearly lost ourselves among the intricacies of the islets), and I went over to the disembocadura, or junction, of the Vermejo with the Paraguay.

One morning as the canoe lay ready for our day's work, a peon came running to my part of the piragua, calling out,—" A tiger, sir,—there goes a tiger !—let us follow him quickly." Down we got to the canoe,—a hatchet was put into my hand,—I was placed in the prow,—and I was told to strike the tiger with my whole force on the head, should we reach him before he got to the shore.　He was swimming lustily across the river, and when he saw us in full chase after him, he cleft the stream with still more mighty strokes of his powerful paws.　The four Paraguayans made the canoe skim rapidly across the expansive tide, and we fast advanced upon our flying foe.　With one foot resting on the extremity of the skiff, I stood with the hatchet in my hand raised aloft, ready to give a death-blow to the tiger.　We pursued, in breathless expectation of the event; but, ere we could overtake our prey, he had got footing in the shallowing stream,—thence he made one tremendous bound to the shore, — and turning instantly round, he glared upon us with fearful ferocity. We had, as nearly as possible, run our canoe right up against the bank on which he stood. We were certainly not six yards from the infuriated animal, and one stroke more of the paddles had brought us into actual contact with him.

After a pleasant, picturesque, and whirling voyage of six days we got to Corrientes, where I soon found that I had escaped from Scylla to fall upon Charybdis; but as it is not our present purpose to speak of the Lord Protector Artigas, but of those matters only which occurred in the republic of the Most Excellent Supreme Perpetual Dictator Francia, I must leave our adventures in the territory of the former to the chance of seeing the light, in a narrative form, at some future period.

Even under all the alarm which the being surrounded by lawless hordes of Artigueños could not fail to inspire, the first words of my brother, when I shook hands with him in Corrientes, were, "Well, thank God, we are both here—beyond the reach of Francia."

Yours, &c.

W. P. R.

LETTER XV.

J. P. R. TO THOMAS FAIR, ESQ.

THE NATURAL PRODUCTIONS OF PARAGUAY.

The Lapacho-tree—Other trees, shrubs, fruit, and vegetables—
Ornithology—Zoology.

London, 1838.

IN this and in a subsequent letter I purpose to
give you some account of the natural productions, commerce, and revenue of Paraguay; and,
in order to exhibit these such as they were when
I first visited the country, in contrast with what
they became, as affected by the policy of Francia,
I shall anticipate a little, in this respect, his
history, leaving its more systematic and uninterrupted development for the close of my con-
tributions to this our Second Series of Letters.

Of the natural productions of Paraguay her
wood ranks decidedly the first in importance.
To say nothing of the yerba-tree (of which a full
account has been given in the First Series), the
lapacho is not only the finest but the most mag-

nificent of all trees. English oak is very fine,
but never to be compared to lapacho. From the
solid trunk of one of these trees a Portuguese
scooped out at Villa Real a canoe, which brought
down to Assumption a hundred bales of yerba
(that is, 22,500 lbs. of Paraguay tea), several
hides made up into balls and filled with mo-
lasses, a load of deals, seventy packages of
tobacco, and eight Paraguay sailors, to manage
the three masts and sails of the large, but yet
elegantly scooped-out trunk of the lapacho-tree.
Of this tree are constructed vessels which, when
fifty years old, may still be called young. Their
frame is not shaken, nor is their constitution
debilitated by all the bumps they have on the
sand-banks of the Paraná, nor by the searching
rays of a tropical sun, nor by the " even down
pours," as the Scotch have it, of tropical rains.

I speak of these ships with reference to the
ordinary course of navigation, under ordinary
repairs,—not in regard to their power of resist-
ing Francia's mode of dealing with them: for
even the lapacho-tree,—indurated, impervious as
it is to external attacks,—is not proof against a
decree or a system which, for fifteen or twenty

years, leaves a vessel to exposure on the beach
of Assumption, without awnings, without caulk-
ing, without watering of the decks, without, in
short, any one of the precautions usually taken
to retard decay, in either river-craft, or ships
that sail on the high seas.

Of this lapacho the grain is so close, that
neither worm nor rot can assail it.   The carts in
Buenos Ayres, and all the rafters of the houses
there, are constructed of it.   Besides the lapacho
there are the urandîg-pitá, the urandîg-irai, of
which the latter is equal in durability to rose-
wood, and exceeds it in beauty.   Then there
is the timbó, the tatayiba, or wild mulberry, the
lancewood, the orange-tree, the carandîg, the
palm-tree, the tataré, and sheraró, all at once
useful and ornamental.   The cebil and curupaî
furnish excellent bark for the purpose of tanning,
while many of the shrubs and plants afford dyes
of the richest hue.   There is one tree of which
the trunk is composed of several stems twisted
round one another, yet so compactly as to form
the appearance of one solid trunk.   There is the
palo santo, or holy-wood, producing odoriferous
gum, and the incense-tree, yielding the delicious

perfume of the pastilla. From the manguasí is produced gum elastic, from which matches are made; and the trees, plants, and shrubs of medicinal properties are rich and various. There is one especially worthy of notice: it is called the palo de vivora, or serpent's-tree, and the juice of its rind, produced by mastication, is an infallible cure for the poisonous bite of the great original enemy of the human race.

One of the many ingenious resources, by recurrence to which the Jesuits conciliated, and won upon the affection and gratitude of their Indian converts, was the successful application, from their botanical science, of many of the herbs and drugs of Paraguay to some of the inveterate diseases of their neophytes. Rhubarb and sarsaparilla grow wild all over Paraguay. The cordage of the vessels there is made from a plant which furnishes fibres of so strong and irresistible a texture, as water has not much power to rot, nor the sun much to destroy. The cotton-plant grows in the greatest luxuriance, and ladies sixty years of age are known to plant, weed, gather in their cotton, separate the seeds (which may be called the weeds) from the downy produce, spin it, weave it, and afterwards tambour it with a taste, richness, and elegance not excelled by any workmanship of Chinese ingenuity.

I sent and brought home several specimens of what were here called *scarfs*, but in Paraguay denominated *towels*. They were worn by some of the most fashionable females in Bath, admired by the shopkeepers there, envied by the ladies who had them not, and confessed by some of the most skilful manufacturers to be altogether inimitable in this country.

Tobacco, coffee, sugar, Indian corn, the yucca-root, melons, oranges, rice, and especially the pine-apple, are all abundant. Of the latter we sent two hundred plants (the cost of the whole being one dollar, or four shillings) to James Brittain, Esq., of Buenos Ayres, who, at great expense, but with much taste and judgment, had initiated there, and successfully, one of the best systems of English gardening. His pines, his hautboys, his peaches, his musk and water-melons, his apricots, his grapes, his celery, his asparagus, his apples, pears, currants, gooseberries, peas, potatoes, leguminous and succulent roots, of every description, might have vied with the best of these delicacies reared at Chatsworth,—and they, I presume, are the best in this kingdom. So much for the vegetable productions of Paraguay.

With birds and animals it is not less redundantly stocked. Azára has described upwards of four hundred new species of the feathered tribe as inhabiting, in his day, the gorgeous woods and dense coppices of Paraguay. Game of every kind is most abundant. The large partridge, the small partridge, the royal duck, and his subordinate train of common duck, wigeon, and teal, the snipe, and the jack-snipe, the water-hen, the diver, the wild swan, wild goose, and wild turkey, the grey and golden plover, the hawk (with his keen eye), an enemy of all these; the vulture, with his curved beak and curved talons, lording it over the hawk; and the eagle, with his imperial glance, carrying fear to the heart of the vulture. Disputing supremacy even with the eagle, comes the king of the vultures,—the stately, cream-coloured bird, with crimson, yet unfeathered, neck, ample and out-stretched wings, beak jet black, and gait majestic, lording it over all his subjects of the sombre race.

Great is the prerogative of this emperor of the tribes of the air,—great almost as Francia's;—and you shall hear how the king of the vultures exercises his sway. With him, as with all tyrants, *gorging* is the principal attribute,—and gorging on blood.

When the vulture-king smells a carcase from afar, or when he pounces with his death-like talons upon an animal endued with life, the imperial bird, nurtured to savage ferocity by such repasts, fills his craving maw with flesh, and slakes his insatiable thirst with blood. All his sooty subjects stand apart at a respectful distance, whetting their appetites, and regaling their nostrils, but never dreaming of an approach to the carcase till their master has sunk into a state of repletion. When the kingly bird, by falling on his side, closing his eyes, and stretching on the ground his unclenched talons, gives notice to his surrounding and expectant subjects that their lord and master has gone to rest, up they hop in hundreds to the carcase. This, in a few minutes, is stripped of everything eatable upon it, and the dry ribs, backbone, eye-sockets, rump, tail, legs and fetlocks, are abandoned for a repast in some other part of the country, on some other animal of the quadruped tribe.

But the most remarkable of all the feathered race in Paraguay is the parrot; and when I speak of him, I include all the varieties of his family, from the cockatoo and guacamayo down to the little parroquet, not more than three inches in length. Though green and yellow are the most remarkable colours in their plumage, yet the Payaguá Indians, with various dyes and poisons, so tinge their wings, pulling out the old feathers, and anointing the new shoots with imperishable colours, that you see parrots in Paraguay of all shades of plumage.

I had two, of which the characters were so curiously developed and displayed, that I cannot refrain from giving you a short account of them. One was a green and yellow parrot of the ordinary size, the other a green parroquet, of a size so small as I have seen nothing to equal of the parrot tribe in this country. It was not larger than a wren; it was perfect in its formation; and it had a voice as shrill, though by no means so disagreeable, as that of a shrew.

With respect to the *parrot*, after living for two years among the Payaguás, and being tinged by their indelible paints with all the beautiful contrast of green and yellow, one of them became the property, first of a lady of Assumption, and afterwards mine. So acute was this bird,—so exquisite his *ear*—so sagacious his perception,— and so strong and instinctive his imitative powers, that I have seen him listen attentively for five minutes to one person's speaking, and then give both the words and tone of the speaker. No mimic more accurate,—no critic more caustic,— no satirist more libellous than this chattering bird. I have heard him imitate the cry of the child, the squeak of the pig, the bark of the dog, and the mew of the cat; and all so admirably, that it was impossible not to class him as a ventriloquist of the first order. He gave the word of command like a drill-serjeant to a company of soldiers; played the trumpet for them, and beat the drum; and then sang the song of " Viva la Patria."

In regard to animals, insects, and reptiles, the soil of Paraguay is also prolific. There are the jaguar, the lion, the ounce, the wild boar, the monkey, the ferret, the stag, the antelope, abundance of horned cattle, horses, asses, and mules. The boa-constrictor abounds in the woods about Villa Real, which are also filled with lizards, rattle-snakes, locusts, beetles, binchucas, mosquitos, and tabanos, with many more, of many other tribes, which, if I should enumerate, the time would fail me. Suffice it to say, that they are all more or less the scourges of our race, and, in defiance of all laws and commandments, are continually shedding human blood.

Yours, &c.

J. P. R.

LETTER XVI.

J. P. R. to Thomas Fair, Esq.

Exports of Paraguay—Destruction of commerce—Revenue of
Paraguay—Expenditure—Francia's imposts—His parsimony—
His opinion of English merchants and manufacturers.

London, 1838.

Most prominent and most important among
the exports of the Republic was the yerba, or
tea.

	Dollars.
Of this there were annually shipped 40,000 bales, containing nine arrobes (of 25 lbs. each arrobe), or 360,000 arrobes, which valued, with duties and charges, at two dollars the arrobe, make	720,000
There were shipped 40,000 arrobes of Tobacco at	240,000
The value of the wood shipped was	150,000
The value of sugar, spirits, sweatmeats, tanned hides, segars, cotton, cloth, &c. &c.	100,000
Dollars	1,210,000
And as the profits on these articles amounted on an average to 50 per cent.	605,000
Paraguay came to receive annually, in the shape of returns for her produce	1,815,000
Or in pounds sterling, at 4s. per dollar	£363,000

This is a small sum, when considered as the amount of a country's commercial wealth. Wealth, however, like everything else, to be properly estimated, must be considered, not in the abstract, but relatively to the circumstances of the country in which it is possessed. The incomes of two English Dukes, and of one English Marquis, are equal to more than the whole commercial returns of Paraguay, though Paraguay is larger than all England, and endowed with natural boons and blessings, incomparably greater than even the most favoured and fertile spots of our beautiful island.

Paraguay then had, though not her Dukes and Marquises, yet her comparatively wealthy classes; and they were those who received and divided among them the annual returns for the produce they had shipped, with its profits, to the amount already stated of about 360,000*l*. There were about 500 families participating in this return, which, on an average, would thus yield to them 720*l*. a-year. Some received much more, some much less; but taking the highest receiver at 2000*l*. a-year, and the lowest at 100*l*., it may be inferred what havoc was made among the aristocracy of Paraguay, when, at one fell swoop, Francia pounced upon and annihilated their commerce.

Nor was it (if I may use the phrase in a country like England) the mercantile aristocracy alone that suffered by his barbarous policy and decrees. All whom the merchants employed,—the yerba manufacturers, the hewers of timber, the ship-carpenters, tobacco cultivators, sailors, growers of the sugar-cane, and even the poor female manufacturers of cigars,—were thrown idle and listless upon the community. If they were not left in a state of starvation, it was only because, even with their nails, they might prepare a patch of ground on which to grow the yucca root; but they were left, to all intents and purposes, denuded of everything beyond the barest, the poorest, means of subsistence. Then for the warehouses which had been used for the stowage of the voluminous products of the country, their roofs fell in upon the rotting merchandise which they could no longer shelter. More than 100 square rigged vessels lay like so many useless hulks on the rivera, or river banks; the sun had made yawning apertures between every plank, and the seams of the deck oped their mouths to admit, as they fell, the copious torrents of rain. The cordage rotted, and the masts decayed. The ruined and dejected owners and masters of the little fleet walked up and down in despondent contemplation of their fast mouldering property.

The revenue arising to the government before this now prostrate state of commerce was, on my first arrival in Paraguay, estimated thus :—

		Dollars.
Duty of Export on 40,000 bales of yerba . .		40,000
,, on 40,000 arrobes of tobacco .		40,000
,, on wood, spirits, cigars, &c. .		25,000
Duties on Exports . .		105,000
Import duty, 4 per cent. on merchandise imported from various quarters, to the amount of 2,000,000 dollars		80,000
Alcabala duty, or duty of re-sale, payable by the purchaser, on produce, merchandise, land; on everything, in short, which passed from one proprietor to another, 4 per cent. The transactions liable to this duty were estimated at 4,000,000 dollars		160,000
Stamps, postages, and property of those who died intestate		30,000
Total revenue of Paraguay, under the old regime		375,000
Reduced to sterling at 4s. per dollar . . .		£75,000

With a military force to maintain, not exceeding 500 men, with no navy to keep up, and with comparatively few public functionaries to pay, this revenue was found sufficient for all the expenses of the State, and even for the ordinary peculations of the Governor and his functionaries.

Let us now see how the account of receipt and expenditure stands as controlled by him who controls all, and especially who holds the purse-strings of his ill-gotten, and even so, diminished revenue, with a miser's grasp.

I take his expenditure first. Though not great, considering that a country larger than our own is kept down by it, it will yet be evident that, the legitimate sources of revenue being stopped by the paralyzation of commerce, measures must be resorted to, characterized by all the grades of tyranny, from the grossest imposts unjustly levied, to the most petty acts of grinding extortion. Francia's great expense consists in the maintenance and clothing of his tools of oppression, the troops.

Of these he has, in the whole country, about 4000; and estimating the expense to him of

Dollars.

each soldier, for food, clothing, and pay at the
very moderate rate of 120 dollars, or 25*l.*
a-year, his Army costs him 480,000
The pay of various public functionaries throughout the Republic (himself included)   .   . 25,000
Permanent expense of preserving the frontiers,
and making incursions upon the Indians   . 50,000
Occasional purchases of arms, ammunition, ordnance, &c. 30,000

Francia's annual Expenditure   .   . 585,000
or Sterling £117,000

If it be considered, first, that the duties on exports and imports, if not extinct, were diminished
to a paltry amount by the non-intercourse policy ;
if it be considered that the four per cent. duty on
re-sale must have undergone a similar diminu-
tion, and that stamp and post-office establishments
never can flourish where commerce is not ; it will
be readily inferred to what different means, and
it will presently be seen to what disgraceful shifts,
the Dictator was driven, in order to raise that
money which was one of the principal sinews of
his power. What sums he derived respectively
from the various sources which produced the
whole revénue it is impossible to say, because
Francia published no financial statements, nor
was there any system or rule laid down for the re-

plenishment of his treasury that was not subject
to the every-day fluctuations of his caprice, or
measured by reference to his projects, or, above
all, modified and violated by the pressure of immediate wants. The data, however, on which the
estimate of his *expenditure* is formed are subject
to no such difficulties. The number of soldiers
he had was matter of notoriety; so was the expense at which he must have kept them. His
wars with the Indians could not be concealed; ·
and his jealous look-out on the frontiers could be
kept up only at a certain and easily ascertainable
expense.

We have seen that, in order to provide for
these various outlays, he *must* have raised upon
the people of Paraguay (after having made them
paupers by his foreign policy, and slaves by his
domestic one) 117,000*l.* a-year. Pitiful as the
sum is, considered in the light of a government's
revenue, it is far from contemptible when viewed
in its relation to all the arbitrary acts, the petti-
fogging schemes, the rigid scrutiny into private
affairs, and the unscrupulous exaction of what
was levied upon the impoverished, and sometimes dying victims of state cupidity or dictatorial necessity.

The following, then, are the sources, permanent and contingent, from which Francia drew (I may say draws) his income:—

First.—While he abolished commerce at large, he was in the habit of granting occasional licenses for the importation, and sometimes for the exportation of property. On all property so privileged he raised the duty from 4 to 30 per cent.

Secondly.—He confiscated the tithes, making them payable to himself as head of the church.

Thirdly.—He levied an annual tax upon every storehouse and shop in Assumption.

Fourthly.—He seized all the municipal revenues.

Fifthly.—From the supercargo of each vessel which he permitted to enter the River Paraguay, the Dictator exacted a copy of invoices, and selected, according to his necessity or caprice, whatever articles he chose, which he either paid not for at all, or years after the purchase; or at prices infamously low, and fixed by himself on principles arbitrary and unjust.

Sixthly.—He levied a duty of 9 per cent. on the few things he allowed to be exported.

Seventhly.—He established laws for fines and confiscations, which brought often the most scrupulous, innocent, and correct persons within their relentless and indiscriminating scope.

Eighthly.—He converted the great number of estates which he confiscated from alleged enemies, or suspected malcontents, into cattle-farms, to manage which he appointed his own overseers. Of these farms, he sold the cattle in the market-place of Assumption, *by retail*, allowing no butcher in the shambles to undersell him; and he thus himself regulated the price of beef.

Ninthly. — The droit d'aubaine, or law of escheat, was levied with a minute and inquisitorial rigour unheard of before. Every one who died in Paraguay, not being a native of that country, forfeited to the state his goods and chattels,—to the last shirt on his back, and to the last penny in his pocket.

No matter how intimately or extensively connected by relationship the poor foreigner might be: he might have a Paraguay wife and ten creole children; he might have lived in the country from his infancy; he might have spread his connexions far and wide; and he might have

benefited the state by the payment to it of thousands of dollars annually;—yet, if he had not
been *born on the soil of Paraguay,* no sooner was
he stretched on a sick-bed, with the remotest
prospect of its becoming a death-bed, than the
unhallowed officers of the revenue, like those of the
church, kept hovering over the carcase of the
dying man; collecting, at first, the *spolia opima,*
but not scrupling, at last, to take from under him
his bed, and out of his drawers everything but
the shirt required for the day. All this, too, was
often done in the presence of the despairing wife,
and of the large family of the dying man. If he
died not so soon as the State (that is, as the Dictator) desired and expected, he was supplied, for
his lingering subsistence, with a daily pittance
from his own means.

M. Rengger observes, that "it was considered
a particular mark of favour from the Dictator that
the funeral expenses of Mr. Joseph Sibibal, a
native of Savoy, had been reimbursed to him
(Mr. R.) and Mr. Lonchamps, who had, in the
first instance, paid for the last sad offices performed
to their friend."

Tenthly.—Forced loans and iniquitous contri-

butions constituted a large part of Francia's revenue. Thus, when he imprisoned the old Spaniards without cause, and liberated them without
either trial or specific allegation of delinquency,
he made them pay, as the price of his returning clemency, 150,000 dollars. Similar exactions,
on a smaller scale, were of daily occurrence.
An unfortunate barrel in front of an old Spaniard's house one day startled Francia's horse.
The owner was sent to prison, and only liberated on payment of a fine to the State of 1000
dollars. All the artizans whom Francia employed were badly, irregularly, and scantily
paid; and yet the " value received" was so nar-
rowly looked into,—measured with such a Shy-
lock's eye, that on one occasion the potent Dictator seized hold of a grenadier's coat brought to
him by the tailor, and taking up a pair of scissors,
a piece of chalk, and a quantity of cloth charged
by Mr. Cabbage as that which had been ab-
sorbed by the fit, showed him, and proved to
him mechanically and mathematically, that he
must have stolen a quarter of a yard. Snip
was sent to the public prison, and the coat was
hung up in the Dictator's audience chamber, as

scarecrow garments are in orchards, a terror to all purloiners.

Not a piece of linen for soldiers' shirts or trousers was purchased without previous inspection by His Excellency; and often, distrustful of Irish and Manchester manufacturers, did he unrol with his own hands the piece of goods submitted to inspection. By application to it of the vara, or yard, he ascertained that it was of the length, 25, 26, or 28 yards, labelled on the ticket. So quick-sighted did he become in the quality of manufactured goods, that finding a great many of them had wide interstices between the threads, filled up with starch, he had one end of the piece washed, and then viewing it through a microscope, ascertained the nature of its real texture. If he found, as it must be confessed he often did, the gaps between the thread to be rather yawning, he allowed the owner half of the prime cost for it, and told him to thank his stars, for that he ought to be imprisoned as a knave and impostor. "This is the way," said he, on one occasion, to an English merchant, " that you hucksters of rags vend your unsound and deceitful manufactures over the world. The Jews are

cheats, but the English are downright swindlers.
With your labels, and your tickets, and your gilt
finery upon your goods, your colours that are
'warranted fast,' and yet fade upon a first wash-
ing, you are the veriest mountebanks and pedlars
that traverse the earth.   There is nothing noble
in your souls ; for filthy lucre, filthily gotten, is
the rotting disease of your heart's core.   Look
ye, Mr. Merchant, for these ten boxes of cotton
platillas, (they were spread out in the Dictator's
audience chamber,) for which you asked me a
shilling a yard, you shall have sixpence ; and
think yourself well off, that I do not send you to
some of the Paraguay looms, (no doubt you understand how to manage a shuttle,) that you
might there learn how to make honest cloth.   I
am not, Mr. Pedlar, like my countrymen, to be
caught by fine outsides, quack commendations, or
the nick-nackery mode of packing up your flash
wares.   Pan, Pan; y vino, vino : * if you think
that, because Francia is a Dictator, he cannot
look after his own affairs, you are a little out
of your calculation.   Go about your business ;

---

* When they say to me "there is bread," let it *be* bread, and
when "wine," *let* it be wine.

and the next time you come to Paraguay with linens, bring them from honest Germany."

Thus I have endeavoured to show you what *was* the commerce of Paraguay, and what now it is. I have pointed out the original and natural sources of revenue of the country; and I have shown you how (having himself stopped these) Francia resorted to knavery and oppression, in order to support his iniquitous government.

Yours, &c.

J. P. R.

LETTER XVII.

Sources of information—Reflections.

London, 1838.

THE preceding letters in this volume, and those which constituted the subject of our first series, have, with a few exceptions, been written from personal observation. They have described things of which we have been mostly eye-witnesses; persons with whom we have been actually acquainted; and scenes in which, either as first or second-rate performers, we have played our respective parts. We have not had to trust to the reports of others for what we have related, and our readers have had no authority better than our own to authenticate the truth of our relation. You and our other readers, therefore, must appeal to internal evidence, and to what you know of our veracity, in order to judge of the verisimilitude of the facts heretofore set down.

The epistles which follow are written from the testimony of third parties. Of these, two were our immediate agents; another, the enterprizing navigator of the Rio Vermejo; and a fourth, the celebrated naturalist, M. Bonpland.

The events to be now recorded came sometimes under the review of the one, sometimes of the other of us; and they embrace, as regards Paraguay, the period between the end of 1815, when we were both banished from that republic, and the middle of 1838, to which our latest authentic information from it comes down.

Of the agents referred to one was the able, accomplished, and amiable son of a highly respectable family in Cambridge,—Mr. Henry Okes. The other was one of the most respected citizens of Buenos Ayres, Don José de Maria. He was forcibly detained in Paraguay by the tyrant, under painful and peculiar circumstances; and he was not only constrained to be the unwilling and shuddering witness of many of the Dictator's worst deeds of blood, but was himself, for a season, the victim of Doctor Francia's illtimed, unjust, and even jesting cruelty.

José de Maria was related to some of the best

families of Buenos Ayres, and married to a
daughter of that Escalada, who was so decided a
friend of the gallant General Beresford. Escalada's younger daughter was married to General
San Martin.

Don Pablo Soria published an account in
Buenos Ayres of his voyage down the Vermejo,
and of his capture, as he entered the river Paraguay, and subsequent detention by Francia.
Soria was a man of great respectability, and in
no possible way could deserve the base treatment
which he received at the hands of the Paraguay
despot. A short analysis of his pamphlet will
form an interesting link in the historical chain of
Francia's cruelties.

There is yet another and important authority
to which we have been beholden for annals
of the Dictator, that of M. Rengger, a Swiss
medical practitioner and botanist, who published, in 1827, a small work on Paraguay.*
We believe it to be now out of print. He states
at page 118 of his book, that on the 25th of

* 'The Reign of Doctor Francia in Paraguay,' Thomas Hurst,
Edward Chance, and Co., 65 St. Paul's Churchyard, 1827. (The
original work is in French.)

May, 1825, he was permitted to quit Paraguay; and at page 120 that "Don José de Maria's ship," that is, our own ship, under the controul of this agent, "sailed the day afterwards."

The news, therefore, brought to Buenos Ayres by M. Rengger and by Don José de Maria had reference to the same period, and the same events of Francia's reign of terror; and we dwell with some particularity on the circumstance for two reasons: first, to obviate the notion of plagiarism from M. Rengger, because the very same facts which he has given to the press we had, as you know, from our own agent, Don José de Maria; and, secondly, to give willing evidence to the unequivocal coincidence of testimony between both, in regard to the cruel character, the ferocious temper, and the despotic sway of the tyrant of Paraguay.

'We may here mention that much of the testimony of both of these unexceptionable witnesses was corroborated to us by Mr. Postlethwaite, a gentleman who acted as our agent in Corrientes; who was residing there when M. Rengger passed up; and in whose house, indeed, the latter stayed for some time.

Lastly, the British subjects who were released through the interference of Sir Woodbine Parish, his Majesty's Chargé d'Affaires in Buenos Ayres, and who came down nearly at the same time with M. Rengger, gave convincing and concurrent evidence, as shall be hereafter noticed, as to the nature of Francia's diabolical career.

Francia endeavoured so hermetically to seal his republic against external observation, as to leave him the hope that his deeds of darkness and of blood might escape the observation of mankind and the records of history. He tried, also, ever and anon, to throw a flimsy covering over his worst actions, so as to hide the atrocity of their nature from the indignant view of mankind; but in vain. The seals were opened by a power which overruled even that of the Dictator. Forth from his savage den have come men of deep science and undeniable integrity,—among them, at last, Bonpland; and the revelations of the Dictator's atrocities, while they have made humanity shudder, have laid up in store for Nero the First of the New World (it is to be hoped there will be no Second) the *anathema maranatha* of all subsequent ages.

It is to be regretted that the grasp of death

snatches from the conscious obloquy of their contemporaries, in this world, those who have spent their lives in loading victims with their chains. But it is to be hoped,—nay we know it to be true,—that there is elsewhere a place in which everlasting chains are prepared for the impious tyrants who have forged temporal ones here, till they have eaten into the flesh of their fellow men.

The force of these remarks, and the truth of these indignant observations will, perhaps, be better appreciated as you proceed in the narrative of Francia's deeds, especially as you shall see him at the conclusion of the volume have the benefit of defending himself under his own signature ; and shall also see that defence submitted, we hope, to a fair and impartial analysis.

Yours, &c.

THE AUTHORS.

LETTER XVIII.

W. P. R. to Thomas Fair, Esq.

MR. OKES'S EXPEDITION TO PARAGUAY.

His character—Suggestion for the voyage of Okes to Paraguay—
His departure—His voyage—The Bajada—His arrival—Francia an Astronomer—Favourable reception of Okes—Permission
to depart—The Sequel—Issue of the Adventure—One of Francia's bloody deeds.

London, 1838.

WHEN we first settled at Corrientes, immediately
after our dismissal from Paraguay, observing the
great beauty and abundance of the cotton crops,
my brother and myself resolved to try, at some
future day, to place the Corrientes cotton in the
Liverpool mart.

The difficulty was to obtain, in Corrientes,
machinery to separate the seed from the cotton,
—this tedious operation being performed in the
country by the hand, which, from the expense of
manual labour there, would not, in the technical
phrase, "pay."

To carry out this scheme my brother, in 1819, being then in England, made an arrangement with Mr. Henry Okes, by which the latter, after visiting Bahia, and seeing the machinery used there, was to go on to Buenos Ayres, and thence proceed to Corrientes. It is enough here to say that, after various experiments made in Buenos Ayres, the scheme was abandoned, as not likely to prove successful.

Mr. Okes, therefore, remained in Buenos Ayres. I do not think that any individual of higher general attainments, of greater depth of mind, of more pleasing manners and conversation, ever visited the shores of La Plata ; and be this slight tribute permitted to the memory of a lamented friend, whose early death was deplored most by those who knew him best. He died in 1821, in his twenty-eighth year; and I may mention that he was the first Englishman who was interred in consecrated British ground in South America.

While we were preparing, as you know, to turn the exercise of Mr. Okes's abilities into some new channel, a vessel arrived to our consignment, called the " Anna Robertson ;" and, among other articles of merchandize, brought an immense box containing mathematical instruments, telescopes, theodolites, microscopes, electrical machines, air-pumps, air-guns, &c., all of the costliest and best description, having been intended originally for India.

" Now Okes," said I, after he had examined them all with a critical eye, "here is a brilliant opening for you. Make a selection of these, and go up with the instruments to Doctor Francia."

That name, even in 1819, began to sound ominously in the ear. Okes looked as if to inquire if I spoke seriously.

" I am serious," I said. "You will have nothing to do with Francia in a political point of view. Your visit to his republic will be wholly commercial, and you must acknowledge that were a merchant to inquire into the political acts of a ruler, before he would visit his dominions, the spirit of commercial enterprise would speedily be extinct. Be assured," I then added, "that, while, with your peculiar abilities " (the favourite study of Okes was that of mathematics), " and with these instruments, you have nothing to fear from the Dictator, you may hope for everything which you could possibly desire in the way of commercial advantage."

Mr. Okes finally resolved to go on this enterprise. We fitted him out with a commodious vessel, a cargo of the value of about 8000*l*., and a large supply from the box of instruments I have mentioned. All the country through which he had to pass was rendered so dangerous by one of the constant civil wars which then distracted the provinces, that Mr. Okes was constrained to go the whole way by water. He sailed from Las Conchas on the 17th of January, 1820, with a British passport, and (to be used in a case of necessity) a British flag.

I wish it came within the scope and compass of this volume to give all Mr. Okes's private letters to me during his sojourn on the Paraná. I must limit myself to here and there an extract :—

" I left you, my dear R.," he commences, from San Nicholas, on the 29th of January, " at Conchas on the evening of the 16th, and, as you may very well recollect, *triste*. Who, my friend, could have been cheerful on separating, for an indefinite period, from those very agreeable, though few, social ties which bound my heart in Buenos Ayres ? Was there any probability I should find on my way, any being with whom I could commune as we have done together ? or in Paraguay any intercourse similar to that in which we have jointly participated ?"

The vessel had gone on before to the mouth of the Paraná, many winding channels intervening between that and Conchas. Mr. Okes followed in his boat.

" At twelve meridian (17th) we had the first specimen of being tied to a tree till the tide should change, and enable us to double a point which we had used every human effort to surmount. In the evening we got alongside of the smack, and soon afterwards we took a departure from Cruz Colorado. Next morning the wind became very squally and contrary, so we approached the bank and tied ourselves to a stump. Our Paraguayans got ashore with their pots and pans, and seemed to be making preparations for a really savage repast, when a heavy shower of rain drove them on board, and although I myself spent the afternoon uncomfortably, the dampness and gloominess of the evening did not hinder our easy and contented peons from joining together round the guitar in singing and dancing. But, oh, heavens ! the charge of musquitoes as soon as the sun had gone down ! To those who, like yourself, have journeyed on these waters, it need not be said how numerous, how large, and how ferocious these insects are. Before we had half finished our supper we were obliged to retreat, and arm, and to defend ourselves against our outrageous foes." . . . . "About ten P.M., we were again tied to a tree. Our Paraguays,—' whose bellies seem to be their God,' —instantly prepared for culinary worship, and were presently to be seen at their unsightly sacrifice." . . . .

"At two, P.M., the wind seemed disposed to favour us a little, when we found we had got aground. The *Soquété* was applied in vain ; the peons got into the water, and tried the force of their shoulders against the hull ; it was still in vain ; and though now six P.M., the discharge of the cargo commenced." . . . . "The physical and mechanical force, such as these people could apply, at last produced effect. At two P.M., the following day, a yell from the Paraguays declared the vessel to be in motion; and at five P.M. we were again under sail." . . . .

They were detained for a whole month at San Nicholas by the confusion of state affairs, and by the jealousy of the authorities there. They did not relish the idea of a vessel's enjoying protection from a British pass, which their own government could not extend to natives. This was so natural, that the wonder is they allowed Mr. Okes and the vessel to go on at all.

They reached the Bajada on the 11th of March; and in answer to a letter which Mr. Okes there received from me, informing him of a domestic affliction under which I suffered, he thus writes:

"It is in morals as in physics, that there are seasons when the mind is held in equilibrium by equal weights of joy and sorrow. How far the particles of either may be compounded of mere animal or rational elevation and depression, it might baffle the united observations and experiments of Aristotle and Sanctorius to ascertain; but the fact, that we are at times thus suspended, and so delicately, too, that a hair would

turn the balance, even we dribblers in physics and
metaphysics may presume to avouch. I am just
now in this moody sort of indecision, like a ship
passive on the glossy surface of an equatorial calm,
waiting for an impulse from any quarter that shall
disturb the wearying aspect of so still a state."

Going on to a happy detail of the means which
a rational mind ought to employ, in order to
enable him to meet the misfortunes and the sor-
rows of life with equanimity, my correspondent
adds: "From the days of Seneca downwards,
all this has been on record; but there is a secret
charm in the counsels of friendship which gives,
even to the most jaded maxims, new beauty and
new strength. I profess no *discovery* in what
I have written, but trusting to the conviction
which I think is stamped upon your mind, of my
wish to promote *your* happiness, I recommend to
you a system which experience and observation
tell me has contributed most to *mine*."

The Bajada was destined to give Mr. Okes
nearly as much alarm as it had occasioned my
brother a few years before. Mr. O. had two or
three pair of pistols, and a couple of fowling-
pieces on board, (not at all intended, however, for

M 2

common military use,) and they did not appear in
the manifest of the cargo. This did not arise from
any necessity for *smuggling* such arms on board
at Buenos Ayres; but from the certainty that if
the fact of arms, even for personal use, being on
board, came to the knowledge of any of the Chiefs
commanding at the places intermediate, between
Buenos Ayres and Paraguay, their cupidity would
be roused ; and perhaps the whole property
endangered. The arms, therefore, and astronomical instruments, belonging to Mr. Okes, were
stowed away ; and we believed that their existence
on board went not beyond the knowledge of the
trusty patrón and of Mr. Okes himself.

False information, however, had been given
that arms for Paraguay were on board. The
vessel was suddenly filled with troops, and poor
Okes was thrown into great consternation. " I
heard," says he, " after I had returned to the
cabin, the order given to open the hatches,
and to discharge the cargo. The work of search
began. For three hours the *tipones* of flour,
cases of merchandise, and bales of goods were
tumbling over my head. The unfortunate Charles,
who constantly heard from his bed-room the

noise of the workman's hammer fitting up the
scaffolding in White-hall, was, I dare say,
less disturbed than I was by the business now
going forward." Nothing, however, was discovered, and they were allowed to proceed to
Corrientes. Here Mr. Okes was kindly received,
by our old friend Mr. Postlethwaite, and no less
so by the Governor Mendez. He was immediately allowed to sail for Paraguay, and, towards the close of April, he arrived at Assumption after a voyage of nearly three months and
a half.

The moment that Mr. Okes landed, he was
marched off in solemn silence to the Dictator.
He was gazed at by all, as he passed along, but
no one ventured to say a word. As soon as
he got to the palace, he was introduced to the
Dictator, who received him in his usual brow-
beating way. "Well, sir," said Francia, "whât
brings *you* here?" "I have come to your republic, Señor Excelentisimo," answered Okes,
"on purely commercial pursuits; and I trust
Your Excellency will permit me to follow them
up." "What do you bring?" then inquired the
Dictator. Okes told him that he had a cargo of

goods, as specified in his manifest, and that over and above, he had some very fine mathematical and astronomical instruments.

"Ah! that is good! that is good!" said Francia, with great glee, and taking a large pinch of Princesa: "I must see them. What are they? when can you get at them? do you understand the use of them?"

Okes answered all these questions satisfactorily; and, before allowing him to go any where, the Dictator hurried him back to the smack, with half a dozen soldiers behind him. The coveted articles were, with great trouble, got out; and that same day they were placed in array before the delighted gaze of the Despotic Astronomer.

"So you are a mathematician?" said he once more to Okes, who assented with a bow. "And you understand perfectly the use of all these instruments?" Okes again bowed. "Very good, very good. I am extremely pleased to hear it. Go now, arrange your business; you have perfect freedom to trade here. You appear to be a man of sense and education. Meddle not with state affairs; mind your own matters; and whenever I may send for you, endeavour to come, and give me a little of your time. Vaya V. con Dios."

All went on as I had anticipated. By his unobtrusive manner, together with the practical lessons which he was able to give to Francia in mathematics and astronomy, Okes established himself in the good graces of his fearful scholar, who at all times endeavoured to show himself in his fairest colours to his new and erudite English friend.

But although Mr. Okes was thus well individually treated by Francia, it required a much less sagacious observer than the former was, to see that this treatment sprung out of purely selfish motives. The general system that he saw going forward, —proscriptions, imprisonments, confiscations, and deaths ; imperious despotism on the part of the governor, terror and dismay on that of the governed ;—made him exceedingly anxious to curtail his visit by every day, every hour that he could. He kept this anxiety concealed from Francia, for if he had not, even the theodolite might not have saved him from Tevégo.

Okes, in the strictest sense of the word, lived alone. He transacted his business in

the forenoon, but beyond the necessary intercourse which that engendered, he had none. He
soon got inoculated with the same distrust of
all the people about him, that they had of
him. At the end of three months, therefore,
Mr. Okes had so far wound up his affairs, that
he was enabled to apply to the Dictator for license
to load his vessel, and return to Buenos Ayres.
Francia granted the permission, and in another
month Okes was ready to depart.

It was with a more sincere reluctance, perhaps,
than he had ever felt before to part with a fellow-
being, that the cold-hearted and selfish Dictator
gave Mr. Okes his passport for Buenos Ayres.

"I doubt not you may have heard," said the
wily Despot, "from my enemies, and you may,
perhaps, yourself be inclined on a superficial
view, to believe, that my government is despotic
and unnecessarily severe. But believe me, Don
Henrique, I had only a choice between this
severity and the anarchy of my country. I preferred the former; and I think I have only prudently
determined to exclude all hope from the enemies
of Paraguay, of producing the latter.

"But my principle is to intermeddle with no

one who intermeddles not with me.* Judge by yourself. You have come here freely ; freely you depart : and while you conduct yourself with the circumspection which you have observed on this occasion, I shall always be happy to see you in this Republic.

"I hope, indeed, Don Henrique, that you will avail yourself not only of my permission, but of my desire that you should return here as soon as you can, and you may depend on the same treatment as you have now received."

In this way did Francia endeavour to allure Okes back ; and, indeed, ere he went, he was made to promise over and over again, that he would return.

But mark the sequel.

Mr. Okes had arrived at so favourable a juncture for the sale of his merchandise, that after loading his vessel with produce, he had still one thousand doubloons, equal to 3500*l.*, in cash, and the value of 4000*l.* in goods and produce. All this property he left in the hands of his agent,

* He may have *begun* with this principle ; but as in all growing despotisms, it was soon thrown aside, and cast into oblivion.

M 3

Don Gregorio Zelaya, a respectable old Spaniard, long resident in Paraguay, with orders to
convert the whole into produce or bills, and send
it to Buenos Ayres as opportunity offered, or as
the Dictator would permit.

The cargo which Mr. Okes brought down sold
to so enormous a profit, that it paid off the
whole of the original investment he took with
him, and left him besides several thousand pounds
as his own share of profits. This was a result
sufficient to tempt any one less philosophic than
Mr. Okes to a renewal of his intercourse with
Paraguay.

Okes arrived in Buenos Ayres amid the hearty
congratulations of his friends, and all expected
he would return to Assumption. But he declared,
as you know, to his partners in the first enterprise,—you and myself,—that be the result what
it would, he should never be tempted back to the
lion's den.   He was sickened of what he was
constrained to see at Assumption, of Francia's
" *necessary* " cruelty, to such a degree as to make
him determine at once to hold no further personal
intercourse with the man.

Six months after his return, the much-lamented

Henry Okes was laid in his grave by many sorrowing friends.

No sooner did the news reach Francia's ear,
(for every thing which passed in Buenos Ayres
he knew,) than in the dead of night he ordered
his myrmidons into the house of Don Gregorio
Zelaya. Seized every paper he had, embargoed
his goods, locked his warehouses;—and all this
to ascertain the amount of the effects of Don
Henrique Okes, the foreigner, whose estate had
reverted to the treasury! All was exacted to
the uttermost farthing ; the thousand doubloons
were paid,—the whole property was delivered to
Francia.

And hereupon the tyrant enacted one of his
bloody tragedies. The examination of the unfortunate Zelaya's books showed the Dictator
that he had a large property under his charge
belonging to a respectable Paraguay citizen, Don
Jose Tomas de Ysasi, to whom Francia had
hitherto shown some favour.

Mr. Ysasi was in Buenos Ayres. Francia made
out a ridiculous series of charges against him ;
Zelaya was called his accomplice in crimes which
were wholly supposititious, and although he was

known as a man of irreproachable integrity.
Without form or process, the unhappy victim,
amid the heart-rending cries of his family, was
dragged to the front of Francia's window, and
there in his sight *butchered* by his Janissaries.
The whole of the property under the murdered
man's charge was confiscated to the state by
the MURDERER.

Yours, &c.

W. P. R.

LETTER XIX.

W. P. R. to Thomas Fair, Esq.

DON JOSÉ DE MARIA.

He visits Francia—A sale of salt—Interference for foreigners by Sir Woodbine Parish—Dénouement of the interference—Effect of Francia's system on the minds of the Détenus—Decree of perpetual silence—Francia's private secretary—José de Maria's imprisonment—The fate of Chilaber.

London, 1838.

I HAVE lingered so long over the sketch of my deceased friend's expedition to Paraguay, and we have yet so much which crowds upon us for the remainder of our volume, that I shall be under the necessity of curtailing much which I had to say of Don José de Maria.

This gentleman was a native of Spain, of the most respectable class of merchants of that country; and in Buenos Ayres he became connected by marriage with the Escaladas, one of the first and oldest families there, and with General San Martin. They both married daughters of Don Antonio Escalada.

In 1817, I finally retired from Corrientes, and established myself in Buenos Ayres. From our knowledge of the trade of Paraguay, we were not indisposed to renew a mercantile connexion with that country; and Don José de Maria having turned his views to the same quarter, he went up with a joint adventure of considerable magnitude in 1818. He was so well received in the first instance by Francia, that he determined to remain for two years, or three at farthest, in the country; and then to wind up our joint concerns, and return to Buenos Ayres.

He was one of the few who benefited by Francia's non-intercourse system, to an extent which, although on a small scale, is perhaps unprecedented in the annals of commerce, and is sufficiently curious to be related here.

We had taken care to furnish Don José with a British passport (the property under his charge being British), got up in diplomatic style, with a wide margin, large seals stamped on an abundant supply of wax, plenty of signatures, and a great display of narrow blue silk ribbon, which tied the two sheets of the document together. It was a splendid-looking affair, and very well calculated to inspire with respect such barbarians as Artigas's lieutenants, for whose especial edification it was intended.

Don José de Maria wanted *ballast* for his vessel, and, at my recommendation, he took a quantity of *salt*, which I knew was always an acceptable article in Paraguay. The salt cost two hundred dollars.

Immediately on his arrival he sold his salt for *four thousand dollars.* Don José Tomas Ysasi, who has been already mentioned, and who was then in Paraguay, had an exclusive license from the Dictator to send off two cargoes of produce, but the difficulty was how they were to pass the Artigueños. Don José de Maria suggested that, if he and his English partners had an interest in the cargoes, he could protect them with his English pass. A bargain was struck. One-third was sold to him, for which he paid a trifle more than the produce of his salt, just sold ; and, after a variety of detentions and disasters, the English diplomatic document brought the two vessels safely to Buenos Ayres. The two cargoes sold for the incredible sum of two hundred and sixty thousand dollars ; and, after a variety of heavy charges and duties paid, the two hundred dollars, worth of salt, taken up by José de Maria, yielded a clear profit of *more than sixty thousand dollars !*

Don José de Maria went on converting his merchandise, of which we sent him a second supply, into produce, and a vast quantity of this accumulated on his hands. But license to ship it, or to leave the republic himself, was now withheld. The strict non-intercourse policy had commenced; and Paraguay seemed destined to be a prison for life to every foreigner who had unhappily not been like my brother and myself— *banished in good time.*

A happy release, however, was at hand for many, brought about in a very unexpected way.

Not long after the arrival of Mr. (now Sir Woodbine) Parish at Buenos Ayres, in 1824, as British Consul General, he concluded a treaty with the government acting in the name of the provinces of the Rio de la Plata, and became our Chargé d'Affaires. He had, from the time of his arrival, entered warmly on a consideration of the best practical means of obtaining the enlargement of the British subjects who were détenus under the unwarrantable system of the Dictator. As, perhaps, no one in Buenos Ayres was better acquainted with the whole question than myself, I had several conversations on the subject with Sir Woodbine, who, taking up the character of Francia with peculiar tact, wrote to him, early in 1825, announcing the treaty which he had just concluded, and hinting at the pleasure it would give to the British Government to be on a footing of amicable intercourse with the Dictator. As a prelude to it, however, Sir Woodbine expressed his confidence that the Dictator would see the propriety of allowing such British subjects as had been permitted to visit Paraguay free egress, should they desire it, from the republic.

Francia was hit in that point in which all men, from the monarch to the mendicant,—however they may try to disguise it from themselves, or from others, are alike vulnerable,—in his *vanity*. We have sufficiently shown, in our two first volumes, how ardently he desired to be a potentate recognised by the British Government; and he now fancied he had at last the ball at his foot.

Immediately, on receipt of Sir Woodbine Parish's clever letter, Francia ordered all the

English to get their vessels ready, taking care to form their crews of foreigners and negroes, and with a strict interdiction against exporting any property but their own.

Unwilling, at the same time, to let it be thought that he yielded to anything like exterior influence, Francia gave license to sail not only to José de Maria (with whom he knew we were connected), but to Don José Tomàs Ysasi, already mentioned, in one of whose vessels Mr. Rengger, on Mr. Ysasi's offer, left the republic.[*] Many other foreigners were at the same time released, among whom were my friends the Mendezes; and some were *banished*, among whom were five friars, released from the state prison, and put on board of the vessel of Don José de Maria. He arrived, to the great joy of his family, in July, 1825.

[*] Mr. Rengger, who was kept in suspense by Francia till the last moment, has the following note:—" Under any other circumstances such an offer would not have been extraordinary; but at a moment when the opportunities were so rare, when the vessels were so overloaded, and when the most insignificant pretext might cause the license to be revoked, it certainly was a very great favour. I, therefore, only fulfil a duty when expressing our gratitude to Don José Tomàs Ysasi, as also to Don José de Maria, who made us the same offer as soon as he received, as the agent of an English house, an order to get his vessel ready."

Francia wrote to our Chargé d'Affaires as plausible a letter as his bad case would permit, in exculpation of his long detention of the British subjects, whom he now released; and in reference to the future, he expressed his expectation that Sir Woodbine would insist with the government of Buenos Ayres on the free navigation of the river, which would lead to a direct intercourse between the independent state of Paraguay and England, and other foreign powers.

The worldly substance of the British subjects detained in Paraguay had been so wasted and attenuated by their long sojourn there, that, with the exception of one or two, they had little but their persons to bring away. Some of them, indeed, were quite destitute, and only enabled, by the humanity of their countrymen, to leave the republic at all. The principal vessels were those of Ysasi and José de Maria ; and these sailed amidst the sighs of a congregated multitude, who had assembled over the novel sight of a vessel leaving their still and silent shores.

The parties liberated by the instrumentality of our Chargé d'Affaires, arrived in Buenos Ayres in March, 1825. They were as men brought back

from the dead; and truly many of them had
ceased to have a very defined notion of their being
still among the living.*

* I have been kindly favoured with the following copy of a
note which Sir Woodbine Parish officially transmitted in 1825 to
Mr. Canning, then Secretary of State for Foreign Affairs:—

"Buenos Ayres, 5 April, 1825.

"List of British Subjects arrived up to this date from Paraguay,
who have obtained their release in consequence of the interference of H. M. Consul General at Buenos Ayres.

Name.	Profession.	Time detained.
1. Constantine O'Rourke	Commerce	4 years
2. Duncan Stewart	do.	4 „
3. Edward Costello	do.	4 „
4. John Lewtas	do.	4 „
5. John Robson	do.	6 „
6. Alexander McGaffy	Cabinet Maker	5 „
7. William Petty	Mariner	4 „
8. James Turner	Carpenter	9 „
10. Michael D'Arcy	Shoemaker	14 „
11. Thomas Wheeler	Mariner	8 „
12. William ———	do.	4 „

"All these persons came away in the schooner 'Martha,' and a
Garandumba: their cargoes consisted of 523 tierces of yerba maté,
and 1200 arrobes (30,000 lbs.) of tobacco. The Garandumba left
Assumption on the 14th of February. Two British Subjects,
John Macfarlane and Alexander James, were preparing to leave
with about 600 tierces of yerba and some tobacco. The smack
(brig) San Josè, the property of Messrs. Robertson, Joseph
Martin, master, was waiting for a license; and Robert Gibson,
another British Subject, with three or four others would leave in
her. There would then remain no British Subject in Paraguay.
Dr. Parlett died shortly before we came away.

(signed)   "CONSTANTNIE O'ROURKE."

One and all, I may say, of the Englishmen who were thus restored to their friends, returned with their minds impaired to a greater or less extent. Their intellects had become numbed, stupified. Not one of them could entirely realize to himself the idea that he was free,—that he might think and speak without fear. One young man, an Englishman of good family, and nephew of a highly respectable merchant in Buenos Ayres, was so paralyzed in his mental faculties, that it was found necessary to send him to England; and till he got there, he did not entirely recover.

Don José de Maria himself, although a man of strong intellect and good education, was pretty much in the same state when he came down; and some time elapsed ere his Paraguay illusions wore off.

Whenever I mentioned Francia's name, he looked suspiciously around him. At 1200 miles distance from Paraguay, he fancied that spies were still about him. As he sat in my room I would sometimes say to him—" Come, Don José, let us talk about Francia." He would instantly cast a glance at the door, and, if open, he rose up mechanically to shut it. He would tell me seriously and earnestly that it was dan-

gerous to talk of Francia; and he was shocked when I laughed at his fears. " My dear friend," I would tell him, " we are in Buenos Ayres; what care we about Francia here?" Then would he shake his head with an unsatisfied look, and say— " In Buenos Ayres or not, believe me our most prudent plan is to say as little about the Excelentisimo Dictador as possible. It is of no use, it may go to his ears; and then we are lost indeed!" By degrees Don José began himself to smile at the strength of his Paraguay associations; till at length they gradually wore away.

Throughout the whole of Mr. Rengger's book, which shows him to be an observing and intelligent man, a latent fear of Francia lurks in the lines. He speaks of him with a sort of cautious respect throughout; and yet the book was written in the solitudes of Switzerland, two years after the botanist's departure from Paraguay.

What a singular illustration is all this of the plastic nature of man! One strong mind,—one cruel heart,—one ferocious individual, by an intense application of his powers, changes, radically changes, the character of a whole community in a few years. Every affection of the soul is blighted, every social tie is cankered, every hope and aspiration of the heart is laid in the dust by the withering influence and pestilential sway of one man. Like the potter, he presses them, one and all, to his own shape,—he casts them in whatever mould he chooses to take up. By one concentrated effort, he uproots from the heart of a nation all the various stems which diffuse life and energy, and love and happiness around; and he plants in their place the deadly Upas of TERROR, which he causes to flourish in frightful and solitary luxuriance, by a constant irrigation of its deepening roots with human blood.

As many of the details which Don José de Maria gave us of Francia will presently be embodied in a general view of his reign, I shall content myself here with a short summary of Don José's residence, and conclude with an anecdote of one of his ill-fated friends.

Don José was one of the few foreigners (the only other exceptions I know of are Messrs. Parlett, Okes, and Rengger) with whom Francia deigned to hold familiar intercourse. He seemed, at first, rather fond of the company of J. de Maria, who was an agreeable and well-informed man. In a conversation which they one day had

on the topic of *Revenue*, Don José, who was a
political economist, understood Francia to desire
him to draw up his ideas on paper, and in that
form to lay them before the Dictator.   Don
José did so; and the following day he was waited
on by one of Francia's messengers, who spoke
thus:—" Sir, here is the paper which you have
had the boldness to lay before the most Excellent
Supreme Dictator : he orders you to destroy it ;
and he commands me to intimate to you ' PERPE-
TUAL SILENCE' on every subject connected with
his or any other government !"

" You may readily conceive," said Don José
to me, " that I troubled the Dictator with no more
of my political essays.   In truth," he added, " I
escaped but too well, as you shall judge by what
I have now to tell you.

" Francia took a liking to a fine young
man of the name of Villarino, and made him
his private secretary.   On one occasion he made
free to advise the Dictator to ameliorate a little
his system of foreign policy, as he believed Francia
would benefit by it if he did so.   The Dictator
scowled, and rising up, ordered young Villarino to quit his presence.   In the dark and
gloomy look of his master the secretary read his

impending fate. He went home and wrote a long letter to Francia, detailing his official career, and showing that he had never been wanting in his duty: ' and he would not,' he said, ' have his name dishonoured by flight, neither would he consent to be led to a prison or a scaffold.'

" He sent the letter to Francia, and an hour afterwards his body was found in the Paraguay, into which the young secretary, in a fit of temporary madness, had thrown himself."

Don José de Maria, although an old Spaniard, was a naturalized citizen of Buenos Ayres; and when an order was given by Francia, that the old Spaniards should assemble in the square, Don José considered that he was not included.

All the old Spaniards who did so assemble were imprisoned, as is hereafter to be told; and as no notice was taken of Don José, he considered he had made a happy escape.

One afternoon, however, as he sat at his widely-opened door (ready to shut it, and lock it if he heard the approach of the Dictator), one of Francia's ominous ministers came up to him.

" Are not you," said he, " *an old Spaniard?*"

The question sounded in the ears of my poor friend as his solemn death-knell.

" I was indeed," he said, " born in Spain, but my adopted country is Buenos Ayres, of which I have been for twelve years a naturalized citizen."

A hideous smile passed slowly across the black and demon-like features of the interrogator. " *Follow me*," he said.

" May I not shut up my house?" asked Don José.

" Follow ME," repeated the other, in a stern voice; and Don José de Maria leaving all his property exposed to whoever might choose to walk in and appropriate it to his use, followed the man of office.

He was somewhat relieved, when he found that he was *only* consigned to the prison in which his unhappy countrymen were already huddled together.

I will not here dwell on his sufferings in prison. He had very nearly died under them ; and while he was yet in a precarious and emaciated state, at the end of six months' confinement he was unexpectedly released. Most of the other unhappy beings remained behind for a much longer period.

Don José's property had been kindly protected; and when he was well enough to move out, he went to the Dictator to express his *gratitude* on being released.

Francia heard him, and taking a large pinch of snuff, which he always did when anything pleased him, he broke out into a fit of laughter! " What!" said he, " Don José; have *you* been imprisoned? Go home! man, go home! Believe me, my friend, *it has been quite a mistake.*"

I must omit whatever further occurred to Don José during the remainder of his sojourn in Paraguay; but here is the awful anecdote which he related to me, and to which I have alluded at the commencement of my letter.

There were two brothers, natives of Santa Fé, whom I knew very well, and with one of whom, a trader from Corrientes to Paraguay, Don José de Maria was intimate. His name was Chilaber.

During the misunderstanding which prevailed between Francia and the neighbouring provinces, some arms had been detained at Santa Fé, which the Dictator alleged were for him. He instantly threw all the Santafecinos in Assumption (some of whom had resided there for thirty years) into prison, and confiscated their property. The Santa Fé Chilaber was a member of the Cabildo there when the arms were seized : the other, unadvisedly ventured to Ytapúa, in Paraguay, to look after some business he had there. He went under an assumed name, but he was discovered by a spy named Ramon Leon. Poor Chilaber was loaded with chains, tied hands and feet on a horse's back ; and, in this way, driven under excruciating pain to Assumption. There, without, as usual, the slightest previous proceeding, his agonies were put an end to by his being shot, mangled, and hung upon a gibbet. The Dictator, with his snuff-box in his hand, gazed from the window of his room on the bloody proceedings which went on before him.

Yours, &c.

W. P. R.

LETTER XX.

DON PABLO SORIA.

Navigation of the Vermejo—Soria's capture—His treatment by
Francia—His liberation, and return to Buenos Ayres.

London, 1838.

IN the year 1823, the first meeting was held, in
my own house in Buenos Ayres, of a few friends
(South Americans of rank) who were anxious to
assist Don Pablo Soria in his great plan of *navigating the Vermejo*.

In 1824 a company, of which I was one of the
Directors, was formed, under the auspices of the
governments of Buenos Ayres and Salta, and
called La Sociedad del Rio Vermejo,—" The
River Vermejo Society."—The small sum wanted
for Soria's operations was easily raised; his own
energy, perseverance, and enthusiasm overcame
all minor difficulties; and on the 15th of June,
1826, Soria sailed from Orán, in Peru, to follow the waters of the Vermejo to the point
where it joins the Paraguay, and thence to de-

scend by that river and the Paraná to Buenos
Ayres.

To give the details of this voyage of discovery,
though both curious and interesting, forms no
part of my present plan. Suffice it to say, that
Soria triumphantly accomplished his purpose;
and on the 12th of August the voyagers disem-
bogued in the Paraguay, near to Neembucú.
This was the moment at which poor Soria thought
his anxieties were at an end, but it was only
here that his real troubles commenced. He was
within the fatal grasp of Doctor Francia.

" On the 12th day of August," says Soria, " at
nine o'clock in the morning, we entered the Paraguay, near Neembucú, and we saw, over the prow
of our vessel, a house on the eastern bank of the
river. With our glass we observed the hurried
movement of men saddling horses ; and three or
four presently mounted, whom we took to be
couriers. It was soon clear to us that this was
a guard-house of our sister province (Paraguay),
—a circumstance which, on emerging from the
barbarous nations of the Chaco, filled us with
joy, and by no means with any such suspicion
as touching on the coast of Africa might inspire.
So we went towards them, till we could hear them

call out from the guard-house, ' Send the patrón
of the vessel on shore.' "

Soria landed and found the place was called
the guard-house of Talli. He was rudely received; every paper, plan, draft, and sketch he
had were taken from him, and *his diaries were
torn up as of no use!* Arms, ammunition, and
money were next taken from him : he and his
people were placed under the custody of armed
men, and information of the whole transaction
was transmitted to the Dictator.

They were next sent to Ncembucú : here their
vessel was tied to a tree under the cliff, removed
from any other. Their canoes were taken from
them ; soldiers were placed over them ; they
were prohibited from speaking to any one but
their guards ; and thus, as Soria says, "separated
from the rest of human kind, we were shut up in
our vessel, which, excluded from the breeze by the
cliff, was a heated oven in that burning climate."

In three days more, 22nd August, a decree
from Francia was intimated to Soria, and it ran
thus :—" *That he was a bold, insolent, and auda-
cious fellow : that by an atrocious and despotic
act he had descended, without previous permission,*

a river which was the dictator's ! that they might return whence they had come, or that he (Francia) would dispose of them all; for DOWN THE RIVER PARAGUAY THEY SHOULD NOT PASS."

Space will not permit me to reflect, as Soria himself justly does, on this precious document, or " discharge of artillery," as he calls it. His answer was this :—" *That it would be as impossible for him to return by the way he had come, as by way of the moon ; and that, therefore, his excellency might dispose of him as he thought fit.*"

Five months Soria and his men remained in this distressing situation, and then, on the 2nd of January, 1827, without any hint as to where they were to be taken, they were, *in less than six minutes,* transferred to a small ship of war, guarded by new troops and by another vessel ; and so, without being permitted to touch at the capital as they passed, they were conducted to *Villa Real,* 80 leagues above Assumption.

Soria's followers were dispersed in Villa Real, after a search of every one of them. They allotted to Soria and to a Mr. Cresser, an Englishman who accompanied him in his expedition, a room to themselves, and then left them at full liberty to go

about as they pleased. They were also supplied
with provisions. After eight months of this life,
the Dictator ordered it to be notified to them
that they might write to their friends, sending
their letters open through the local authorities.
I wish I had room for Soria's two letters.

On the 15th of January, 1831, the commandant
of Villa Real intimated to them, " by supreme
order," that they should hold themselves ready
to depart on a second notice. On the *3rd of July*
they were ordered to embark. Soria had brought
with him 300 hard dollars; but two-thirds of this
sum, which he still retained, he was compelled to
leave in Neembucú, and take yerba in exchange
at the government's own price.

On getting to Neembucú, Soria was ordered to
engage his passage by the brig Carmen, with a
threat that if he did not do so he should speedily
return to Villa Real. Honest Soria lost no time
in fulfilling the injunction. " It was also notified
to us," says he, " that we returned, *because it was
Francia's will ;* a fact of which the truth, justice,
and kindness it is not possible for a moment
to doubt. By Francia's will we came—by Francia's will we went; and, God knows, had his will

so been, he might have deprived us of our liberty for ever."

" In short," says Soria, " well treated in the vessel of war which brought us, without being allowed to touch land from Villa Real to Neembucú, and there only to adjust our passage-money by the Carmen, which was waiting for us, we sailed in her for Corrientes on the 20th of July, 1831, escorted, till we came to the frontier of Paraguay, by a serjeant and six men: and, to conclude, we arrived in Buenos Ayres on the 27th of August following."

Thus Soria and his men were detained in Paraguay five years ; and then he was dismissed after being robbed of his vessel, his charts, his plans of the Vermejo, his diaries, of everything save the 200 dollars which he had brought with him.

" Esto, sí," exclaims Soria, " se llama perder á un hombre !" " Truly this is the way to ruin a man !" and assuredly so it was. But, in the art of ruining his fellow men, Soria had fallen in with an adept not easily to be surpassed.

Yours, &c.

W. P. R.

LETTER XXI.

W. P. R. to Thomas Fair, Esq.

Monr. Aimé Bonpland.

Ilis arrival in Buenos Ayres—He proceeds to Candelaria—His establishment there—Its total destruction by Francia, and massacre of his people—Horrible cruelty—Francia's own account of the transaction—Santa Maria—Attempts made to procure M. Bonpland's release—Failure—His colony at Santa Maria—His philanthropy—Dismissal from Paraguay—Return to Buenos Ayres.

London, 1838.

I THINK it is so long ago as the year 1817, that Monsieur and Madame Bonpland arrived in Buenos Ayres from France. The fame, the talents, and the science of the one,—the accomplishments and fascinating manners of the other,—and the *savoir faire* and unaffected urbanity of both, — made their society to be generally sought in the capital of the provinces of the River Plate. From the early period mentioned, my own acquaintance with Monsieur and Madame Bonpland commenced.

About 1819 M. Bonpland determined on proceeding to some of the interior provinces; and he finally settled at or near Candelaria, in the Misiones, and on the southern bank or Entre Rios side of the Paraná. This part of the Misiones is under the jurisdiction of the province of Corrientes.

M. Bonpland had not only a fine field here for his pursuits in botany and natural history, but he proposed to rear extensive plantations of the yerba tree, so as to provide the provinces with the tea, of which such scanty and precarious supplies were now received from Paraguay.

For about two years M. Bonpland prosecuted, in peace and retirement, but with all the energy of an active mind, his philosophic and useful avocations; and success the most complete promised to crown his judicious labours. His little colony was a model of industry, order, and happiness. The docile Indians were the Naturalist's labourers; and he pursued a system with them which, with all the virtues, had none of the vices that characterized the rule of the Jesuits. A law inseparable from the nature of M. Bonpland, was the desire to elevate whatever portion of humanity surrounded him; and his gentle manner, his unassuming deportment, and his fund of good sense and acute observation withal, carried a great sway with him on every hand, and more especially endeared him to those whom he employed in his service.

On such a man as this,—one of the benefactors of the human race, and one of the most amiable of his kind, — did the ruffian Francia turn his scowling looks,—and that was equivalent to the ruin of Bonpland.

In the midst of what he considered to be complete security, — in a territory, the authorities of which respected and venerated their guest,— in a territory at peace with Paraguay,—in the pursuit of objects which were yet to add to the stock of knowledge possessed by the world at large,—did M. Bonpland follow up, not merely his harmless, but his highly beneficial career; and, were it not of FRANCIA that I have to speak, the world would not believe what I have now to relate.

The despot waited till *time* had removed, if there ever had existed, even a shade of suspicion of him in the mind of M. Bonpland. Then, with the stealthy creep of the tiger, Francia approached, and sprang upon him. At midnight, a body of *four hundred men,* which had been gradually and silently gathered on the opposite shore, passed over in canoes from Ytapua to Candelaria. With drawn sabres and loaded muskets they rushed upon the colony of M. Bonpland. Amid the cries and shrieks of the inmates, the soldiers *massacred* all the male Indians. of the establishment; they beat and wounded the women; they set fire, in every direction, to houses, implements, crops, plantations,—and reduced the whole to a heap of black and smouldering ruins; they stunned M. Bonpland with the blows of their sabres; they loaded him with irons; they dragged him from among the corpses of all the faithful servants, who, three hours before, had surrounded him in health, happiness and affection; they mocked his mental anguish on witnessing the horrors which surrounded him; they heeded not the agony of his bodily sufferings; but, pushing and thrusting him on board of a canoe, they carried him across the Paraná to the town of Santa Maria.

Fancy not that I have here given you any exaggerated account communicated to me by M.

Bonpland himself, or that the picture takes its colouring from my own imagination. Hundreds of witnesses have attested the truth of my narrative, and in the province of Corrientes the precise facts, as I have detailed them, are familiar to the whole population. And in reference to M. Bonpland himself it is worthy of remark, that he always spoke in very moderate terms of all that had befallen him through the orders of Francia.

I have put down, then, a true and faithful relation of what Francia did to Bonpland; and sure I am that I carry along with me the feelings of my readers,—one and all,—when I say that this act alone is more than enough to consign the name of the tyrant to the execration of mankind.

The following is Francia's *own* version of the story to M. Rengger, as given by the latter :—

" M. Bonpland formed an establishment for the preparation of the herb of Paraguay, with the Indians who, after Artigas' submission, settled themselves in the ruined Misiones of Entre Rios. He wanted to establish relations with me, and came twice for the purpose to the left bank

of the Paraná, opposite Ytapua, with despatches
from the Indian chief, written in his own hand
Now, I could not allow the herb to be prepared
in those countries, which, besides, belong to us "
(they do no such thing); " it would injure the
commerce of Paraguay; and I was under the
necessity of sending four hundred men there,
who destroyed the establishment, and brought
away several prisoners, among whom was M.
Bonpland."

"From what I have since learned," adds M.
Rengger, very truly, " I perceive the Dictator
told me only half the truth;" and then our author supplies the history which corroborates what
I have myself set down.

M. Bonpland, then, was carried in chains to
the Paraguay territory. It appears that some of
the Indians, when the indiscriminate massacre
took place, were roused, in their despair, to resistance, and, ere they were all murdered, some
of Francia's soldiers were wounded. Forgetting
his own barbarous and savage treatment, M.
Bonpland, who had some skill in surgery, dressed
the wounds of his enemies,—even while he wore
the chains with which they galled his own lace-
rated body.

The whole of these proceedings were communicated to Francia, and, after a time, his usual mock humanity came into play. He commanded the fetters to be removed from M. Bonpland, and ordered him to be kept a prisoner at large in the town of Santa Maria; or rather he drew a circle of a few leagues around it, within which M. Bonpland was allowed to move.

The great Naturalist, always enthusiastic in his scientific pursuits, solicited permission of Francia to visit Assumption, and to travel in the republic; but this the Dictator peremptorily refused. Bonpland, therefore, with philosophic resignation, but undaunted by his misfortunes, settled at a small place called the Cerrito, or Little Hill, between Santa Maria and Santa Rosa.

The detention of M. Bonpland in Paraguay soon became matter of notoriety, not only throughout South America, but Europe, and several distinct attempts were made to procure his enlargement. They all, unhappily, only tended to fortify the dastardly Dictator in his resolution to keep his prisoner where he was.

The first of these efforts to induce Francia to liberate M. Bonpland was made by the country-

men of the latter resident in Monte Video; and
the court of Rio Janeiro next ineffectually interfered.

I must here remark that Francia, dreading,
about this time, from the returning tranquillity
of the surrounding provinces, some combined
attempt on their part to interfere with his rule
and system, opened a communication with the
Brazilians, who then had possession of the Banda
Oriental. He wrote to General Lecor, the Portuguese governor of Monte Video, and a treaty
of commerce and amity, of a Chinese-like nature,
was ultimately concluded. Ytapua, in the Paraguay Misiones, was made the new South American Canton, to which point, and not beyond it,
the Brazilians were to carry on their traffic. The
treaty answered neither party in effect, and, ere
long, sunk into desuetude.

It was through the medium of this General
Lecor,—a fine old gentleman who served under
the Duke of Wellington in Portugal and in Spain,
—that the application on behalf of M. Bonpland
was made.

The next step taken in favour of M. Bonpland
as by the Institute of France. That body sent

M. Grandsire to solicit, at the hands of Francia, the enlargement of their celebrated countryman. But, though M. Grandsire penetrated to the Paraná, and did all that could be done, his mission was unsuccessful.

Our own Chargé d'Affaires, Sir Woodbine Parish, after his successful interference on behalf of the British détenus, resolved also to make an effort in favour of M. Bonpland.

I have stated that Francia, on liberating the British subjects, demanded the free navigation of the river Plate up to Assumption, a claim which, of course, it was totally out of Sir Woodbine's power either to initiate or to sustain. When he thanked Francia, therefore, for the liberation of the British détenus and their property, he politely showed the Dictator that the British Chargé d'Affaires had no power to interfere in the inland navigation of the United Provinces of the river Plate; and it was when he gave this explanation that he made an appeal in favour of M. Bonpland.

Nothing could exceed the rage and disappointment of Francia when he found that all his

towering prospects of a free inland navigation,
and diplomatic relations with Great Britain, had
crumbled into dust,—and this, too, after he had
allowed the last British subject to escape from
his malignant grasp. I fancy I see his savage
aspect, as he paced up and down his den with
Sir Woodbine Parish's letter in his hand;—and
I think I see him doing all that his rage would
here allow him to do,—enclosing Sir Woodbine's
letter in a fresh envelop, and re-directing it to
" The English Consul at Buenos Ayres."

The last, and most interesting, effort made
to recover the liberty of the companion of Humboldt was by Madame Bonpland.

Not long after he went first to Corrientes,
Madame with her interesting daughter returned
to France; and it was from Paris that in 1826,
she set out, on the noble but melancholy task
of endeavouring to move the tyrant of Paraguay
in favour of M. Bonpland. The history of
Madame Bonpland's exertions to attain her
object would form of itself a volume of no common interest; and at the close of this one,
hampered, as I am for space, I cannot consent

to mutilate the story here.   Suffice it to say that
Madame never was able to attain her object ;
and that Bonpland, therefore, remained a prisoner till Francia's own black time arrived.

I return to the little establishment of our
détenu at the Cerrito, where he established himself towards the close of 1821.

M. Bonpland is in the most exalted sense of
the word a cosmopolitan.   His maxim is, Exert
yourself for the improvement and the happiness
of mankind.   In whatever corner M. Bonpland
may be situated, he considers that it is a section
of the world of which he is a citizen.   Place him
where you like, he will forget self, and turn
instantly to employ his energies, his knowledge,
his science, and his philanthropy, for the benefit
of those who surround him.

No sooner, accordingly, did he find himself in
the enjoyment of a certain degree of liberty in
Paraguay, than he set about ameliorating the
condition and improving the habits of the simple
people among whom (albeit per force) he had
taken up his residence.

He had considerable medical skill; he became

at once the surgeon and physician of the district, and in particular, he became the head of Francia's medical staff in that quarter. He would ride leagues to attend on any sick soldier who required medical attendance. Had the *Great Gaoler* of Paraguay himself been stretched on a sick-bed, and within Bonpland's reach, he would have returned good for evil, and brought his enemy to health if he could.

At first he had some difficulty in even procuring a livelihood for himself by his own labour; but as his character developed itself among the warm-hearted Paraguayans, their kindness grew into affection and reverence, and Bonpland gradually prospered and became the father of the people.

His means, by his unceasing industry, increased, and he led the way to the progressive advancement of every one about him. He showed them the best way of cultivating their ground; he introduced a spirit of active industry among them. He gave gradually a greater extent to his own farm; as he did so, he employed more people. He introduced the cultivation of the humbler arts; he added first a carpentry shop, then a blacksmith's, to his own premises. He had carts made, implements improved, and roads mended. The agriculture of the country assumed a more flourishing aspect under his paternal guidance; flocks and herds increased; and his own establishment assumed, year by year, all the growing importance of a thriving and increasing colony.

While M. Bonpland thus advanced in his useful career, and began at last to reap himself the sure benefit of his judicious plans; when all the country round could do nothing but speak of the benefits which it derived from the labours of the good Bonpland; the demon of destruction, like an ill-omened bird, was once more hovering around him.

Useful as he was to the Dictator, the distrustful and envious ruler began to get jealous of the increasing popularity of his prisoner. He could not but feel that his own proceedings offered a sorry, but a most startling contrast to those of Bonpland; and of Bonpland, therefore, he determined to get rid.

It is not easy to say, as regards that amiable

man himself, whether his *capture* or his *dismissal*
was the basest.

It was, I think, in the commencement of the
year 1831, that M. Bonpland, now in the midst
of well-earned comfort and prosperity; no longer
looking upon himself or looked upon by those
around him as an exile; beloved, respected, re-
vered " by all the country round ;" accumulating
his stock of botanical and natural specimens and
curiosities; it was under these circumstances that
the Dictator reduced M. Bonpland for a second
time to beggary.

He was visited one evening by the commandant of Santa Maria, or one of his officers, with a
few men, and he was told that an order had just
come down from Assumption to remove him from
Paraguay, *that very night*. He was allowed to
take with him a few clothes, as much money as
would pay his expenses to Corrientes, and *nothing more*. All the rest of his property was
abandoned; and to this day he has never received
a farthing of it.

He was conducted in darkness and in solitude to the banks of the Paraná; a canoe
lay ready to receive him; he was taken across

to the Entre Rios side, under the escort of
soldiers: there they landed, and there they left
him.

Such was the conclusion of M. Bonpland's nine
years' detention in Paraguay.

He remained for some time in Corrientes, but
returned to Buenos Ayres in 1832. He there, in
May of that year, paid me a visit of two or three
days at Monte Grande, a little Scotch colony
situated a few leagues from the city, which I was
then superintending; and it may be imagined
how much of our conversation turned on Paraguay and Doctor Francia. The details of his
residence at Santa Maria, at which I have here
merely glanced, were replete with interest. And
so far from having quitted Paraguay with that
feeling of abhorrence of Francia, which his proceedings might naturally be presumed to inspire,
M. Bonpland spoke of him with philosophic
serenity, and only regretted, over and over again,
that there was no chance of the Dictator's *allowing
him to return to Paraguay.*

He is now in Corrientes, actively engaged once
more in agricultural plans ; and it is ardently to

be hoped that he may yet delight Europe with
an account of his residence in Paraguay, and of
the United Provinces of the River Plate.

Yours, &c.

W. P. R.

LETTER XXII.

To THOMAS FAIR, ESQ.

J. P. R. RESUMES AND CONCLUDES THE SERIES AND
THE VOLUME.

The three salient points in Francia's history—His fear of assassination—His prying and minute organization of his troops—
He sows jealousy of each other among them—His minuteness—Military impertinence encouraged — Anecdotes of his
cruelty and caprice—Courts-Martial—Increase of dungeons
and prisons—The public prison—Treatment of the prisoners
—Females not excepted—State dungeons.

London, 1838.

THERE were three remarkable and salient points in
the history of Francia's despotic career : first, the
wily cunning in which it commenced; secondly,
the cautious and gradual steps by which it proceeded; and, lastly, the unrelenting cruelty by
which it was consummated.

Of the first point you have seen sufficient in
the early series of these Letters. I purpose now
to dwell a little more in detail on the second,
particularly to show you how the oppression of
the citizens of Paraguay proceeded hand-in-hand

o 2

with the increase of the military power; and how
systematically Francia ensconced himself, in his
work of progressive tyranny, spoliation, and
caprice, behind this bulwark of his insolent security.   Every company added to his grenadier
corps emboldened him to new outrage; and most
deserving, at the same time, of observation is the
Machiavellian spirit, by which he sowed discord
and distrust among the armed Janissaries upon
whom he depended for the maintenance of his ill-
gotten and worse-used power.   As tyrants are
proverbially afraid of poison in the very meat by
which they exist, so Francia was desperately afraid
of the swords and bayonets by which his political
existence was supported.

Let us see the means by which the astute
and jealous despot endeavoured to parry any
thrust that might be made at him from this
quarter.

His first care was to call in, and to have repaired under his own immediate inspection,
every straggling musket and rusty blunderbuss
which could be collected.   The number of
Guards, or Quarteleros, so often mentioned heretofore, was augmented, and all higher rank than

that of captain abolished.   The Dictator himself
became general, colonel, paymaster, quarter-
master, and head tailor to the regiment.   Not a
musket was delivered out but by his own hands.
Grenadier hats and coat trimmings were not
only devised, but fitted, stored, and distributed
by himself.   He held personal communication
with every man in his regiment of Guards : he
pampered, flattered, paid, and caressed them.
At the same time he diffused among them a
spirit of constant and ever-jealous rivalry, and of
aspiration to his favour and countenance.   He
began his system of indulgence with the private,
and diminished it as he went through the grades
of corporal, sergeant, ensign, lieutenant, till it
faded into nothing with the captain.   The superior rank of this last was thus counterbalanced
by the personal favour more openly shown by
the Dictator to the captain's subordinates.   But
the feeling of importance thus created in them
was again counteracted by Francia's exaction,
from the soldiers and subalterns, of a passive
obedience to the captain's orders.

Without knowing how, the captain thus felt
himself in possession of actual command divested

of moral power; and the soldier, as little knowing how, felt that, although he must obey his captain and other superior officers, the turn of a straw, the nod of the Dictator, might reduce the captain to the ranks, and raise the private to the command of a company. The jealousy thus excited in every superior officer toward the one next subordinate to him, and *vice versâ*, created a prying and malicious vigilance of the conduct of each into that of the other, and produced, as a never-failing result of misbehaviour, a report of the case to Francia. Again, the hope of advancement fostered, by the Dictator, in sergeants, corporals, and privates, kept them within the sphere of duty on the one hand, and on the alert to report, at head-quarters, any dereliction of it on the part of their commissioned officers. At the same time, an *esprit de corps* was not only encouraged but inculcated, in virtue of which every man in the regiment considered himself superior to any mere civilian. By this distinction in favour of his soldiers, the Dictator meant at once to soothe the feverish feeling to which all were subjected by the system of discipline enforced; and to try at what ratio of acceleration he might proceed to extinguish every lingering spark of liberty among the people.

Machinery, with such "a wheel within a wheel" of complicated powers for the destruction of all the institutions and laws of pity and humanity, was never, perhaps, before put in motion.

Nothing can be more indicative of the penetration and address by which Francia has beaten down the people of Paraguay than the fact, that though they are 300,000 in number, his whole regular force has seldom exceeded 3000, never 4000 men. But the same system of discipline and distrust, founded upon the agitating principles of our nature—hope and fear,—which he introduced into his regiment of Guards, he diffused throughout the community, and extended to every department of the State. In addition to this, he dispensed with all assistance in his Government, except what was merely mechanical, and could be rendered by low individuals of narrow education.

He was his own minister of finance, secretary-at-war, collector of customs, and keeper of the strong box of the State. No petty commandant of a petty village could pay his drummer and fifer without an order express from the Dictator. **He** was the axis upon which every piece of the **State** machinery turned,—the centre of attraction, toward which everything gravitated,—the mainspring which kept in motion all, even the minutest parts, of the working system of his government.

At this period, 1816-17, it became impossible to walk the streets without being intentionally jostled by every soldier you met. He obliged you to take off your hat to him, laughed and sneered at you, and demanded money. No home was safe from the invasion of those insolent mercenaries ; and not many could escape the contagion of their lawless vices. Francia *occasionally* checked them ; more to let his soldiers feel his power over even the military license which himself had created, than with any view to a mitigation of the sufferings it entailed upon the population. Some time after the ineffectual application in favour of Echagüe, by his wife (as mentioned at pages 299, 300, of vol. ii., first series), another, but more distant relation of his, having been employed in some matters by Francia, ventured once more to intercede for the imprisoned, enchained, and dying man. " Sir," said the Dictator, " I have permitted you to approach my person, not because you deserved it, but because I chose it. You now pretend to *dictate* to me, and, by interceding for your friend, impugn the judgment by which he has been consigned to perpetual imprisonment and chains. Go where he is, and there, like a dog, as you are, rot and die in the contiguous dungeon." The friend of Echagüe thus rotted and thus died.

A lieutenant of the name of Iturbide, presuming upon the Dictator's fancied partiality for him, disobeyed, upon some trivial occasion, his captain, and assigned as a reason for doing so, that he was a greater favourite of the Dictator than the captain himself. This boast came to Francia's ear. He said not a word to the lieutenant, but ordering a muster of the Quarteleros, he went up personally to the officer, collared him, and pulling him out of the ranks, addressed him thus :—" I found you a beggar, and I made you an officer. I now find you an ill-behaved officer, and I send you back to be a well-behaved beggar. If you are not that, I shall put you in the stocks, or in a worse place." So saying, Francia had the officer stripped of his uniform, clothed in the filthy habiliments of a mendicant, and drummed out of the regiment.

In something of the same style were all the courts-martial of the Dictator conducted. Not even a drum-head was required around which to assemble them. Francia's *dictum* was omnipotent, and the execution of it imperative, irreversible, instantaneous. Never was a single instance known of commutation of sentence, or of mitigation of punishment.

As the Dictator multiplied his barracks and added to his troops, so he increased the number of his dungeons, augmented the number of his prisoners, and took less and less pains to hide from public gaze the unheard-of cruelties to which he subjected them. He seemed rather to thrust his dungeon system on the notice of the enslaved people, as a constant exhibition held up to them *in terrorem*, and indicative of the fate that awaited the slightest demonstration of enmity to his government, or the remotest indication of disapproval of his measures.

Of the prisons constructed for Francia's victims there were two kinds ; one was styled the "public prison," and was a large building 100 feet square,

divided into eight compartments, on a ground
floor. The other class, and by far the most
terrific, went by the ominous name of " *state
prisons*." Of these latter there were several, all
in the different barracks, and under the rigid
surveillance of the troops quartered there.

To proceed first with a description of the " public prison." It was destined to receive inmates
of every class, save and except political delinquents. The court attached to the prison had
an area of about 12,000 square feet; and in
each confined, dingy, suffocating apartment, there
were crowded promiscuously together from thirty
to forty human beings. There was not room in
these apartments to accommodate, outstretched
upon the floor, so many wretched inmates; and
those who could not find room to rest there, were
suspended in small hammocks, hung one over
another. The narrow windows of these crowded
cells scarcely deserved the name of air-holes, although in a climate in which the thermometer of
Reaumur ranges generally from twenty to twenty-
eight degrees, under a roof literally *baked* in the
sun, and barred against egress to the prisoners
during twelve hours out of the twenty-four. The

perspiration of the inmates hence arising, and
the pestilential effluvia combining with the filth,
coarse food, miserable clothing, disease, and in-
action of the prisoners, rendered the scene so
loathsome and pitiable, as to forbid the possibility
of referring you to any other like it.

Many of the prisoners were daily led forth to
work for the state; and though the clanking of
chains proclaimed their wretched condition, and
grillos, or iron rings round their ankles, joined
by a cross bar, rendered walking at once painful
and difficult,—though hard work, under the hot
rays of the sun, exhausted the frame,—and
though the captive was obliged to eke out, by
beggary, the scanty supply of provisions allowed
him by the state,—yet his condition was comparatively happy; for he had at any rate air and
exercise, from the want of which the closely pent-
up "prisoner of state" languished, pined, and
died.

To this general treatment there was no exception. High and low, rich and poor, male and
female, were alike subjected to it. Here were the
robber and the just man, there the black and the
white, bound together by one chain. The re-

spected citizen and the unprincipled gambler, the guilty highwayman and the hospitable philanthropist, were all under the same ruthless régime. They had their abode together, and together clanked their galling chains. Not even was the respectable female,—nay, she that had been torn from her home in a state of pregnancy,—was not exempted from the common lot of the worst of the male prisoners. If such females, however unconsciously, however innocently, had excited the tyrant's suspicion, alarmed his fears, or, under whatever frivolous pretext, incurred his displeasure, they were immured in the dungeon.

There was one sole alleviation of misery to the inmates of the public prison: they had a humane gaoler; and his humanity was exercised as far as it could be by any one of Francia's functionaries in favour of his prisoners. He had himself, for some years, been an inmate of the abode of which he was now forced by Francia to be the keeper. Experience of the wretched lot of its inhabitants had no doubt softened his heart into feelings of sympathy and commiseration. Like the keeper of the prison of Philippi, Gomez, who kept that of Assumption, set meat before his prisoners, and " washed their stripes."

Such was the "*public* prison," and such were its inmates; but what were the horrors of the one, or what the sufferings of the other, to those of the " state prisons," and to the appalling spectacles of human wretchedness within them? The public prison was a palace, the sufferings of the prisoner enjoyment, in the one case, as compared with the other; but as I have already too long detained you, in one letter, over the cruel and complicated means adopted by Francia for the ruin of his enemies, the terror of his subordinates, and the consternation of every inhabitant of Paraguay, I shall defer, till my next, a description of other parts of the machinery of government, at once invented and constructed by Francia, to enable him to work out the ruin of his country-men, and his own unenviable elevation.

Yours, &c.

J. P. R.

LETTER XXIII.

J. P. R. to Thomas Fair, Esq.

State dungeons—Their inmates—Tevégo made a place of exile—
The torture chamber—Use made of those instruments of ty-
ranny—The Pelado—His fate—Horrible mode of conducting
executions—Fearful progress of the reign of terror—Case of
the shoemaker—The tradesmen's gibbet—Generalization—
Application of it to the shoemaker's case—Dark prospects—
Anecdote of a jury—Inference drawn—Applicable to Francia—
Hazael, Nero, and the Dictator.

London, 1838.

I HAVE described to you, among other things, in
my last letter, the "*public prison*" of Assumption.
I proceed now to describe, as distinguished from
that, the "*state dungeons.*" These are narrow
cells, constructed under ground in the different barracks. They are small, damp, vaulted
dungeons, of such contracted dimensions, that to
maintain an upright posture in them is impossible, except under the centre of the arch.

Here it is, that loaded with irons, with a sentinel continually in view, bereft of every comfort,

left without the means of ablution, and under a
positive prohibition to shave, pare their nails, or
cut their hair;—here, in silence, solitude, and despair, the victims of the Dictator's vengeance, and
often of his mere displeasure or caprice, are constrained to pass a life to which death would be a
thousand times preferable. The feeble light
admitted to these dungeons, contrived by this
demon of relentless cruelty, is by a door left
half open during the day, but closed at sunset.
After this time, the wretched, and in most cases
innocent, victim is left to pine away his hours of
darkness and of solitude. He has not a spark
of consolation to illumine the gloom of the present, nor a ray of hope to cast a shadow of light
on the dark horizon of the future. He is still a
living, languishing member, or rather outcast, of
the world. But entombed alive,—cut off from all
human intercourse and sympathy,—he drags on
a hated and loathsome existence, till, stricken to
the soul by anguish, or a victim to disease, or in
the convulsions of madness, he yields to Him who
gave it, a soul into which the iron has so deeply
entered as to make him receive, as the best of
boons, at the hands of his God, a release from his

earthly woe. Thus died my friend and companion
Gomez; thus died my friend Dr. Savala; thus
died Padre Maiz; thus died the old Governor,
General Velasco; and thus his faithful butler.
Thus died Machain; and thus, or on the banquillo,
perished almost every kind and simple-hearted
friend I ever had in Assumption. Thus, especially, perished every man who excited the Dictator's jealousy by reason of some glimmering of
better understanding than his neighbour,—of a
thought of independence,—or of a spark, were it
but a latent one, of liberty in his soul. The irreversible decree was, —" Off with him to the dungeon; or away with him to the gibbet or the banquillo.*" " Off," in short, " with his head! and
so much for Buckingham."

But even all these modes of punishment were
insufficient to allay the despot's fears, satisfy his
vengeance, appease his wrath, or quench his malignity. *Exile* was one of his favourite inflictions;
nor, considering all the dangers and privations
attendant on it, one of the least terrible. With
a small population of abandoned men and women

* The banquillo is a low stool or form on which, in a sitting
posture, delinquents are shot.

of colour, he laid the foundation of a colony called Tevégo, near Fort Borbon, and distant about 100 leagues northward from Assumption. It is a place, of which the atmosphere is one great mass of malaria, and the heat suffocating,— where the surrounding country is uninterrupted marsh,—where venomous insects and reptiles abound,—and where the fiercest and yet unsub-dued tribes of Indians are making continual in-roads. No huts but those constructed by the boughs of trees, or by a few hides and mats, are to be seen; no provisions are to be obtained but from the Portuguese, or the chase; and no pro-tection is afforded but that of a small guard of militia, to awe and tyrannise over the colonists. Many would have preferred confinement in the public prison to banishment to Tevégo.

When shall I have done with the account of Francia's tortures and inhuman ingenuity in multiplying the means of increasing human misery,—of initiating in Paraguay a system, of which the least almost that can be said is, that it is a type of the worst sufferings to which the worst of men are likely ever to be doomed in another world?

Come forth to light the last, the worst, the
most heartless, yet most characteristic, of all his
institutions : one which with impious mockery and
derision of suffering humanity, he called "THE
CHAMBER OF TRUTH." This was neither more
nor less than the "TORTURE CHAMBER," a dark
den of iniquity, in which blows or stripes on the
back of an alleged delinquent were ministered by
sturdy arms, and to the number of from 200 to
500, till either the Dictator was satisfied with the
extorted confession, or the miserable victim in his
fidelity, or in his inability to answer the questions
put, perished under the thong of the executioner.
Francia, the man who had boasted of the annihilation of the inquisition, established for supposed
political offences, a school of torture of which the
cowled ministers of the " Holy Office" would
have shrunk to. become members. Of them
there were, at any rate, *many* who sat in judgment upon a supposed culprit; and where there
are many, the chances are that the voice of
humanity will be heard in one or more of them,
if not to refuse assent to all punishment, at least
to plead in mitigation of it. In Francia's case
there was no such compassionate diversion in

favour of mercy. It was Francia, the jealous, the cruel, and the vindictive, who alone had to award the torture, and Francia, who was never known to relent, who alone and uncontrolled was to order execution to be done.

You have now seen on what principles, and by what complex manœuvres and intrigues Francia organised his corps of Jannissaries. You have seen, when fortified and upheld by these, how he fell upon the inhabitants of Paraguay with all the worst scourges of the worst of tyrants. He had, as described—

First, his " PUBLIC PRISON;"

Secondly, his " STATE DUNGEONS;"

Thirdly, his " GIBBET;"

Fourthly, his " BANQUILLO," or bench for execution ;

Fifthly, his " TEVÉGO," or land of exile ; and,

Lastly, and worst of all, his " TORTURE CHAMBER," impiously called his " CHAMBER OF TRUTH."

Let us now see how he proceeded to render these practically subservient to his own views.

In October, 1817, the dictatorship, to which in 1814 he had been elected for three years, expired. He was now, by the same means of a Congress, but with much less difficulty than on the former occasion, elected " DICTATOR FOR LIFE," or rather "DICTADOR PERPETUO," "PERPETUAL DICTATOR."

From this moment he threw off all disguise. As a first exercise of his capricious tyranny, take the following anecdotes.

Some caricatures and pasquinades appeared against him, the work of some of his own American political antagonists in Paraguay. Upon mere suspicion, several individuals were arrested, and without either ceremony, or form of trial, consigned in chains to the " State Dungeons."

Shortly afterwards it was rumoured, that a person of the name of Valta Vargas, a Paraguayan, harboured treacherous designs; and he, and a number of alleged accomplices, were again escorted to the " State Dungeons." The demon of suspicion began now to stalk abroad; and a word, a hint, a look, ay, even the inauspicious meeting of the Dictator in the streets, if misinterpreted by his jaundiced temper and jealous soul, were sufficient reasons why the culprits should be dragged from their families, and left to languish in chains in the prisons, or to drag out a miserable existence in exile.

Having in these, and in other similar cases,

given practical intimation to his own countrymen, how he was about to proceed in *their* case,
Francia proceeded to give an ominous, a terrible
evidence to the old Spaniards, of how he had
made up his mind to deal with them.

There was an old Spaniard* who lived next door
to me, and whom I had known from my first arrival in Paraguay. He went by the *sobriquet* of
" El Pelado," " the bald man." He was an inveterate enemy of the creoles, and a great bigot;
but under a salutary respect for the law of self-
preservation, he lived for many years in Paraguay, without intermeddling in political affairs,
and denying himself, as much as he possibly
could, the privilege of even gossiping about them
with his most familiar friends. To my brother
and myself he sometimes opened his heart, because he knew he was in safe hands; but we
never heard him speak, especially dilate, on
such subjects without admonishing him of the
danger of its perilous tendency. He was a man
of a fiery, irritable temper; but still, he was a
man under the check of practical prudence, and
being a mere shopkeeper, from whom most people
kept aloof, because of his forbidding manners, he

* See Page 25.

was, perhaps, of all the men in Assumption, the least formidable to the Dictator. But this personage did not deem his enemies those alone who were capable of doing him an injury: a word uttered to his disparagement, a thought expressed unsuited to his momentary caprice, however impotent the party who might utter it, was the signal for banishment, chains, or death.

When Francia proceeded to annihilate or debase the monastic orders, he converted into barracks some of their monasteries. This so exasperated the poor Pelado, especially as his hopes at the time were raised to a great pitch of excitement by a false report of a Russian squadron being on its way to Paraguay, that he gave loose to the following remark :—" The Franciscans have gone to-day; but who can tell that Francia's turn to go may not be to-morrow?" By some busy and malicious tongue this short, but fatal speech was conveyed to the ears of the Dictator. He summoned the Pelado to his presence, and addressed him in these terribly emphatic words :—" As to when it may be *my* turn to go, I am not aware; but this I know, *that you shall go before me*." Next morning the Pelado was brought to the banquillo, placed not far from Francia's window; and the Dictator delivered, with his own hands, to three soldiers, the three ball cartridges with which the unfortunate man was to be shot. The aim was not effectual, and the executioners were ordered to despatch him with their bayonets. Upon the whole of this scene of barbarity and blood, Francia looked from his window, being not distant more than thirty yards from the place of slaughter.

You will ask me how the Dictator came to limit the number of men who were to do the work of execution on the Pelado to three; and as little facts are often illustrative of great, sad, and horrible things, I will answer you. He was too economical of the powder and ball, upon which he mainly depended for protection, to give it out in the necessary quantity to render even execution a work of comparative humanity.

In no subsequent case did he deviate from this practice; so that in the great number of executions which followed that of the Pelado, in all cases where the ball did not reach the heart, or penetrate the head, the sufferer was reduced to a mangled corpse by the process of stabbing him with the bayonet. Of all such executions, too, Francia was an exulting spectator ; nor were the bodies, which had been consigned to death in the morning ever permitted to be withdrawn till the evening. At frequent intervals, during the day, the Dictator came to his window and stood gazing on them as if to glut his eyes with the work of murder, and minister fiendish satisfaction to his revenge, by the view of the mangled carcasses of those whose alleged enmity he had thus made to lick the dust. Not content with this in the case related of the Pelado, Francia seized all his property, and sent his wife and children forth, though Creoles, mendicants upon the bounty of their neighbours.

An execution precisely similar to that of the Pelado, and on almost similar grounds, viz.—some wish expressed by a European, not favourable to the despot,—took place a few days afterwards. From henceforward the reign of terror may be said to have commenced, and that under circumstances which left neither doubt nor conjecture as to what was to be the filling up of the dark picture of Francia's sway.

Deeming now the dungeon and the gibbet to

be the only means of effecting reform, and that
not in matters of political concernment alone, but
of those which were merely mechanical, the Dictator had a special gallows erected for the inti-
midation of his workmen and artizans.   The best
of them had never been initiated into the principles or mysteries of mechanics, and their practical
blunders often roused Francia's irritable temper
into uncontrolable harshness and asperity.   But
as all he did was ever done systematically, he
gave no indication for some time to his blun-
dering workmen of his displeasure further than
by telling them that he was not pleased with
their work.   Finding this remonstrance of little
effect, the erected the special gibbet in question.   In came, according to custom, one afternoon, a poor shoemaker, with a couple of gre-
nadiers' belts, neither according to the fancy of the
Dictator. "Sentinel,"—said he,—and in came the
sentinel; when the following conversation ensued:

Dictator :—" Take this bribonazo," (a very
favourite word of the Dictator's, and which, being
interpreted, means " most impertinent scoundrel"),—take this bribonazo to the gibbet over
the way; walk him under it half a dozen times :

and now," said he, turning to the trembling shoemaker, " bring me such another pair of belts, and instead of *walking* under the gallows, we shall try how you can *swing* upon it."

Shoemaker :—" Please your Excellency I have done my best."

Dictator :—" Well, bribon, if this *be* your best, I shall do *my* best to see that you never again mar a bit of the State's leather. The belts are of no use to me ; but they will do very well to hang you upon the little frame-work which the grenadier will show you."

Shoemaker :—" God bless your Excellency, the Lord forbid ! I am your vassal, your slave ; day and night have I served and will serve my lord ; only give me two days more to prepare the belts ; y por el alma de un triste zapatéro (by the soul of a poor shoemaker) I will make them to your Excellency's liking."

Dictator :—" Off with him, sentinel !"

Sentinel :—" Venga, bribon :" " come along, you rascal."

Shoemaker :—" Señor Excelentisimo : *This very night* I will make the belts according to your Excellency's pattern."

Dictator:—" Well, you shall have till the morning ; but still you must pass under the gibbet : it is a salutary process, and may at once quicken the work and improve the workmanship."

Sentinel :—" Vamonos, bribon ; the Supreme commands it."

Off was the shoemaker marched : he was, according to orders, passed and repassed under the gibbet; and then allowed to retire to his stall. Whether the electric shock which he had undergone strung his nerves anew, or whether his genius was quickened by a keen perception of the danger of being a sloven or an ignoramus, in a vocation so important as that of beltmaker to his Excellency, it is very certain that the shoemaker appeared the next morning before Francia with a couple of belts, so entirely to the Dictator's fancy, as to save the operator's neck from the halter, and to procure for him the station of belt-maker general to the army.

The example was so salutary that blacksmiths, gunsmiths, architects, tailors, tambourers, capmakers, all became better tradesmen. The " Tradesmen's gibbet" was the terror of them all, and a single peep at it, even in the dis-

tance, sent every man home to his respective
calling, with a combination of alacrity, fear, and
dexterity, which I doubt much if any other stimulus, however exciting, would have produced.

What shall we *say* to this ? That " facts
are stubborn things" is an axiom which all are
ready to admit ; and yet, if I were here to raise
a question (which God forbid I should) as to
whether man is a being who, to be trained to any
useful purpose, must be awed by the gallows or
the thong, instead of being inducted into industry
and civilised life by the legitimate means of
education and of competition, what a hive of
controversialists, reasoners, and theorists, should
I not at once have buzzing about my ears !

It has been said that the authors of " Letters
on Paraguay" are deficient in powers of generalisation. Considering that these are the highest
powers with which the human mind can be endowed
—powers which can legitimately be exercised
by such men alone as Bacon, after all individual
observation and all specific science have been exhausted, we (I mean my brother and myself)
may well acquiesce in the truth of the charge. But
another truth is, that we have not set ourselves

up *as* generalisers. We did not think our subject much required it. We have been content to state facts, and to draw from them, as we conceive, no very remote, far-fetched, or elaborate deductions. That task I leave to abler heads, and in the mean time you may solve, according to your own notions of generalisation, the curious matter-of-fact problem, by which the shoemaker at once saved his neck from the halter, escaped the wrath of such a despot as Francia, and got himself promoted to the rank of belt-maker-general to the " Dictator of Paraguay."

" A soft answer," says Solomon, " breaketh the bone." In the shoemaker's case, a pliant disposition did more than this : *it turned the Dictator from his purpose.*

But passing from considerations which, if followed up, might raise a passing smile, I am compelled once more to rivet your attention upon scenes in which there *cannot* be the relaxation of a smile; upon scenes which Imagination with her darkest pencil could scarcely trust herself to depict ;—pieces which Tragedy, armed with her blood-stained dagger, would scarcely dare to act. Yet are they true, " as proof of holy writ;" and to those who, from their respect for human nature, and the difficulty of believing it can be so *very* bad, would be inclined to doubt their authenticity, I would address the following anecdote, which must yet be fresh in the recollection of many of my readers.

A very few years ago, a trial for *crim. con.* took place in an English county. At this trial, the guilt of the defendant was so clear and indubitable, that by all *reasoning* parties on the evidence adduced, one only inference could be drawn; and that was, that the criminal act had indeed been committed. But certain virtuous, and *not*, perhaps, very reasoning members of the jury, came to the conclusion, in *spite* of the evidence, " *that the thing could not be.*" " The circumstances," they said, "are too atrocious;" "it is not in *human nature* to believe that criminality so glaring should have taken place."

Very well. The defendant was acquitted; but the plaintiff, convinced that he had been grossly betrayed, brought up on a following term, and upon a motion granted for a new trial, such a host of witnesses as to the truth of the allegations against his wife, that the latter, with all her effrontery, and even with all the zeal of her advocates, (justifiable, I suppose, in any case where a client is to be defended,) left the injured husband master of the field.

The short inference I would draw from this illustration is, that in Francia's case, as in the one related, and in every other, we are bound to look at the evidence; and if that bear out the allegations, no matter what new and unheard-of atrocities they may involve against human beings, we *must* allow them to form part of our estimate of the family of man. It is a very awful thing, to be sure, to be obliged to admit that many of the miscreants who have darkened the pages of history were of the same species as that to which ourselves belong. Yet they were. One was Tiberius, another Caligula, another Nero, another is Francia. They were monsters, and he is one, if you will; but still human monsters; and it is our wisdom, in contemplating their characters, not to reject the hideous points of them, as untrue, but to study them till they inspire us with salutary horror of such practices, and with not less salutary dread of such principles, lest any particle of them, leading to the same detestable results, should creep unawares into our *own* characters, and, though not destined to be developed so broadly as in Francia's case, make part of our own moral nature.

There is more instruction in Hazael's question to Elisha, and in the prophet's reply, than we sometimes think. The latter having predicted all the evil which the former would bring upon the children of Israel, " But what," said he, " is thy servant a *dog*, that he should do this great thing ?" " And Elisha answered, The Lord hath shown me that thou shalt be *King over Syria.*" Had Hazael never been king of Syria, Caligula never emperor of Rome, nor Francia ever Dictator of Paraguay, the world would have been spared a great deal of tragical and revolting record. As it is, we now see that the germ of ruthless tyranny must have taken deep root in the hearts of all those monsters, and that, nurtured by the quickening stimulus of power, it sprung up and bore most bitter fruits to mankind.

I purpose, in my next Letter, to give you some account of the atrocious and terrible inflictions by which Francia's career began now to be deeply

stained, leaving in its sanguinary track anguish
and despair, as the sad lot of almost every family
in Assumption. There is scarcely one of any
respectability which does not mourn the bereave-
ment of a father, husband, brother, or more distant relative, and always of that member of
the family who was considered its greatest orna-
ment.

Yours, &c.

J. P. R.

LETTER XXIX.

J. P. R. TO THOMAS FAIR, ESQ.

Francia's growing terrors of assassination — Conspiracy against
him—The conspirators betrayed—Wretched consequences—
Fate of the conspirators—Further precautions taken by
Francia—The intrigues of Ramirez, an Artigueño colonel—
Executions and torture — Executions continued — Female
heroism—Change of the national character—Fate of Don
Andres Gomez — General effects produced by the Reign of
Terror.

London, 1838.

It is of all things the most unlikely, even among
a people so passive and so trodden under foot
as the Paraguayans, that a tyrant like Francia
should have pursued his career, without the
penalty ever paid by such men, of being haunted
by the dread of assassination. His whole mode of
life showed that he was no exception to the rule :
poison and the dagger were for ever before him.
Every cigar he smoked, though made by his own
sister, was carefully unrolled, to see that it contained no suspicious-looking drug. His pro-

visions he examined with like scrupulosity; and no one was permitted to come into his presence with even a cane in his hand. Every one who obtained an audience was obliged to stop short at a distance of six paces from the Dictator, and to allow his hands to hang down by his side.

Mr. Rengger states, that having, in ignorance, omitted this ceremony at his first interview with Francia, he was gruffly challenged with a design to assassinate him. Loaded pistols, and unsheathed sabres were always within the Dictator's reach; people were driven by his dragoons from the deserted streets through which he rode; and he changed his place of rest (if rest, indeed, the jealous and alarmed soul can ever be said to enjoy,) from one abode to another. Sometimes he slept in his own palace, sometimes in one of the Quartels in the town, and sometimes in the cavalry barracks in the country. The scowl of distrust was seldom off his countenance; and he moved about like a demon, ready to spill human blood on the turn of a straw.

He was not long without a pretext for the gratification of his savage designs, and for the bringing into awful and practical use the machinery enumerated in my last letter, by which he was prepared to support his ill-gotten power, appease his restless jealousy, and give full effect to all his tortuous designs.

It is not,—or it scarcely is,—in the nature of things, that Francia should have exercised his tyrannical sway in the manner described, without having something more to combat than the mere *phantoms* of enemies conjured up around him by his own restless fears.

When we consider that he was ruling, on principles at once relentless and capricious, a country filled with his enemies,—with men whose pride he had humbled, of whose offices he had deprived them, and whose honour he had laid in the dust, to make way for the low and despised tools of office, through whom he at once insulted and oppressed all the men of family, education, and wealth in Paraguay,—and this for a period of more than six years;—our wonder cannot be that plots and conspiracies should have been hatched, but that they should have been so long in breaking the shell.

At length, a solemn league and covenant was entered into by a number of the most respectable citizens of Paraguay, to overthrow Francia's government, if not to do vengeance on his person.

Puyerredon, then Director of Buenos Ayres, co-operated with the malcontents, and sent his emissary, Valta Vargas, to scatter the seeds of discontent in Paraguay. But the imprudence of this person soon led to his arrest, though not, fortunately, to the detection of the conspirators. These followed up their plans with a secrecy almost incredible, when it is considered that they were two years in maturing them.

At length, the day of Good Friday, 1820, was fixed upon as that on which the enemies of Francia determined to rush in upon him in his palace, rally the troops, appeal to the citizens, and risk everything for the chance of emancipation from the galling and relentless thraldom of the tyrant.

But it was not registered in the decrees of fate that it should so be. The ill-omened star of Francia was still in the ascendant; and, during the latter days of Lent, a caitiff of a conspirator revealed the whole plot to his Franciscan confessor. The penitent was ordered, at the peril of his soul, to go and deliver up a full account of

the whole matter together, with the names of all
the parties concerned, to Francia. So the traitor
did, and on that night the groans of the state
dungeons were augmented by the wailings of
more than fifty of the best inhabitants of Assumption. Every member of the former Junta was
arrested, and every friend and relation he had.
Their property was confiscated, and the house in
which the conspirators had held their meetings
was razed. The blacksmith could not forge
chains fast enough; the rigour and privations
of a system of imprisonment, already sufficiently callous, were augmented; all that demo-
niacal ingenuity could devise, or fear, hatred, and
jealousy wrought to a pitch of phrenzy, could
invent, was had recourse to; the cup of bitterness
held up to the prisoners was drained to the dregs;
terror and consternation were spread among those
who escaped the dungeon. The Dictator felt his
arm strengthened by the detection of the plot,
while at the same time it offered to him a plausible pretext for the multiplication of every pre-
caution which jealousy could suggest, and every
cruelty which revenge could devise.

Francia now saw in those who approached him

only traitors and assassins; and all the inhabitants of Assumption, as well those accused, as those who were not, were put beyond the pale of the laws.

One motive, and only one, prevented Francia's doing instant execution upon the conspirators. *He was still afraid.* Connected as they were with every family of distinction in Paraguay, he feared to draw down upon him the odium, or to raise the rebellion that might, and probably would, be consequent on the wholesale slaughter of his enemies. He left them, therefore, to languish in the state dungeons, unshaved, unshorn, unwashed, badly fed, wretchedly clothed, without communication with a human being, with their nails unpared, and their bodies fœtid from filth, till death, as he paid his frequent visits, was received, even by the greatest lover of life, as a welcome guest. Many of them joyfully answered his summons. Without medical assistance, without the presence of friends, without the consolations of religion, and without even the decency of burial, they yielded up the ghost. But they escaped the grasp of the tyrant; in many cases with exultation, in all with thanksgiving, and they returned their souls to Him who gave them. Sad,—sad pass in the history of human wretchedness, when death comes to be considered our best friend;—the cold, and even unconsecrated tomb, our most coveted abode !

The Dictator now rode about, conscious of the enmity and distrust of every good man, and with a breast boiling with hatred toward the few respectable ones he had left at large. A man's being seen in the streets within 100 yards of him was an unpardonable offence : it was generally visited with imprisonment or exile. One day his horse shyed at an old barrel in front of a house; instantly the owner of it was arrested.

An informer told him there were still conspiracies hatching, and that there was an intention on the part of the conspirators to murder him as he rode through the streets. Instantly all houses in suspicious situations were levelled with the ground; lanes were pulled down, and orange trees, shrubs, and other places of concealment were indiscriminately uprooted. Yet would the gloomy tyrant, at night, sometimes prowl about the streets in disguise, and alone. He was unable to confide, except to his own quick ears, and sharp eyes, the

work of tracking the machinations of his supposed enemies, of prying into dark and suspicious recesses, and of listening at the doors of
those houses in town, whose inhabitants he most
suspected.

At length, in 1820-1, an event occurred which,
by hastening the execution of many of Francia's
state-prisoners, put an end at once to their sufferings, and to some of his own fears.

Artigas became, about this time, so reduced
as to be constrained, with about a thousand of
his followers, to seek refuge in the territory of
his old enemy Francia.   The asylum sought was
granted, and the marauding chief,—once the
Most Excellent Protector of thousands of miles of
territory, and of all its inhabitants,—was pursued
for his life by one of his own rebellious lieutenants.   This was a gaucho colonel of the name of
Ramirez.   Artigas fled to Paraguay.   He was there
admitted by the Dictator, but banished to Curu-
güatí, with an allowance of thirty dollars, or eight
pounds a month, and liberty to spend in quiet
misery the latter part of a life, of which the former
had been devoted to plunder, pillage, smuggling,
robbery, and every species of turbulent and law-

less outrage.   Such was the melancholy, but instructive, fate of Artigas.

No sooner, however, was the quondam protector thus placed in political limbo and seclusion, than Ramirez, bent, like all his predecessors, upon aggression, disturbed by intrigue, and menaced by a force collected on the eastern bank of the Paraná, and in the Misiones territory, the republic (oh, prostituted name!) of Paraguay.   He initiated a correspondence with the conspirators confined in the dungeons there, and with other malcontents ill-disposed towards Francia.   Into the hands of this last fell a letter of Ramirez, addressed to Don Fulgencio Yegros, President of the first Junta of Paraguay.   This was the signal for the outpouring of blood.   The bearer of the obnoxious letter was shot without ceremony, and the prisoners were one after another subjected to the awful ordeal of the "CHAMBER OF TRUTH," in order to establish their innocence, or to prove their guilt.   The leather-thong produced such numerous confessions of the existence of other culprits and accomplices, that every successive day saw the "state dungeons" gorged with fresh inmates.

.. Three demons were alone accessory to the in-

quisitorial investigations of the CHAMBER OF
TORTURE,—Francia himself, a legal functionary,
and a registrar. No one but these ever knew the
result of the examinations. That result was
only revealed to the public by the corpses of
the prisoners, as day after day they perished on
the banquillo,—glutted the eyes of the despot,—
tempted to voracity the birds of prey,—and, after
exposure to these for a whole day, were conducted in the evening,—often mangled,—by
their despairing relations to a dark and silent
grave.   Poor Don Fulgencio Yegros was first
shot, and then bayoneted ; Don Fernando
de la Mora followed in the same way ; Gal-
van, Yturbide, and fifty others, all went in
succession.   Then came the turn of Don Pedro
Juan Cavallero, the second member of the original Junta, and the most beloved by the troops
of all the officers in Paraguay.   The sentinels
came into his cell in the morning to drag him
forth to the banquillo,—but he had eluded their
clutches, and bidden defiance to farther tyranny.
He had managed to strangle himself during the
night, and, on the morning destined for his execution, was found a ghastly corpse under an

epitaph which, in these words, he had written
in charcoal upon the wall of his dungeon—" *I
know that suicide is contrary to the laws of God
and of man,—but the tyrant of Paraguay shall
never exult in having spilt my blood.*"

These bloody scenes were re-enacted over and
over again till the middle of 1822. One notable
instance of heroism is worthy of record. The
wife of one of the conspirators having attempted,
on the day of her husband's death, to rally
around her some of the men who even *yet* deserved to be called men in enslaved Paraguay,
was detected,—thrown into a state dungeon,—
and loaded with heavy chains. The only words
she was ever afterwards heard to utter were
these,—and, day after day,—hour after hour,—she
repeated them, " Had I a thousand lives to lose,
I would risk them all to destroy this monster."

The desolation of Paraguay was now complete.
The ruin and prostration of its simple and
good-hearted inhabitants was sealed with the
seal of irrevocable despotism. With a crown of
iron on his brow,—and an iron sceptre in his
hand,—the gloomy tyrant moved about, to the

terror and dismay of his subjects,—or issued his irreversible and cruel decrees for their extermination.

From being the most open, frank, and kind-hearted people in the world, the Paraguay-ans became the most sordid, low, and hypo-critical of the human race. The demons of discord, jealousy, and distrust took possession of every habitation in the land. The overruling passion of self-preservation cooled or deadened all the softer feelings and affections. The bro-ther informed against the sister, the wife against the husband; the son betrayed the father, or the father the son; and the bosom friend of yester-day became the vile spy and informer of to-day. All the hinges of society were out of joint. No inhabitant of Paraguay could say that the man who had broken bread with him to-day, might not be the instrument of his destruction on the morrow.

My next Letter will open up to you some view of the manner in which Francia, after having laid in the grave all the aspirants to power that remained among his own countrymen, dealt with those who were no aspirants to power, but whom he had determined to fleece, the Old Spaniards.

Before doing this, however, I must shortly relate to you the fate of my excellentand intelligent friend, Don Andres Gomez, honourably mentioned throughout these Letters.

MM. Rengger and Longchamps write thus of him. Speaking of the stupor which had seized all the inhabitants of Paraguay, M. Rengger proceeds to say:—" We did not much participate in those feelings, until one morning, all of a sudden, a friend of ours, Don Andres Gomez, with whom we lived for two years under the same roof, was apprehended. We were all at breakfast when a grenadier of the Dictator's guard entered the apartment, and took him into custody. From that moment he has been kept in chains, without any clue whatever being given to the motives of his arrest."

Wretched man ! he was torn from his mother and his sister, both of whom depended on him for their subsistence, and only valued life as it was cheered by his kindness, enlivened by his wit, and solaced by his affection. He soon became a maniac, died

with his fetters upon him; and his mother and
sister, both the most interesting women I had
known in Paraguay, and both broken hearted, followed,—the one her son, and the other her brother,
—to the grave,—in the same state of mental alie-
nation in which Gomez,—immured in one of Francia's dungeons,—had expired. The mother, prohibited from seeing her son,—the sister, forbidden to
visit her brother,—drooped, and languished, and
died.   They died without a friend to close their
eyes, except an old and faithful female domestic;
—for it was one of the curses of the Dictator's
reign, that, when he had once declared his displeasure against an individual, his frown extended to all who dared to approach either the
victim or his relations.   Those who did were
instantly arrested; and among this number were
several honourable women, who, in their wretchedness, had ventured, through iron gratings,
to exchange a few words with those husbands,
whose misery, sufferings, and separation from
them they had long, and in despair, bewailed.

So cheap did Francia, at this time, hold human
life, that when a woman, in a fit of jealousy,
accused her lover to the Dictator of having

spoken disrespectfully of him, it was ordered that the unfortunate and innocent man should receive a hundred stripes. He prayed that he might be shot rather than be subjected to so degrading an infliction; and, with cold and callous indifference, the despot, telling him he should have the benefit of the alternative he preferred, ordered him to be shot.*

Thus it was throughout the country,—for Francia's tools, and agents, and satraps, in the provinces, were not more scrupulous nor backward than their great tyrant-in-chief in the infliction, upon their respective prisoners, of the most cruel and vindictive punishments. Thus, also, it came to pass that a people, proverbially the most humane, united, hospitable, and enduring in South America, were converted into a community of beings in whom fear and distrust obliterated all traits of their original character. Every man, and almost every woman too, became an isolated member of a silenced society.

* It has been said that Francia never *commuted* his decreed punishments. This instance, however, must be recorded as an exception; for where the Dictator had only awarded *stripes*, he changed the sentence to that of death.

The guitar was laid aside,—parties there were none. Each person saluted his neighbour as he passed him with chilling frigidity; and, in the anxious desire of every individual to preserve the unenviable life he was still permitted to hold, the concerns of all others,—their fears, perils, sufferings, and even death,—were viewed with cold indifference, or only thought of as lessons of salutary warning.

Yours, &c.

J. P. R.

LETTER XXV.

J. P. R. to Thomas Fair, Esq.

Measures adopted against the old Spaniards—The unfortunate
mason—False accusations and cruelty—Imprisonment, murder,
and mockery—General Velasco—His history—His humming
birds—His butler—The fate of both—Fate of the Bishop
—Fines imposed on the old Spaniards—Orders to shoot those
who looked at the Government House—Solitude around the
Tyrant's abode.

London, 1838.

With few exceptions, Francia's acts of deliberate
cruelty and bloodshed had been hitherto confined
to his own countrymen. But with the threefold
purpose of avoiding sinister interpretations of his
conduct in this respect,—of filling his coffers by
confiscation, and of satiating his now pampered
love of barbarity and oppression,—he opened
upon the old Spaniards the flood-gates of his ire;
and while he annihilated some, and laid prostrate
others, he broke down the spirit, enfeebled the
frame, and consigned over to hopeless disease, or
other protracted modes of death, many more.

The signal for all this multiplication of misery upon the natives of Spain was quite in character. A poor mason of that country made some blunder in a trifling work committed to his charge. "Off with him," said Francia, "to the Banquillo;" and in less than an hour from the time of the order having been given, the ill-fated mason was a corpse. This was in June, 1821. Two days afterwards a proclamation was issued, by which all the Spaniards in Assumption, and within a league of it, were peremptorily required to present themselves in the large square, in front of the Dictator's palace. The accusations contained in this official document were not less numerous than they were without even the semblance of foundation. The poor Europeans were accused of not only harbouring many designs against the government, but of obstructing its proceedings. That their *thoughts* were,—must have been,— anything but friendly towards a government by which they were only oppressed and harassed evermore, it were not easy to deny; but for their actions, they were innocent, harmless, and,— for any purpose of obstruction to Francia's lawless career,—they would have been as impotent

as those of the babes in the cradles of their respective families.

More than three hundred, however, of these
alleged Spanish culprits were collected in the
square early in the forenoon, and were there left
standing, exposed to the rays of the sun till it
was setting. Francia deigned not to take the
slightest notice, or to give a single order respecting them, till the captain of the guard came in
and asked him, what was to be done? " Oh, by
the bye," said the Dictator, affecting to have for-
gotten his Bando, or proclamation of the morning, "now I think of it, I did order those picaros
(rascals) to assemble in the square this morning.
Well, well, take them all to prison, and to-morrow
I will determine what is to be done."

The trembling and unoffending Spaniards were
marched off to the public prison.   They were
there huddled together in thirties and forties in
each apartment, and augmented by these numbers the incarcerated inmates already choking
and dying within the straitened walls.   There
was but one door and one small aperture in each
room for the admission of scanty and unwhole-
some air.   Day after day, night after night,

weeks, months rolled over the heads of the unhappy men, and yet no announcement was vouchsafed to them, either of the *cause* of their imprisonment, or of the probable issue of it. Meantime
their business went to wreck and ruin; their families pined away in solitude and were gradually
reduced to poverty, while their situation was rendered indescribably wretched by the daily terror
in which they lived of hearing that a husband,
father, or brother, had expiated his imagined delinquency on the Banquillo. The prisoners, many
of them, languished in disease, and died without
medical aid; and yet, subject to all these horrors, the Dictator would not allow his captives
to be styled *" Prisoners."* He mocked and insulted them by ordering that they should be
called his " *Recluses ;*" and this on the score of
what he considered a humane indulgence, that
of allowing them to walk about, in community of
woe, during some hours of the day, in the yard
of the prison.

Among the victims who fell a prey to this system of prison discipline was the late amiable and
venerable Governor of Paraguay, General Velasco.
Allusion has been made to him in the first series

of these Letters; but as his character was so primitive and engaging, and his end so affecting;—as
I long enjoyed the honour of his friendship, and
was witness of the simplicity of his habits; and
as the barbarous treatment he experienced,
moreover, was illustrative of the indiscriminating
rigour of Francia,—I shall transcribe to these
pages an account of it from a paper which I wrote,
and which appeared some years ago in a form
less calculated, than a connected account of Francia's reign, to attract attention.

General Velasco was a man of most amiable
and interesting character.   Descended from an
old family in Spain, he had for some time held
his government under the Viceroys of Buenos
Ayres.   With a person tall and erect, and a
military air, he had, nevertheless, in his countenance, that which indicated humanity, kindness, and affability, to be the leading features
of his character.   His venerable figure, his grey
locks, and the remembrance of his unassuming,
humane, and even-handed administration of justice, had conciliated at once the affection and
respect of all who knew him.

When his authority was superseded by that of

the Junta, composed of Yegros, Cavallero, and Francia, his very enemies respected him so far as to leave him unmolested, at liberty to live where he would, and to move about as he pleased.

I was introduced to him soon after my first arrival in Paraguay. He was then about sixty years of age. His mode of life was simple, frugal, retired, and unostentatious; but yet there was something of the *je ne sais quoi* of the old Governor about him. Every part of his attire was scrupulously clean. Everything in his humble dwelling had an air of neatness and arrangement, which showed rather diminished means than superseded habits of elegance and taste. The scanty supply of plate spread upon his table, which never admitted of more than one guest, was kept very bright. His repast was laid out upon a napkin snowy white; pure and cool water in a sparkling caraffe showed that to be his principal beverage, for the wine stood on a small sideboard to be helped only when called for. An old, faithful, and favourite butler, stood with demeanour more respectful, and waited with attention more reverential, than it was possible for him to have done during

General Velasco's governorship. All this I saw when I occasionally dined with him, preparatorily to our going to shoot partridges in the cool of the evening. He was a keen sportsman and an excellent shot. With his Biscayan barrel, inlaid with silver, and a conspicuous but capital lock, he took his graceful aim, and seldom missed his bird. Often did we go forth to our two hours' sport, in the most lovely country on which Nature ever lavished her beauties. With our favourite dogs* and our two servants, one to hold our horses while we were in the enclosed grounds, and another to alleviate our slight fatigue, by handing us a glass of what was there a great rarity,—English porter,—General Velasco and I spent many an afternoon together.

We afterwards returned, with our ten or twelve brace of birds, to his or to my house, and there, in the open court, smoked our cigars under the clear moon and in the refreshing coolness of the evening breeze.

One only other amusement, the simple yet dignified General had — he was very fond of

---

* I have mentioned General Velasco as the first introducer into Paraguay of the Malvinas pointer.

humming birds; and half-a-dozen cages stocked
with them were hung around the walls of his
sitting-room.   There he fed them,—there he bred
them; and as I often walked in upon him early
in the day, I saw him, in his morning gown, surrounded by numbers of the little flutterers,—some
sipping syrup from one small quill in the General's hands, some from another.   They flew about
his ears, hovered round his mouth, buzzed and
fluttered about his head and hands, with all the
endearment of complete confidence and love.
When tired, he shook his hands in the gentlest
possible way in the midst of them, and the rich
and gaudy little tribe dispersed, each member
to its respective cage.   Scarcely had it taken
possession, however, of this, when poising itself
upon its wings, within its pretty tenement, the
little flutterer looked toward its kind feeder, and
was soon again hovering around him.

General Velasco was supported by the cheerful, voluntary, and honourable donations of his
countrymen, the old Spaniards.   They ministered
to his wants in a way so delicate, that it deserves
to be recorded.

The butler had been a servant in the General's

family in Spain; and, in order to accompany the member of that family whom he most loved, he embarked with him from the Peninsula for South America.

This butler had the entire superintendence of General Velasco's domestic affairs when he was governor. When he *ceased* to be governor, the General insisted upon the butler's providing for himself, by means of another situation. The butler remonstrated thus :—" Is it possible, Sir, that after having been a favoured servant of yourself and your family during twenty years of prosperity, you should now humble me so far as to thrust me from your presence in the bleak day of adversity ? *What* have I done to deserve this ?"

As Ruth to Naomi, so Benito (that was the butler's name) " clave " to his master. Most *honourable* butler ; he *would* not go free. " Entreat me not," he said, " to leave thee, or to return from following after thee : for whither thou goest I will go ; and where thou lodgest I will lodge ; thy people shall be my people, and thy God my God: where thou diest will I die, and there will I be buried: the Lord do

so to me, and more also, if aught but death
part thee and me!"

Benito and his master were *not* parted but in
death and chains. It was to Benito's care and
kindness that all the neat arrangements about
his master's domestic establishment were to be
traced. In order to effect this, Benito first spent
his own little fortune, earned in the Governor's
and in his family's service; and he told his master
that the money thus supplied came from the old
Spaniards. When Benito had no more to give of
his own, he went among the General's countrymen,
and soon found them not unwilling contributors
to all his master's wants. The good butler, and
faithful steward, was not the General's servant
merely,—he was his guardian angel.

"They were lovely in their lives, and in their
death they were not divided;" for, though it may
be supposed if *any* history could have softened a
despot's heart (that of Dionysius, we know, was
softened by one scarcely more pathetic) that of
General Velasco and his servant might have
softened Francia's. Alas! no. Velasco perished
of starvation, filth, and neglect,—perished, too,

ın chains; while Benito, stretched at his master's feet, survived him but one day.

The fate of the Bishop was not less tragical. I had often met him, and was always politely received; and when I considered how strong were the prejudices of Catholics against Protestants, and especially how strong were those of the dignitaries of that church in that remote region, I not only felt obliged by the Bishop's civility, but wished that a similar deference to the rules of external decorum between contending and rival sects were a little more attended to in our own enlightened country.

Harassed, jaded, insulted, and alarmed by Francia's daily invasions of the prelatical jurisdiction, by his open ridicule of the church, and by his hostility to its members, the Bishop was driven to insanity, superseded by a vicar-general,* and died in a state of mournful imbecility and destitution. As for the mass of the old Spaniards who were imprisoned, those who survived their captivity were liberated at the end of eighteen months, upon payment, within three days, of a

---

* Paî Montiel, now the humble and subservient agent, by whom Francia ruled the Church.

contribution of a hundred and fifty thousand dollars by the richer class of prisoners; while the poorer, or rather the absolutely destitute class, were banished from Assumption. The Paraguayans forgot, on this occasion, their natural antipathy to Europeans; and a transient gleam of the olden hospitality of the country shone forth in kind assistance and relief of the poor exiles.

Thus did Francia proceed, without a check in his career, till the beginning of 1825; and how little the character of the despot was changed then, even after he had been for ten years the scourge of his country, and, for five, had been imbruing his hands in its blood, the following anecdotes may show:—

A poor woman, ignorant of any other mode of approach to the Dictator, went up to the window of his room; and not only was she consigned, for the rash act, to prison, but her husband, though altogether ignorant of what had been done, was punished in a similar manner. To prevent the recurrence of any incident so outrageous to the dignity of the Supremo, he ordered that thenceforth every person observed gazing at the front of his palace should be shot in the act. " Here," said he to the sentinel, "is a bullet for the first shot; and here," giving him another, "is one for a second, should you *miss* the first; but if you miss the second, be assured I shall not miss you."

This order being made known, you do not need to be told what gloomy solitude reigned around the walls of the tyrant shrouded within them. A fortnight after the order was issued, a half-naked Payaguá Indian, in his ignorance, stood gazing and gaping upon the forbidden sight of the palace walls. The sentinel fired, but fortunately missed; and the report of the musket having brought the Dictator out before a second aim could be taken, he countermanded the order, and pretended never to have issued it.

But I fear I have too long detained you over details, of which the nature is so gloomy as to forbid their being draped in aught but the language of execration, or accompanied by any other imagery than that of the horror which it is their nature to excite. Still these details were necessary, in order to bear us out in the character we have attempted to draw, and have yet to sum up, of this modern Nero, who has (we are sorry we cannot yet write of him in the past tense, all the cruelty, with at least an equal share of the wantonness and frivolity of his predecessor.

Yours, &c.

J. P. R.

353

LETTER XXVI.

J. P. R. To Thomas Fair, Esq.

The Dictator's various occupations—General of dragoons—His
military attire—He gives the word of command—He turns
land-surveyor—Lays off a town—Demolishes the old one—Endeavours to build a new one—The job proves a failure—Francia
finds that he cannot make successful war upon the elements
—His sites are staked off, but not built upon.

London, 1838.

It was one of the wisest sayings of one of the
wisest of men, "that all he knew was, that he
knew nothing ;" and if he had never penned
another word, this little sentence would have im-
mortalised him. Our Dictator, in his estimate of
himself, reversed the sober judgment of the sage ;
for, in every action and every word, the Supremo
proclaimed to all beholders and all hearers—
" this I know, that there is nothing which I do
not know." You have seen him acting the various
parts of lawyer, legislator, secretary of state,

farmer, paviour, philosopher, linguist, algebraist, astronomer, intriguer, recluse, beltmaker, gunsmith, director of customs, chancellor of the exchequer, paymaster-general of the troops, inspector of barracks, master of the horse, and of the ordnance too, drill serjeant, tailor, trouser and cartouche-box maker. You have seen him also in the parts of gaoler and executioner; and, finally, in that of president of the detestable "CHAMBER OF TRUTH," the very designation of which, as combined with the iniquitous purposes to which it was appropriated, implies an amount of despotic impudence, and of phlegmatic daring, to which it would not be easy to find a parallel.

You shall now have the Supremo exhibited to you in three more of his characters, and those, except the parts of executioner and gaoler, his favourite ones. You shall see him, first, acting as general of cavalry, and, with a fierce countenance, leading a couple of troops to a charge against empty space. You shall next see him playing the land-surveyor, and with his theodolite mal-adroitly measuring angles, acute and obtuse, till, in order to complete his lines, he found it necessary to pull down three-fourths of the houses of Assumption. Lastly, you shall have the Supremo exhibited to you in his character of architect, attempting to repair the breaches made by him in his capacity of land-surveyor.

First, then, I am to present the Dictator to you as a dragoon. For this purpose you must no longer think of him in the black suit of a diplomatist, in which he was drawn in our first series. His sable coat was exchanged for that of a Spanish general,—his round hat for a towering and menacing cocked one, with a stiff red feather and gaudy cockade in it ;—on his left breast he wore conspicuously, what some called a star, and others a breast-knot. It partook of both, for some rich embroidery made it look like the former, and the intermixture with this of tri-colour ribbons,—red, blue, and white,—made it look like the latter.   The whole constituted a huge and barbarous badge, the design of which he had adopted from a caricature engraving of Buonaparte, perpetrated by a German artist, at Nuremberg, in defiance of every law of propriety and even credibility. The Dictator dragoon cherished into stunted growth two mus-

tachios on his upper lip, which were plentifully
manured with princesa; and he is said much to
have regretted that the soil of his face was not
adapted to the growth of whiskers.

To these appurtenances of military costume, he
added a cavalry sabre, in a steel scabbard, and a
pair of holsters covered with crimson velvet, in
which were two double-barrelled pistols. He wore
also a blue silk, or rather satin, sash (color de la
patria), with a tassel at either end of it, not unlike
the tassel of a modern bell-pull. But the Supremo, even arrayed in all his military glory,
was too much of a civilian entirely to lay aside
the honourable insignia which distinguished the
learned and diplomatic members of that body.
Of these insignia, silk stockings, gold buckles,
and thin shoes were indispensable parts; and a
still more notable emblem of civic authority was
the yellow cane, with the gold head and black
tassel. The Supremo, therefore, kept all these
as indispensable parts of his costume. To boots
he had a rooted antipathy, and boasted of never
having worn them since he was first admitted an
abogado de derecho, or jurist. Over his silk
stockings he had thus fastened his military spurs;

and so, half soldier, half lawyer, a more refined centaur than any one of the crew which took me to the Bajada, did Francia sally forth to drills, inspections, and reviews.

Conceive him now, with his civic cane slipped into a receptacle for it in his holsters, and his right hand wielding a not over brightly burnished sabre, at the head of two troops of cavalry, and prepared to lead them on to the charge. "*A paso lento, mā-ā-ār-chén*," cried the Dictator—" move on, at slōw-ōw-ōw time ;"—"a paso redoblado ;"—"at *quick* time ;" — "Cárguen á galope;" — " charge at full speed." Like Hannibal, son of Hamilcar, he then led his men over some of the sloping Alps of Paraguay. "*A-ā-ālto*," after half an hour's gallop, cried the Dictator—" *hā-ā-ālt :*" and then he ordered his aides-de-camp to beat with their sabres any man who had fallen out of the ranks, or whose horse had stumbled over the burnt trunk of a palm-tree.

I never heard that the Dictator's military feats went beyond such as those I have described, except when he sometimes inspected his foot-guards in the square ; sent every man whose belt was awry to the stocks, and awarded to every one, whose best coat was a little soiled, a number of stripes, graduated by the humour of the moment.

I am now to present to you this dictatorial jack-of-all-trades (pardon the lowness of the expression, I can find no other to suit) as land-measurer and surveyor.

Behold him, then, in addition to his usual escort of three dragoons, with two foot-soldiers behind him, one carrying on his shoulders a theodolite, and another the chains by which the territory destined for his scientific operations was to be measured and laid off. He had with him, besides, two or three of his best masons, and a clerk to note down results, distances, alterations required, and projected improvements to be made. The territory on which the Supremo proposed to operate was no other than the entire site on which the ancient city of Assumption stood.

I have, in the first series of these Letters, described Assumption as an irregularly and ill-built town, every way inconvenient, with sandy instead of paved streets, and frequent springs gurgling up in the midst of the pathways. The Supremo had determined to remedy all these things, by the practical application to them of his own acute, original, and scientific genius. He had determined, in short, to lay off a *new* town, which should wholly eclipse the old one; and though this would have been no difficult matter for a sixth-rate artist in this country to have accomplished, it turned out, in the hands of the first artist in Paraguay, to be an onerous, operose, cruel, and despotic undertaking to carry into effect.

His plan was to lay out the city in capacious streets, intersecting each other at right angles, and in straight lines, in a direction of due north-west and south-east. Like Hamlet, the Dictator thought that when the " wind was southerly, he knew a hawk from a hand-saw." Three new squares were to be built on sites now covered with houses; and one square was to be altered and enlarged. Salient angles were to be lopped off; narrow streets were to be made wide; lanes were to be abolished; orange-trees were to be hewn down; fences were to be exterminated; for huts there was to be no commiseration; while babbling springs were to be choked, and gurgling rills to be dammed. Against brooks and stagnant waters a war of extermination was

declared, and the sandy surface of Assumption
was to be overlaid by granite brought from many
leagues' distance.   ↲

Dictatorial power may accomplish much; and
the Supremo soon showed that it should lose none
of its omnipotence in his hands. Down went the
theodolite, and down for its management came
the Supremo from his horse. The very first line
marked out in the direction of north-west swept
off a dozen houses all standing obtrusively in the
way. The next line in the transverse direction
called for the annihilation of twenty dwellings
more. These two first measurements a little
staggered the land-surveyor; but his one invariable appeal to himself was, " Am I not Supremo?"
Soon were his scrupulous objections to his own
original plans silenced. " The houses *must* come
down," said he to himself; and he proceeded on
his survey without misgiving and without remorse.
His first afternoon's work devoted eighty tene-
ments to destruction; and another week's use of
the theodolite and chains marked out a hundred
more habitations for immediate demolition.

So far was the land-surveyor's conscience from
being moved by a contemplation of the misery

which such a step must entail upon the inhabitants of the devoted dwellings, that he looked
upon every one of them as enemies to the ameli-
oration of the city, and as obstructing and
thwarting his plans for its improvement. With
his usual impetuosity and haste, he issued orders
to every one of the owners of the obnoxious
houses immediately " to quit," and not only
so, but to be themselves the demolishers of their
own dwellings, free of all expense to the state.
One poor man applied to know, " what remu-
neration he was to have ;" and the Dictator's
answer was, " a lodgment, gratis, in the public
prison." Another asked, " where he was to
go," and the Supremo's reply was, " to a state dungeon." Both culprits were forthwith lodged in
their respective new residences ; and their houses
were levelled to the ground.

The surveying department, or rather the sur-
veyor-general, after devoting upwards of five
hundred dwellings to demolition, sent the inmates
to substitute for them huts in the woods, and
left every inhabitant of Assumption unequivocally
to infer, that if his house interfered with the lines
of north-west and south-east, especially if any

objections were made to the projected plans, that
he (the objecting tenant or owner) must be prepared at once for ejectment and for banishment.

Consequently, no further remonstrance was
made ; and the levelling theodolite, under the
scientific hands and unscrupulous conscience of
the Supremo, proceeded on its angular and recti-
lineal process of destruction.

Here a beautiful, but impertinent cottage
offered some impediment to the plan of the
new city, and there a goodly mansion had an
awkwardly projecting angle in the way of a north·
west street. "Down with them both," said the
Supremo; and down they came.

So much for Francia, in his capacity of land-
surveyor. Let us see him now in that of architect,
endeavouring to repair the ruin and havoc which
in his other vocation he had produced.

A celebrated ruler of olden times boasted,
" that he had found Rome a city of brick, and
left it one of marble." This can never be our
Supremo's boast. He found Assumption an
awkwardly built city, it is true ; but how has he
left it ? " Like a lodge in a garden of cucumbers."
It is a half deserted, half built, flimsy specimen

of crude designs planned in ignorance; of fantastic structures, reared without skill; of nodding, tottering edifices, at intervals, few and far between, and built with single reference to their being kept upon the lines of due north-east and due south-west. Gaps of one, two, and three hundred feet intervened between many of the houses; the squares had one side and a half, or one and three quarters completed; all the rest being masses of rubbish of the houses which had been thrown down to make way for houses that were never to be built. Wherever a public building occurred in the architect's two favourite lines, he allowed it to stand, no matter how far it projected, or how much it receded. Every *private* house that interrupted the fatal line was unmercifully sacrificed : nor was this all. ´

The mathematical science of the Dictator was so scanty, that before he could fix the *true* lines in which the new houses of the projected city were to run, he was obliged to demolish a great many buildings, which the result of his final admeasurement showed him might as well have been left standing, inasmuch as they would not have interfered with the contemplated symmetry of the embryo capital of Paraguay. The result was, that the *first* demolitions of brick and mortar were adopted as mere preliminary steps to pave the way for a more accurate mensuration, and a more complete destruction. The surveyor's work being finished, except as regarded the engineering department, which was of course still under the direction of the Dictatorial Πολυτεχνης, he proceeded thus to prepare for carrying into effect his great architectural projects.

The streets of Assumption were not only streets of sand, but were often formed into ravines by the heavy rains, and in all cases rendered by these, and by numerous springs and brooks, of a very unequal surface. In order to remedy this obvious defect in the thoroughfares, our engineering, architectural land-surveyor, caused all the rubbish and debris of the demolished houses to be cast into the gaps and chasms, and ravines of the *old* streets, so as to approximate them to the level on which he had determined that the new houses of the new city should be built. Little hillocks which stood in the way of this levelling process were cut down, and little valleys which offered an obstruction

to it were choked with rubbish. At length the
site of the intended city was made as level as
the engineer deemed it possible to make it; and
to work went all hands to raise the superstruc-
tures which were to embellish it. Four hundred
wretched prisoners in chains were set to work as
bricklayers, masons, and carpenters; the carts,
horses, asses, and mules of every labouring man
were pressed into the service; no pay was ever
awarded to them ; the Dictator observed that
they ought to be proud of serving the state gra-
tuitously, since he condescended personally to
superintend the erection for them of a city destined to be the most beautiful and important in
the new world. .

Onward pressed the Dictator in his great undertaking, scattering the population of Assumption, pulling down their houses about their ears,
sending them to seek for shelter where they
might best find it, obliging many of the more
substantial inhabitants to build houses in sub-
stitution of those which he had made them demolish, and on spots selected according to his
fancy.

Slowly, however, even with all the Dictator's

potency, did the work of reconstruction proceed; for though he was master of many Paraguayan slaves, even the Congress had not been able to confer upon him the power of contending with the elements, of changing the course of nature, or of evoking at his nod the waters from the dry land.   Besides, in his anxiety to rear a superb superstructure, he overlooked the essential point of laying a solid foundation.   A tropical storm of one night often swept away the works on which five hundred men had been engaged for a month.   As the streets were not paved, the torrents of rain swamped and undermined all the rubbish that had been lavished upon them.   The old cataracts, chasms, and ravines were re-opened; the springs which the mighty engineer had choked in one place burst forth in another; the houses were no longer level with the streets; the windows of some of them were choked with mud and sand forced up against the walls by the impetuosity of the roaring torrents; and the foundations of others were laid bare by the sweeping streams by which they were inundated and undermined.

Many of the smothered streams found vent in

the very heart of the rising edifices; and, seeking
a level, spouted forth with irresistible impetus,
till reaching the elevation of the mortar-built
walls, back fell the water to its mother earth.
The *jets-d'eau* were beautiful,—not finer some
of those at Versailles; but water having a tendency, where there is nothing but newly-laid brick
and mortar to resist it, to make awkward in-
roads, the mortar was attenuated, the bricks
were loosened, and next day exhibited to the
Dictator, as he rode along with his plumb-line,
theodolite, and square, so many chinks and apertures, as convinced him that the half-constructed
edifice must come down. In some cases he set
his men to the work of demolition; in others,
nature saved him this trouble; so that, what
between the development of the destructive
organ in the Dictator, in the elements, and,
above all, in the contumacious springs, the city
of Assumption was no sooner half built than it
was laid wholly prostrate. Nodding and tottering to its fall stood every edifice: the backs of
many of the old houses were turned upon the
new streets, as if in contempt of the Dictator's
operations: crumbling to the ground came one

day half a dozen structures ; crash the next came
half a dozen more ; and all-persevering as was
the besotted architect, yet, after five years' labour, not one-fourth of his edifices had attained
the security afforded by a roof ;—whole streets
were laid off with stakes of dry reed, not marking
where a house *had been*, but where houses *were
to be;*—the town presented the appearance of
having sustained a lengthened bombardment ;
and though, by degrees, *after* his five years of
frustrated plans and disappointed hopes, Francia succeeded in having some tolerably good
houses erected, yet of the man, and of his whole
undertaking, it may be safely asserted that there
never was, nor is ever likely to be, so remarkable,
and especially so literal, a fulfilment of the latter
part of a striking parable :—   *   *   *
"He shall be likened unto a foolish man, which
built his house upon the sand : and the rain
descended, and the winds blew, and beat upon
that house, and it fell ; and great was the fall
thereof."

Yours, &c.

J. P. R.

LETTER XXVII.

J. P. R. TO THOMAS FAIR, ESQ.

Reflections preparatory to the closing Review of Francia's Character—Charges brought by Francia against Mons. Rengger, "That he is a wretch, assassin, poisoner, seducer, and intriguer;" "that he wants to marry a Paraguay lady;" that he is "a mendacious miscreant;" "that his work is an essay of lies;" "that he is an ungrateful vagabond."—His Letter about Buenos Ayres—The Dictator's contempt for him.

London, 1838.

WE now draw to a close,—and I confess gladly,—of the bloody history of perhaps one of the worst, as well as most contemptible, of living men. This letter and my next will finish the account which it has fallen to me to give of the tyrant; and in accordance with my promise that Francia should have a privilege which himself never extended to a human being,—that, I mean, of self-defence,—I now proceed to insert a document translated from a copy of his own MS., published by his own command in a periodical of Buenos

R 3

Ayres, entitled the Lucero, and of which MS. the copy is now in the possession of Sir Woodbine Parish.

In further fulfilment of my promise, my next letter, the concluding one of the series and of the volume, will present to you an analysis of this document; and wind up with a short, but comprehensive *résumé* of the awful charges, which fairly, freely, without exaggeration, and supported by the most undeniable evidence, I have laid at Francia's door.

The account is now between him and his God. He cannot, in the course of nature, long cumber the ground; and I think it would have been a culpable omission in the annals, horrible, humiliating, but yet instructive,—of bad men, to have allowed this one to descend to his grave without the scorn, contumely, and reproach of all good ones. What safeguard have we against a repetition of the same infamous practices which have characterized Francia's reign, but the exposure of them? Men may frame local laws, and tyrants may execute them; but the press can circulate far and wide, and promulgate from generation to generation, the account of deeds

which shall instil salutary fear into the minds of
future legislators, and yet more salutary distrust
into those of the masses that are to be legislated
for.   After all, I fear, it is to the control of those
masses,—educated, I mean, (and what a process
of centuries is national education!) that we must
look for stability of institutions,—virtue in the
executive power,—patriotism in the soldier and
sailor,—integrity in the judge,—charity and simplicity in the minister of the altar,—impartiality
in the magistrate,—uprightness in the merchant,
—and common honesty, industry, and independence in the labouring classes themselves.   I speak
not of Tories, Whigs, or Radicals,—of Moralists,
Religionists, or Theorists,—of any one sect.   I
speak of the family of *mankind;* of the oblique
tendency of his nature; and of the fearful exem-
plifications of this tendency, as illustrated by the
history of such men as Francia.   Above all, it
is to be hoped that such an exposé will cause the
South Americans to look about them, and try to
detect and to displace any incipient Francia,
that it is just possible may at this moment be
planning among them such another career as
that of the despot of Paraguay.

I proceed now, without further preface, to give you a correctly translated copy of the document to which I have referred.

" NOTES MADE IN PARAGUAY, BY THE DICTATOR FRANCIA, ON THE VOLUME (FOLLETO) OF JOHN RENGGER.

" THE Swiss, John Rengger, came to Paraguay with his companion and countryman, Marcelino Longchamps, to establish himself as a physician. It was not long before Rengger leagued himself closely and seditiously with the old Spaniards, and with the Frenchman Saguier, a notorious spy of the royalists, and who established himself here as a so called botanist. It was shrewdly suspected that they had both been banished from Europe. Here, Rengger occupied himself in the poisoning of such American patients as he could lay hold of ; and, among others, no sooner had the Treasurer Decoud swallowed the deleterious beverage than he fell into mortal agony, while the wretch of a physician from that moment abandoned his patient, nor would return to see him, in spite of repeated solicitations to this effect.

" During the two months in which Rengger attended the barracks of the regiment of men of colour, he despatched more than twenty of them, and was on this account sent about his business ; when at once the mortality ceased.

" No wonder that the fellow (el Bribon) avoids in his volume all allusion to this barbarous massacre. He knew well he should not find his account in making that public.

" In imitation of Rengger, the old Spaniard Baiguer set himself up to administer poison ; and was, in like manner, forbidden to exercise his vocation of quack.

" Himself bitterly inimical to the cause of America, Rengger did all in his power to seduce others into his own views. He persuaded the Saxon, Gustavus Leman, an' ally and correspondent of the patriots, to desert them, and take part with the old Spaniards, on the allegation that he would receive better treatment at their hands, than at those of the Americans.

" But there are other things which show Rengger to have been a precious rogue. He tried to inveigle the old physician Narbaez, who, in mockery of the system of the Swiss, practised

with success in several of the barracks. Rengger's object was cunningly, through the influence
of Narbaez, to raise himself in public opinion,
and to attain, through him, a knowledge of the
medicinal herbs and plants of the country.

" The Dictator, at length, in order to avoid the
necessity of sending this wretch to a scaffold, this
assassin, this poisoner, this seducer, and intriguer
with factious enemies, refused to grant the request which he made, that the government would
allow him to remain in Paraguay in the exercise
of his medical vocation. His principal object,
however, in desiring to remain was not this, but
that he might marry the daughter of the rich old
Spaniard Antonio Recalde. Of that lady, the
poor doctor was desperately enamoured; but see
if in his book he says anything of the rejection of
his addresses, and consequent discomfiture of his
marriage plans. The object of such omission is
clear; it was to lull suspicion as to his mendacity
in the fresh piece of iniquity of which he has been
guilty, in attempting to pass off as history a
tissue of abominable falsehoods : and in doing
this, and stamping himself as an unblushing liar,
he has done exactly what was wanted to complete

his character. So odious in Paraguay had this barbarous Atheist made himself,—so well had he established his character for perverseness, that the Paraguayans in mockery and derision gave him no other name than that of ' *John Rengo*.'* Some people who were walking on the banks of the river, and saw him embark, called aloud, also, ' *Adieu, pill-doctor !—Adieu, purger !—Adieu, poisoner !*'

"Chafed and enraged, not less from being unable to effect his marriage, on account of the Government's prohibition, than from being banished the country and mocked by the patriots, the malicious Rengger left Paraguay like a dog with an old kettle tied to its tail. This is the man who, coming into the country and cloaking over his secret mission, has published a pretended historical essay, of which the object evidently is to undermine the reputation of the Dictator; but the raving and contemptible volume ought rather to have been styled an Essay of *Lies*. It may, without exaggeration, be affirmed that, as regards Paraguay and its government, it contains not a word of truth.

* A bad pun upon Mons. Rengger's name, and signifying " John the Limper." or " Lame Man."

"Even in those parts in which there is some foundation of reality, every thing is changed, disfigured, distorted. All is dressed up with fictions, and evidently meant to lower the character of the Dictator. Things the best known and best authenticated are, with malice the most perceptible, and disingenuousness the most culpable, slurred over, or altogether kept out of view, simply because they do not dovetail into Rengger's plan. There is ample evidence on the face of the book that it is made up of disfigured accounts, slanderous tales, impostures and stories not only accommodated to the taste of Europeans, but invented by them, in revenge for the frustration of their repeated conspiracies, machinations, and plots. Take, for example, the mad brained, or rather, ridiculous fiction of the Marquis of Guaraní, envoy to Spain; and other hidden schemes, by which they thought to lay prostrate the Dictator, with whom they are at rancorous variance, because he is a firm and decided patriot,* and viewed by them as an insuperable stumbling block in the way of their particular theories and

* This word " patriot," not a little prostituted in modern times, appears with singular audacity and reckless impertinence in the mouth of such a man as Francia.

plans. Rengger, as being accredited with them
for every species of iniquity, has lent a helping
hand to increase the catalogue of such stories;
and that by means of his fresh lies, fictions, mis-
representations, and of the pure inventions of his
own fantastic imagination.

" He has given himself up, without a blush, to
the infamy of acting the mendacious and calum-
nious impostor; and this because of his engagements with the Europeans,—of his declared
aversion to the patriots,—of his desire to revenge
himself for the denial of his application to
government,—and of the contempt and mockery
which he suffered in consequence of the frustration of his connubial plans.

" These were likewise the causes which impelled
his impudence to the pitch of inventing sayings,
and of forging conversations of the Dictator, which
never took place. We are in no ignorance, now-
adays, of the objects and implacable malice of
such men. The single object of these rascals,
devoid of soul, is to disburthen themselves of vile
passions; and for this purpose they avail themselves of sinister machinations and intrigues. It
is a vain and even a risible effort in this ungrate-

ful vagabond and low calumniator to speak about that of which he understands nothing.

" Rengger, foreseeing the charge of falsehood which would be brought against him, hastens, in the preface of his ' *Essay of Lies,*' to adduce as a witness of the truth of his impostures the person of the name of Longchamps, already mentioned. But this man is neither more nor less than the countryman of the other, and took up his miserable abode with him in a hut, as his Gaucho companion, and as an accomplice in all his iniquities.

" The malignity of this calumniator has not been confined to Paraguay : it has extended to the patriots of other states. After his departure from hence, two letters of his were intercepted which he wrote from Buenos Ayres, on the 20th of September, 1825, one to the wife of the Recalde already mentioned, and the other to her daughter Angelica. There are some curious things revealed in them. To the mother he writes in these studied terms :—' *In Buenos Ayres, I do not feel at home. The Porteños have adopted the bad qualities of all the European nations, without one of their virtues. This city is like a house in*

*ruins, which they have painted outside like whited
sepulchres, while within all is hollowness and
decay.'*

" Who knows but that in Buenos Ayres, he
flattered and gratified many by abusing the Paraguayans, at the very moment when he was writing
to Paraguay in vituperation of the Porteños and
of their city.

" These short notes shall suffice to give an idea
of the character and depravity of this infamous
impostor and villainous man, who, emerging from
the mountains and crags of Switzerland, actuated
by an innate perversity of disposition, and desirous of making a figure, and of giving to himself
an adventitious importance, dares, with insolent
brutality, to interfere with the Government of
Paraguay !

" If it were necessary, it would be easy to show
in detail the impostures and falsehood which pervade his whole volume, for the enlargement of
which he has after all been obliged to have recourse to impertinences and despicable frivolities,
all the progeny of his own perverted brain. But
the best answer to malevolence, to its abandoned

authors, to scoundrels, and to traitors, is that of contempt."

[Here follows the rubric of the Dictator.]

Yours, &c.

J. P. R.

LETTER XXVIII.

J. P. R. to Thomas Fair, Esq.

ANALYSIS OF THE PRECEDING DOCUMENT, AND
CONCLUSION OF THE SERIES.

Scurrility of Francia's Exposé—Notoriety of the Facts alleged
by Rengger—Lowness of Francia's Imagery and Language
—Mons. Rengger's Forbearance—Reason assigned for this—
Credit given to Francia by Mons. Rengger—Investigation of
Francia's Charges—Their Refutation—Address to Francia,
containing a Résumé of the Charges against Him.

If anything were wanting to enable me to complete the sketch with which I am now to conclude,
of Francia's character,—anything beyond the too
well attested record of his infamous deeds,—it
would be found in the document under his own
signature, which precedes.

By an appeal to facts, of which not only the
truth, but the notoriety has been attested in
America by many witnesses, and proclaimed to
Europe by not a few, he has been traced to his
den of iniquity. His actions have been dragged

forth to the light; and this, as in a dark place, has shone in upon his deeds of despotism, of hoped for concealment, and of fancied seclusion. He is destined, we may trust, henceforth to stand out in such bold relief on the page of history as shall mark him for one of the most cruel and yet most contemptible of tyrants that ever swayed the destinies of his fellow men.

When I say that Francia has lent his own signature to render more palpable his own condemnation, and that in a way which could scarcely have been otherwise accomplished, I allude to three points, the most prominent, as they strike me, in the document referred to.

One is the personal abuse, scurrility, and low language which pervade it.

No gentleman could have adopted such language as his own without a deviation from all the usages of decorous writing. The imprimatur was issued by himself, and shows to what a pitch of vulgar wrath he must have been roused before he could deliberately have committed such an ebullition of it to paper.

Another point is, the allegation against Messrs. Rengger and Longchamps of falsehood. Of this, all who knew and were witnesses of Francia's deeds in Paraguay (and such witnesses were many), would readily attest the Swiss writers were never guilty in anything they said of Paraguay. But no such attestation is required: the low terms, the evident pique, the mean, petty, paltry, and unmanly tone, in which the accusations are couched, are the best evidence that can be offered at once of the Dictator's malignity, and of the innocence of the Swiss gentlemen whom he ranked as his enemies, and would have consigned to everlasting obloquy, because " *they told him the truth.*" That was a sound which never perhaps, except in this case, saluted his ears, after his elevation to the Dictatorship: and what was to be expected but that the first sound of so unwelcome and hated a tocsin should cause them to tingle and himself to rave?

Another remarkable feature of Francia's document is the palpable omission of the denial of any one of the specific accusations laid to his charge by Mons. Rengger. The facts which Messrs. Rengger and Longchamps muster in fearful array against him were too well attested for even the impertinence of Francia to gainsay. One thing, and one alone, he has denied, a story about the Marquis of Guarani; but that very story is recorded by those gentlemen, not only as a mere report, but as one utterly devoid of probability and truth.

I shall address myself shortly to the points of accusation in question; I shall draw out a brief analysis of the whole charges against M. Rengger; and I shall then wind up, by an appeal to the despot of Paraguay himself as to the truth of the charges laid at his door.

The first thing which, on a perusal of Francia's tirade against Messrs. Rengger and Longchamps, strikes the reader, is the lowness of the imagery, and the unscrupulous accommodation to it of the language in which it is couched. I have heard Francia make use of violent, and sometimes even of coarse expressions; but they were as isolated words in his discourse, which on the whole was pleasing and gentlemanlike. Such language, however, was no longer suited to the confirmed tyrant, and especially (as he conceived himself to be) the insulted man.

No stronger evidence of the change in Francia's character could have been offered to me than that adduced by the coarse outpouring of the vials of his wrath upon the peaceful, unobtrusive, and respectable natives of Switzerland, who, in pursuit of objects exclusively scientific, had left their native mountains for tropical regions, to which the unbounded luxuriance of nature invited their research.

The accusations against those gentlemen of their being mountebanks, murderers, poisoners, conspirators, rebels, and spies, are too ridiculous for confutation. As if Francia would have tolerated without punishment of any kind, and that for six years, the residence of such men within his blood-stained territory! It is a bad thing, often, to prove too much; and the Dictator's peevishness and ire undoubtedly led him in the case in question beyond the licence, and especially beyond the prudence, of cool or credible advocacy of his own case.

It would be curious, if it were not horrible, to hear the man who had sent hundreds of his own countrymen to dungeons, chains, exile, and the gallows, turn all at once so scrupulous as to say, that in order to save such an alleged political and moral wretch as Mons. Rengger from the scaffold, he had allowed him to depart from Paraguay.

The whole tone of Mons. Rengger's book is one of subdued impartiality and of simple historical truth. Of the South Americans, generally, he speaks with great favour; and of Francia, if not with partiality (that were no easy task), yet with a forbearance, which all who read the book must perceive, and perhaps regret.* Such men, as this Dictator, ought to be viewed as scourges, affording profoundly awful lessons to the family of man; and he who has an opportunity of observing such pests of his race, and does so, with too much lenity, with a softened revelation of their iniquity, or with a mitigated expression of abhorrence of

* Take the following as a specimen:—" We thus, after a sojourn of six years, during four of which we were forcibly detained, were granted permission to quit it. It is only justice to state, that during all that time Dr. Francia never directly threw any difficulties in the way of our researches; but, on the contrary, gave us more than once proofs of his good will. Would that I could speak as favorably of his administration! To the conduct of the inhabitants of Paraguay, both Creoles and Spaniards, towards us, we can only allude in terms of praise; and we shall always recollect with gratitude the hospitable reception which they gave us."—*Messrs. Rengger and Longchamp's Account of the Reign of Dr. Francia*, part I. page 120.

their atrocities, however much he may be entitled
to our admission of his forbearance, can scarcely
exact our acquiescence in his historical justice.
How are we to learn what is the *nature* of man,
but by a study of the *history* of man ?

Mons. Rengger may well, however, stand excused for having given to the world, in regard to
the actions of Francia, only what he has, and for
doing this with a palliative judgment, which it is
the duty of those who follow a little to correct.
The truth is, that Mons. Rengger, like all who
left Paraguay in 1826, left it under feelings
of fear and trembling that cannot well be conceived, except by those who, in a small and
petty society, have lived for years under the
jealous glance, and subject to the capricious
tyranny of such a petty despot as Francia. They
know that every word, they are convinced that
every action, they dread that every thought of
their hearts may come to his knowledge ; and
they are too well aware that the caprice and not
the justice of the tyrant will decide the merits of
their case. When they lie down at night, they
say " Would God it were morning;" and when,
disconsolate and without hope, they arise in the

morning, they say, " Would God it were evening." This, I believe, to have been the position,
and those the feelings of all who resided in Paraguay at the time of which I speak. The minds
of Francia's subjects were so filled with appre-
hensions of what his tyranny might any day
dictate, that even when beyond his reach, at
Buenos Ayres, or still further beyond the effects
of his thraldom, in Europe, those who had once
lived under his iron rule were yet afraid to trust
the evidence of their own senses as to their safety.
Francia stalked before them in their dreams;
nightmare, with the gibbet by her side, chilled
them with horror; the dungeon, the dagger, and
the banquillo, were their waking thoughts, and
their sleeping imagery; so that when they came
to write, or to speak, of the man who had kept
them in this state of mental and bodily agitation,
they could not readily forget their long-felt im-
pressions of fear and of distrust.   In proportion
as the apprehension of Francia was vivid and
terrific, just in that proportion did Mons. Rengger
perhaps find it impossible to trust his mind, his
memory, his imagination, or his fingers, with the
revelation of the whole truth.

His book, therefore, is a very subdued account of Francia's reign of terror ; and credit is given to this man for many principles as being just, which were altogether false ; for many actions as being creditable, which were characterized by selfish, short-sighted, inflated, and ignorant views.

Take, as an example, Mons. Rengger's account of Francia's *agricultural* policy. Great credit is bestowed on the Dictator for his sagacious and enlightened improvement in this branch of national prosperity.

Now, what are the facts? Paraguay was a mercantile community ; and though her commerce, like that of all other countries, depended essentially on her agriculture, and on the productions of her native and immense forests, yet Francia rendered abortive all these sources of wealth by shutting her out, on principles of purely political jealousy and personal expediency, from intercourse with the whole world. The natural and superabundant produce of Paraguay was the yerba, or tea, the tobacco, the juice of the sugar-cane, and the noble trees felled in her forests. By shutting his ports, Francia put an end to the exportation of all those valuable commodities, and gave the *coup de grâce* to the abundant imports which were received for them in manufactures, flour, and specie. Hundreds of vessels decayed in his ports; thousands upon thousands of bales of yerba and tobacco rotted in his warehouses; rafts of timber were no longer floated down the river; and merchants, traders, sailors, wood-hewers (making together a very large proportion of the inhabitants of Paraguay), were thrown back in listlessness upon their impoverished homes, and forced upon the cultivation of the soil as a mere mode of providing scantily for the means of subsistence, which before had been abundantly supplied by the medium of commerce. One season, a plague of locusts laid waste the cultivated grounds of the republic, and left the inhabitants in a state of starvation. Francia ordered a second crop to be sown by the disconsolate members of his isolated community. A second crop *was* sown; and, to the astonishment of all, produced an abundant harvest. This harvest, however, afforded no more than a simple supply of provisions for each member of the community; and yet Mons. Rengger, upon this fact, gives Francia credit for important improvements in the agriculture of the country.

Shortly to recapitulate the charges brought by Francia against Mons. Rengger, they may be reduced to eight:—

CHARGES.	REMARKS.
1. That he leagued himself with the Old Spaniards against the Creoles.	Let any one in his senses ask himself if Francia was the person to allow the man against whom he believed such allegations to go scot free, after having him for nearly six years under his thumb?
2. That he poisoned these last, and especially the treasurer Decoud, and more than twenty of the Dictator's soldiers.	
3. That being bitter against the cause of America, he seduced others into his views.	
4. That he endeavoured to inveigle an old Paraguay practioner to teach him (Rengger) a knowledge of the medicinal herbs of Paraguay.	Admitting these to be facts, they *may* have involved (I dare say they did) in Francia's estimate charges of high-treason; but I hope, for the honour of science, and of the holy state of wedlock, that he would get very few men to agree with him.
5. That Rengger wanted to marry the daughter of Mr. Recalde, a rich old Spaniard.	
6. That his book is a tissue of falsehood.	An assertion contradicted by every witness worthy of credit that has come forth from Paraguay.

7. That he invented the story of the Marquis of Guaraní.	Mons. Rengger, in his book, expressly states the story of the Marquis to have been one without foundation; while his remarks on Buenos Ayres are so favorable, not to say partial, that I fear it may be some time before she ever have such another historian.
8. That he wrote against Buenos Ayres.	

So much for the only tangible part of Francia's vindication of himself, or rather of his accusations against Mons. Rengger. All the rest is such a tissue of low and rabid abuse, conveyed in language only fit for the pen of him who used it, that it shall stand, without further comment, as a true index made by himself, and better made than it could be by any other, to show the workings of his coarse and pampered mind. But it remains to be asked of Francia, in reference to this strange document, *what he has to say for himself, and what to offer in his defence?* Aye, where is his defence, or even his denial of the specific charges brought against him by Mons. Rengger?

Had *I* the putting to him of those interrogatories, I should do it in this wise :—

" Sir,—By your own admission, you have *read*

all the charges brought against you by Mons. Rengger. What! have you not a single case, then, which you can prove ought to be expunged from the awful catalogue compiled by your accuser? Are you tongue-tied on an occasion so solemn as this? Could you not deny the execution of Yegros, of the Pelado, of your poor Mason, or of any one of more than forty of the most respectable individuals of Assumption, sacrificed to your bare suspicion and jealousy? Could you not deny the yet more cruel and lingering death inflicted by you on the old and innocent General Velasco, and on his faithful butler, or that on the equally innocent Gomez and Zavala? Could you not say that the story of your " CHAMBER OF TRUTH " was a fiction, and that there were no such places in Paraguay as either state prison or state dungeons? Has Tevégo no existence? Was not the average of your prisoners, in Assumption alone, five hundred, and of your exiles three hundred? Is it possible that this can be more than a twelfth part of the whole population of your capital and its suburbs? What should we say here, if such a proportion of the inhabitants of London,—that, too, the most respectable,

and, in a great majority of cases, the entirely
innocent inhabitants of London,—were clanking
their chains, or dying in misery and filth, or
eking out a scanty and horrible existence in
exile, and in such a place as Tevégo? Why, the
number of slaves, prisoners, and exiles of London,
in the case supposed, taking the population at
two million, would be a hundred and sixty-five
thousand; and, if the case ran entirely parallel
to yours, all this misery would have been brought
upon the inhabitants of London in the course of
a few years. What a calculation! Can you read
it without trembling? And if you can, why don't
you show (it is a simple question of figures) that
it is founded on false allegations?

" Where are your ships? Is it true, or is it
not, that they are all rotting on the beach of that
capital which you pulled down in caprice, and
attempted in vain to rebuild in ignorance?

" Why are the thousands and tens of thousands
who were wont to consume your tobacco, and tea,
and wood, which constituted the best riches of
Paraguay, getting these productions from other
quarters? How did you behave to Mons. Bonpland? Was it as stated by Rengger and con-

firmed by the companion himself of Humboldt?
If not, why don't you deny the charge?

" Coming a little nearer home, what are your
claims, more immediately personal, to respect?
Have you not, in your early years, been repeat-
edly guilty of seduction, and have you ever provided for any of your victims, or for one of your
illegitimate progeny? I have seen them walking
about the streets of Assumption, in destitution
and in beggary. I have seen a woman, who
attended you assiduously for eight years, languishing in penury, and dying of slow disease.
I have seen your beautiful daughter patrolling
the streets of Assumption, at once with her
person exposed, and on her head, for sale, a
bundle of cigars; this, too, while her father was
first consul of the republic of Paraguay. Where
are your bowels of compassion? You were a
rebellious son, and you have been an unnatural
father. Do you ever hear now of mirth-making,
festivity, or conviviality in Paraguay? No.
Hushed is every sound of hilarity,—silenced the
guitar,—dimmed every eye with tears,—throb-
bing every heart with sorrow. The hyena laughs
when he contemplates destruction and death.

Your smile is like his, ever portentous and deceitful: it is at once the expression of your ferocity and the precursor of blood.

" Then, sir, for your attainments. What are they? Great in Paraguay, no doubt; but there is not a Cambridge *freshman* that would not laugh them to scorn. Such a blot upon humanity, such a disgrace to letters, such a technical quack, so daring a villain, and yet so plausible a knave, where shall we find? Search the world over; and not till you get to one of its remotest corners (Paraguay) shall you see such a man.

" If you think on the face of such allegations, so substantiated as these, that the world will believe that no such disgrace to humanity as Doctor Francia has ever had an existence,—that it will be content, upon your bare assertion, to found belief, 'that to the scoundrels and traitors who thus charge you, the only answer is that of contempt,'—you need not lay the flattering unction to your soul.

" Look at the papers which have already proclaimed your bad name far and wide; and if this book meet your eye, as that of Mons. Rengger did,—if you desire to blot out one record of your multifarious cruelties,—if you would not go down to your grave with the accumulated maledictions of mankind upon your head,—stand forth :— answer the questions that have been put to you, rebut the facts that have been stated in this book, show that you are not,—that you never have been,—the man you are now represented to be, and you may still achieve a triumph which will rescue your name from eternal obloquy."

———————

Such, my friend, are the tone and style in which Francia ought to be addressed; and it must be abundantly evident to you and to every one else, that no mere general declamation of his can make void charges of so public and specific a character. They must be rebutted seriatim ; and that not upon the personal testimony of the tyrant, but by public appeal to those who have been witnesses of his cruel career.

Yours, &c.

J. P. R.

CONCLUSION.

As the first series of these letters went to press, a report of the death of Francia, which was afterwards found to be devoid of truth, obtained general circulation in this country. It is somewhat curious that again, when we have concluded our account of the Dictator's reign, letters from Buenos Ayres announce that a rumour is there afloat of Francia's having gone the way of all living. The statement rests on a communication from a small port on the Paraná, called the Esquina, in the jurisdiction of Corrientes; but, as our newspapers say of many other similar and dissimilar reports, "it wants confirmation."

The probability is that every illness of Francia, at the advanced age of at least fourscore, is construed into his death, and the *certainty* of his demise is substituted for its *likelihood*.

Our details of Francia's reign only reach to 1826-27; and the little episode of M. Bonpland brings us to 1831.

After the departure of all the foreigners detained in Paraguay, there has been no means of obtaining detailed accounts of the latter years of Francia's government; and if there were, they would probably be uninteresting. By his executions and cruelties from 1820 to 1822, every shadow of opposition to his authority was removed; and in fact there remained no *elements* on which he could further wreak his vengeance. He then completed his system, and ever since a monotonous gloom has settled on the land.

Francia continues to supply himself with such necessary articles as he requires, from Buenos Ayres or Montevideo. They are sent in the first place to Corrientes, and thence transhipped in small vessels to Neembucú. That is now the Canton of the Republic. Not only does no stranger pass that point, but, as it may readily be supposed, no one has any inclination to do so. The isolation and the desolation of Paraguay are complete.

It is rather a curious fact, which we have omitted to mention, that Francia, on some Englishman going up to Paraguay with a British passport, would not allow the vessel to discharge

till he had so far mastered the English language
as to be able to read and comprehend the document.

No doubt the Dictator, who has considerable
powers as a linguist, has advanced in his knowledge of the English idiom.

In *this* view we cannot help indulging a hope
that he is not yet dead: we should be glad
that he still lived to " read and comprehend" the
terms in which his character, on the most undeniable evidence, is here drawn; and that he
should thus know, ere, " amid curses not loud
but deep," he breathed his last, the estimate
which is likely to be formed of him by POSTERITY.

THE AUTHORS.

THE END.

Lightning Source UK Ltd.
Milton Keynes UK
UKHW04f0620181018
330753UK00001B/149/P